Self Help Group and Women Empowerment

About the Authors

SWAPAN SHAW (*b.* 1979) is a professional social worker, working in various fields of social work. Presently, he is working with the Central Social Welfare Board, New Delhi under the Ministry of Women and Child Development, Government of India as a capacity of Welfare Officer. He is having experience of working more than 15 years in the field of developmental sector. During his work he is having opportunities to work under many colossus personalities. He has gained lots of experience while working with the various exponents of social work. He was awarded M.S.W. and Doctoral degree in social work in the year 2003 and 2013 respectively from Visva-Bharati University. Prior to be associated with CSWB, New Delhi he worked with a reputed Christian Voluntary Organization where he learnt real life field experience with techniques of finding solution towards the problem with the help of the client. After that, the academic career motivated him in the field of research work. Both the exposures helped to conceptualize and internalize various social issues and social work principles, values and ethic to address them. He gained good amount of communication and interpersonal skills working through different segments of people. From time to time he extends consultancy services and closely associated with number of social action bodies. He has published many articles in various reputed journals.

DEBOTOSH SINHA (*b.* 1962) currently is a Senior Professor in the Department of Social Work, Visva-Bharati.

Apart from classroom teaching, fieldwork supervision, guiding Ph.D. students and other administrative assignments he has to his credit a number of articles and papers published in different reputed journals along with contribution of chapters in various books. He also authored five books on social work.

He was also a visiting faculty from time-to-time to University of Tampere (Finland), University of Stockholm, University of London and Glasgow, University of Dhaka, Shahjala University of Science and Technology and Rajshahi University of Bangaldesh. Recently he was visiting fellow in the University of York, Toronto, Canada. He also visited a number of countries (Italy, Norway, China, Indonesia, Hong Kong, Malaysia, Thiland, South Korea and so on) to attend seminars, conferences or for some other academic purposes.

Dr. Sinha had also conducted a number of research projects sponsored by his own university as well as Ministry of Social Justice and Empowerment, National Human Rights Commission and other Ministries of Government of India. He is also been closely associated with number of social action groups and voluntary bodies.

Self Help Group and Women Empowerment

A Discourse

Swapan Shaw
Debotosh Sinha

CONCEPT PUBLISHING COMPANY PVT. LTD.
NEW DELHI-110059

ISBN-13: 978-93-88937-69-6

First Published 2021

Published and Printed by

Since 1974

Concept Publishing Company Pvt. Ltd.
A/15-16, Commercial Block, Mohan Garden,
New Delhi-110059 (INDIA)
T : 91 11 25351460, 91 11 25351794
E : publishing@conceptpub.com; *W* : www.conceptpub.com

Cataloging in Publication Data--Courtesy: D.K. Agencies (P) Ltd. <docinfo@dkagencies.com>

Shaw, Swapan, 1979- author.
Self help group and women empowerment : a discourse / Swapan Shaw, Debotosh Sinha.
pages cm
Study conducted in Bīrbhūm (District) of West Bengal, India.
Includes bibliographical references and index.
ISBN 9789388937696

1. Women in development—India—Bīrbhūm (District) 2. Women in development—Government policy—India—Bīrbhūm (District) 3. Self-help groups India—Bīrbhūm (District) I. Sinha, Debotosh, author. II. Title.

LCC HQ1742.S53 2021 | DDC 305.42095414 23

Dedicated to
our Revered Parents, Beloved Wives
and our Children

Preface

Women constitute half of our population and play a vital role in the development of the family, the community and the nation. It has been widely recognized that unless women's potential is properly developed, no transformation and economic development is possible. So, to accelerate the growth and prosperity of the nation, it is very important to create opportunities for socio-economic development of women in rural India. In fact, since independence, it has been felt that women experience poverty to a great extent than men do. The benefits of poverty eradication intervention programmes targeted towards the head of the households have failed to trickle down and reached the women. Since then, the Government of India (GOI) has been emphasizing the need for designing separate development programmes for women and to earmark a specific percentage for women beneficiaries in other rural development programmes. However, it was only in the year 1975, the year declared by the UN as **International Year of the Women** that the situation began to improve significantly.

The GOI's policy on women development has undertaken various shifts of emphasis since Independence. The most significant changes occurred in the mid-1980s with the Seventh Five Year Plan, which started a move towards equality and empowerment rather than development. This included the evolution of **Department of Women and Child Development** under the **Ministry of Human Resource Development** and its counterparts in the states. In addition, Women's Development Corporation were set up in most states to implement the new strategy of economic development by facilitating access to training, entrepreneurship development, micro-credit, technical consultancy services and marketing facilities. The Eighth Five Year Plan marks a further shift towards empowerment of women, emphasizing women as equal partners in the development process. The Government continued advocacy for sustained equitable growth opportunities for women in the subsequent five year plans including the Twelfth Five Year Plan period which is reflected below in its mandate.

1. Increased participation by women in local governments and decision making processes.
2. Greater spread of community-based organizations, including women's group.
3. The promotion of income activities and thrift and credit through self help groups for women.
4. Recognition of the need to sensitize all levels of bureaucracy, legislators, and law enforcement agencies to gender issues.
5. An increasing focus of poverty alleviation programmes for women, a mandate to eliminate discrimination against girl children and adolescents in matters of food, health, education, and child labour.

The term women empowerment and Self Help Group are closely interwoven. So before going into the brief discussion on SHG, let's have a glimpse over the connotation of the term women empowerment both from the theoretical as well as operational point of view.

Theoretically empowerment defined as the processes by which women take control and ownership of their lives through expansion of their choices. Operationally women empowerment has also defined as a mental state where the processes have been identified as resultant of two basic components. The first is **social mobilization** and secondly **social security**.

The origin of SHG during early 1980s and continuous attempt was made in the neighbouring country of Bangladesh by Dr. Md. Yunus to encourage landless and marginalized women known as beggar to undertake pity trade with little loan given from his own pocket at the initial stage. This effort was turn into an effort of a grand success with its renovation approach to motivate. The rural poor and disadvantaged women to inculcate banking habits through small savings and credit activities.

Under this canopy we made an attempt to see the relationship between Self Help Group and Women Empowerment. The **first chapter** is introductory where all the concepts, objectives, values and implications have been glossed over. In the **second chapter** we try to see the history of feminism both from the point of view of Eastern and Western culture. The **third chapter** deals with review of literature in the related field. Methodology of the study has been described in the **fourth chapter.** The **fifth chapter** reflects Results, Discussion and Analysis. In the **sixth chapter** we have discussed how social work profession can play a role in this area. The major findings of the study have been separately described in the **seventh chapter** followed by conclusion and suggestions in the **eighth chapter.**

Swapan Shaw
Debotosh Sinha

Acknowledgements

May we make use of this occasion to express our deep gratitude and sincere thanks to Block Development Officer, Bolpur-Sriniketan Community Development Block; Pradhan and members of Gram Panchayat for field level support.

We acknowledge our indebtedness to all the members of Self Help Groups, Bank Officials, Panchayat and Block Officials and Staff of Microfinance Institutions for their kind cooperation during the time of data collection.

Swapan Shaw
Debotosh Sinha

Contents

List of Tables, Figures and Charts

LIST OF TABLES

LIST OF FIGURES

LIST OF CHARTS

1

Introduction

In recent years the paradigm of women empowerment has attracted significant attention while **'self help group'** and **'microfinance'** have formed over the years and these two important subtexts of the 'empowerment' help to enhance the woman's status in the male dominated patriarchal society. But interestingly while all these three have been studied separately as well as finding the correlation among them, elicits strange results—of which one is: a self help group based only on the operational mode of microfinance sustains itself and when pursued to the full, delivers empowerment. The present study has been undertaken to address a number of allied themes of SHG such as Microfinance and Empowerment to accomplish this pending task.

A broad overview of such task could be described through intensive study of our earlier research on self help group, microfinance and empowerment which helps our intended task to address women related issues and thus makes our assignment fruitful for the society. The best beginning could be an appraisal of the status of women in India necessitating the question of women empowerment and how through self help group and microfinance; helps to empower the women need to be tested carefully.

Conceptual Background

The conceptual background of the study itself carries a lot of significance in order to explain the study perspective clearly. Women in this regard are the essential part of every aspect of any economy. All-round development and complete growth of a nation could be possible only when women are considered as integral and equal partners with men in progress. Empowerment of women certainly is achieved when we recognize the harness the women labour in the mainstream of economic development. Empowerment of women is a holistic concept and multidimensional in nature. It must cover socio-economical, political, cultural, psychological and spiritual aspects. Among all these aspects women empowerment is very much determined by economic empowerment of any woman. Economic empowerment should be given utmost importance in order to achieve a long lasting and sustainable development of any society. In this context self help group and microfinance definitely play a pivotal role to remove economic hardship. A requisite of microfinance is an important means for attaining women empowerment through self help group.

SHGs are the voluntary organizations which disburse micro-credit to the members and facilitate them to enter into entrepreneurial activities. Formation of SHG of women in India has been recognized as an effective strategy for the empowerment of women in India.

Microfinance intervention is a well accepted mechanism for poverty alleviation throughout the world. It helps to improve socio-economic status of rural poor. In India too, microfinance is making progress in its effort for reducing poverty and empowering rural women. Microfinance through the network of cooperatives, commercial banks, regional rural banks, NABARD and NGO has been largely catering micro credit to the poor rural women for entrepreneurship.

So, this study will highlight how SHGs and Microfinance are instrumental for women empowerment in the study area the researchers have adopted.

Key Terms Defined

The key terms defined involve both theoretical and operational interpretations of the specific terms used in this study by the researchers to project the degree of parity between the theoretical and operational perspectives. The key words used in this study are **'Self Help Group'**, **'Microfinance'**, and **'Empowerment'**.

Self Help Group

Theoretically, Self Help Group has been defined as a small, economically homogeneous and affinity group of poor rural women, which voluntarily agrees to contribute to a common fund to be lent to its members as per the decision of the group which works for groups' solidarity, self and group awareness, social and economic empowerment in the way of democratic functioning.

Operationally, Self Help Group is an organization of socio-economically backward people who are primarily looking to explore possibilities for income generation because money is traditionally known as power. The role of the Self Help Group member in decision making in family life and as a community member has been operationally taken as empowerment in this study.

Microfinance

Theoretically, microfinance may encompass any efforts to increase access to, or improve the quality of; financial services for poor people currently use or could benefit from using. It refers to the provision of financial services to poor or low income clients, including consumers and the self-employed. The term also refers to the practice of sustainable delivering those services.

Moreover microfinance not only gives a poor chance of access to the credit but also to cover savings, insurance and fund transfers. Marguerite Robinson (2001): *"microfinance refers to small scale financial services for both credits and deposits that are provided to people who farm or fish or herd, operate small or micro enterprises where goods are produced, recycled, repaired, or traded; provide services; work for wages or communication; gain income from renting out small amount of land, vehicles, draft animals, or machinery and tools; and to other individuals and local groups in developing countries, in both rural and urban areas."*

Microfinance (described here as small scale financial services to clients that are economically active in various urban and rural areas) is an effective tool to fight against the poverty by providing entrepreneurs with the necessary capital to start and expand their entrepreneurial activities. Microfinance is also associated with a positive impact on social and human development such as household income, savings, children's education, health and nutrition and women's empowerment.

Empowerment

Empowerment is manifested as a redistribution of power; whether among nations, classes, races, genders or individuals. The goals of women's empowerment are to challenge patriarchal ideology (male domination and women's subordination); to transform the structure and institutions that reinforce and perpetuate gender discrimination and social inequality (the family, caste, class, religion, educational process and institutions; the media, health practice and systems, laws and civil codes, political processes, developmental models, and government institutions); and to enable poor women to gain access to and control of both material and informational resources.

Operationally, a growth of women's self-confidence, in their knowledge of their rights, their willingness to participate in public action and even the reduction of domestic violence may have occurred as a result of women's participation in the new forms of social relationships embodied in the credit organizations. It includes the following components: women's sense of self-worth; their rights to have and to determine choices; their right to have the power to control their own lives, both within and outside the home; and their ability to influence the direction of social change to create a more just social and economic order, nationally and internationally.

While we have designated the key terms of our study most categorically; it is needed now that we approach them discursively, i.e. the specific discourses to which these terms belong should be spelled out elaborately which would hint at their implication. We begin with the status of women.

Women: From Ancient Under-description to Modern Underdevelopment

The status of women in India has been subject to many great changes over the past few centuries though the literature that describes this is said to have been spare. Scholars believe that in ancient India, the women enjoyed equal status with men in all fields of life. Works by ancient Indian grammarians such as

Patanjali and Katyana suggest that the women married at a mature age and were probably free to select their husband. She was not only honoured in the home itself but an equal respect was shown to her in other fields of social and intellectual life. In most areas they held their own status.

In the social and religious field no *'Havana'* (sacred fire), 'Yoga' (union with God) or religious occasion were considered incomplete without her. In the ritual of *'Purna Ahuti'* (casting sacred things and jewels to the fire), the offerings are done by the joined hands of husband and wife. The old rituals are continued even today, though not with proper appreciation of its meaning or significance.

It was during the age of the **'Sutras'** and the **'Epics'**, i.e. period between 500 B.C. to 500 A.D. that position of the women started deteriorating. The various socio-political factors such as the invasions of the foreigners and the misinterpretations of the old religious books were some of the causes of women loosing the respect and the positions they held earlier. The practice of child marriage is believed to have started from around sixth century. The Indian women's position in the society further deteriorated during the medieval period. *Sati,* child marriages and ban on widow remarriages became part of social life in India. The Muslim conquest in the Indian subcontinent brought the *Purdah* practice in the Indian society. In some parts of India, the *Devadasis* or the temple women were sexually exploited. Polygamy was widely practiced especially among Hindu Kshatriya rulers. Beside that the lethargy of women of this period was also an immediate cause of this worsening trend.

By 700 A.D. the theory of perpetual tutelage of women formulated by Manu, a codifier of society, became prevalent. The laws of Manu do state that whenever women are honoured, Gods are pleased. But the laws he enunciated, he gave to women a place of very low status, depicting women as a vile being that should be held slavery.

The position of women, which once started deteriorating, continued till 1850 A.D. In this period even saints and religious minded people also denounced them as the root cause of all evils. Along with these there were also the inhuman and oppressive social and religious practices, such as infanticide, foeticide, dowry etc. which show the women's position was nowhere in male dominated society (Saraswati Mishra, 2002).

Beside the women in India are victims of a multiple socio-economic and cultural factors, and represent a vulnerable group. Vulnerability helps us to understand the dynamics of poverty. Poverty is not a static condition. Population, households and individuals face various risks that can plunge them into poverty. Society has to take steps to reduce their vulnerability and to cope with the effects when shocks occur. Vulnerability indicates exposure to hazards and the livelihood that the welfare of an individual or a household falls below minimum consumption level. In the framework of sociological analysis of vulnerable poverty, inequality and backwardness of weaker section including women, the main underlying assumptions in socio-economic handicaps rooted in social, economic and religious institutions have rendered certain groups of society several disadvantages.

Throughout history and in many societies, inequalities of women and men were part and parcel of an accepted male dominated culture. One of the basic factors unequal shares of women in development relates to the division of labour between the sexes. The division of labour has been justified on the basis of the childbearing function of women and this is biologically important for survival. Consequently, distribution of tasks and responsibilities between men and women in the given society has mainly restricted women to the domestic sphere. Mass poverty and general backwardness have further aggravated the inequalities. While the women's childbearing and child-rearing functions are respected in many countries, there has been very little recognition of women's actual or potential contribution to the economic, social and cultural status. The role of women within the family combined with high level of unemployment and underemployment of the population in general, has led to the unequal state of priority to men in matters of employment.

Apart from these, the effects of the long term cumulative process of discrimination against women have been accentuated by underdevelopment. Graphically, while women represent nearly 50 per cent of the world's adult population and one-third of the labour force, they labour nearly two-thirds of the total working hours but receive only one tenth of the world income and own less than one per cent of property. The story of over worked women in the rural areas of the developing and underdeveloped countries is too well known (Maithili Viswanathan, 1994).

In every modern state of the Nineteenth and Twentieth centuries the concept of welfarism has taken a prime place in the government's objectives. Since the states declared themselves as welfare states, they have responsibilities of amelioration of various programmes for the vulnerable sections of the society. The dawn of independence has given a chance to propose several programmes. The Government of India evolved several economic programmes. One such programme is that self help programme.

A significant outcome of the broad policy debates in the Seventies was a shift from viewing women as target of 'welfare' policies in the social sector to regard them as 'critical agent' for development. This was recognized by the Sixth Five Year Plan, which for the first time incorporated a chapter on Women and Development. The subject of women's development is multi-dimensional, multi-sectoral and multi-disciplinary. In the recent past, awareness about the contribution of women at the level of family and community has been on the increase. As the issue of redistribution with growth was considered threatening, this was subverted around mid 1970s by a call from meeting 'the basic needs of the poor directly' along with efforts towards promoting economic growth. Basic needs encompassed health, nutrition, water, sanitation, shelter, education etc.

Besides these attempts, the Government of India prepared the National Perspective Plan (1988-2000) which envisaged a multipronged strategy for integrating women into the mainstream. 'Shramshakti' in 1988, a comprehensive report of the National Commission for self-employed women and women in the formal sector, examined related issues concerning women workers in the formal sector and made valuable recommendation for improving their status.

Paradigm-Shift from Development to Empowerment

The early Nineties saw the reshaping of strategies of socio-economic development and the emphasis shifted from 'development' to 'empowerment'. There was a realization that women have limited access to capital market, education, skill training, extension education and active participation in the decision making process. In the Constitution 73rd and 74th Amendments Acts of 1992 constitute a major milestone on the road to empowerment of women as the amendments ensure one-third of the total seats and the position of the chairperson in rural and urban elected bodies.

Twenty-first century is considered the era of "women rights". Feminist approaches believe in the right of women to have political, social and economic equality with men. It is a discourse that involves various movements, theories and philosophies which are concerned with the issues of gender difference, advocate equality for women and campaign for women's rights and interests.

Paradigm Localization: From Women Development to Women Empowerment

Whether empowerment is really achievable and how? In connection with this issue Amartya Sen (1993) explained that the freedom to lead different types of life is reflected in the person's potential set which depends on a variety of factors including personal characteristics and social arrangements. Moreover, the full accounting of individual freedóm goes beyond the potential of personal living. Say for example, if we do not have the courage to take decision on a particular issue which one should have to take by himself/herself, then we can not say that they really capacitate with empowerment process. Another important point made by A. Sen (1997) is that evidence of inequalities is underlying when one denied certain universally measureable value added functioning like proper nourishment, good health and shelter which are the basic fundamentals of survival and well-being regardless of gender.

The World Bank has suggested that women should be the main thrust of women empowerment process to achieve success in social development programme (World Bank, 2001). The National Policy for the Empowerment of Women (2000) stated that "The women movement and widespread network of NGOs which have strong grassroots presence and deep insight into women's concern have contributed in inspiring initiatives for the empowerment of women. The United Nations (2001) defines 'empowerment' as the process by which women should have an authoritarian role in taking decisions, having control on their property and ownership of their choices.

Kabeer (2013) emphasized distinction of choice, and the focal point necessarily has to be on strategic life choice, that is choices that shape the livelihood. The expansion in the range of potential choices available to women includes three interrelated dimensions in the form of indicator and hence its validity as a measure of empowerment. These dimensions are: **(1) Resources**—Women must have access to material, human and social resources which are necessary to be able to exercise choices; **(2) Agency**—The process of decision making, including negotiation, deception and manipulation that allow women to act upon their goals; and **(3) Achievement**—The combination of resources and agency helps women to experience their well-being.

Mayoux (2001) explained empowerment as a process which is "a multidimensional and interlinked process of change in power relation". It consists of **(1) "Power within"** which enables women to articulate their own desires for change and strategies for change. **(2) "Power to"** which enables women to upgrade necessary skills and tap the matching resources with the matching needs to achieve their desires. (3) **"Power with"** which enables women to articulate their collective interests through organizing them, to achieve desired change. **(4) "Power over"** helps to change the underlying inequalities in power and resources that constrain women's desires and their ability to achieve them. These power relations operate in different spheres of life, e.g. economic, social and political and at different levels, e.g. individual, households, community, market and institutional.

United Nations Development Programme (UNDP) has identifies two fundamental routes for empowerment. The first is social mobilization and collective efforts using agency setting, as poor women often lack the basic capabilities and self-reliance to counter and challenge existing disparities and barriers against them. Often, change agents are needed to catalyze social mobilization consciously. Second, the process of social mobilization needs to be accompanied by economic security. Until and unless their economic deprivation and livelihood secured, they will not be in a position to mobilize for mainstreaming (UNDP, 2001).

However empowerment is a process of helping people to gain

control over their lives through raising awareness, taking action and working in order to exercise greater control. In other words, empowerment facilitates changes and enables to do what one wants to do. Empowerment is the feeling that activates the psychological energy to accomplish one's goals. The following approaches can attain meaningful women empowerment.

When a woman moves forward, the family moves, the village moves and the nation moves. This is the central theme in the socio-economic paradigm of the country as it is an accepted fact that only when women are mainstreamed, the progress of any economic and social development is meaningful. So empowerment and emancipation of women in the society are to crying call of the day. A few indicators of women empowerment become very important to look into.

Educational Empowerment: Education is the key factor which opens the door to life, develops humanity and promotes national development. Education can be an effective tool for women's empowerment. It enables rural women to acquire new knowledge and technology required for improving and developing their task in all fields.

Economic Empowerment: Female's role are seen as reproductive and domestic in support of the male bread earner of the family and these practices have conditioned women to accept a subservient role. The fact is that women, though largely absent from the formal workplace and hence from official labour statistics, are nevertheless heavily engaged in subsistence agriculture and informal sector of economy. Women are considered only reproducer but not producer and their efforts are always neglected by the family members. Economic independence is a major indicator for women empowerment. The various dimensions of economic empowerment of women are:

(a) *Access to resources:* The rural women need to have control over limited resources like land and livestock, so that they could take decisions and implement them in any way that is required. Ownership and control over productive assets will create a sense of belonging and owning.

(b) *Access to input and credit:* Access to productive resources is critical for enhancing women's economic choices. Since, formal credit institutions rarely lend to the poor, special institutional arrangements may become necessary to extend credit to those who have no collateral to offer their enterprise. The policy challenges into support effective grassroots credit schemes and intermediaries and ensure that low income women have assured credit from formal financial system.

(c) *Access to cooperatives and local women's organizations:* Collectivization has been recognized as a tenet of women's empowerment. It has been defined as a process of bringing a group of women together at a base to become an integral part of an economic activity. Organizational efforts should be made for integrating rural women into development.

Social Empowerment: Empowering women contributes to social development. Economic progress in any country whether developed or under-developed could be achieved through social development. Hence women's empowerment cannot be ignored, while devising various policies for rural and socio-economic development.

(a) *Status of Women:* Every country has made progress in developing women's capabilities, but inequalities continue to exist between women and men. The low status of women is the outcome of a variety of causes in which patriarchal values reinforced by traditional media and other socio-political institution play a major role. Thus the institutional bases of women's oppression have to be sensitized to accept the gender equality and moreover, women's perception of themselves would also need to be changed.

(b) *Gender Bias:* Cultural traditions and economic necessity have always meant a significant role for women in agriculture. In India it is not uncommon that women do not have control over the land. Even, where women constitute a large share of agricultural producers, but, there are cultural constraints to easy communication between men and women, because almost all extension workers are males. Therefore, the role of agricultural extension worker is very significant. Besides, cultural norms have to be addressed before we tackle other dimensions.

(c) *Health and Nutrition:* Health and Nutrition are two very important basic needs for empowerment of rural women. To achieve real and quicker development in health sector an extensive as well as intensive **"Health Education and Awareness Campaign" (HEAC)** needs to be given topmost priority and it should mainly stress on nutritional education, benefits of immunization, family planning etc.

Physical Empowerment: Women in the Third World Countries perform their dual role in the field as well as take care of their children and homes. Until and unless we recognize their physical hardships endured by women while meeting their productive and reproductive responsibilities and make noble efforts to improve upon their health status, other advancement will have limited impact for them. Thus, physical empowerment is very much dependent on other dimensions.

Psychological Empowerment: It is believed that women in Third World countries undermined their own position and their economic contribution in the family. Due to cultural view of the low position of women in many societies, the women themselves often have a negative attitude towards their potentials and importance.

Technological Empowerment: Though most of the women in the Third World countries are involved in almost all farming operation, still they have inadequate technical competency due to their limited exposure to outside world. They are compelled to use age old technologies. Appropriate technology can empower women by giving them additional time and energy for greater and more efficient participation in other economic and social activities.

Empowerment Incorporated: Government Plans and Programmes

Since independence, the Government of India's policy on women's development has undertaken various shifts of emphasis. Empowerment of women has consistently been one of the major objectives of Indian policy. Time and again, the policies and programmes need to address abject poverty of deprived women. The journey of Five Year Plan get rolling with nominal welfaristic programmes to more definite right based approach with some kind of true development. India has embarked upon a series of Five Year Plans, each containing some kind of poverty eradication and social justice component or the other. In the 1980s, the problem of poverty, particularly the rural one, was brought into sharper focus. Both the Sixth and Seventh Plans emphasized growth and social justice, with special focus on women's empowerment. The purpose of women's empowerment is to enable them to gain access to decision making process through capacity building, so as to cope with the requirement of life more efficiently. The period since then has witnessed greater employment generation through the diversion of investments into sectors and sub-sectors with a higher employment potential. It is widely recognized that empowerment of women not only helps them to improve their living conditions, but also contributes to the upliftment of the family as a whole. To achieve greater gender equality, it is indispensible to meet the gender needs, which comprise broader economic, social and political aspects, like division of labour, equal wages and legal rights, besides political issues of gender right and relations. This would help them to promote economic growth, alleviate poverty and improve health. Targeted gender expenditure has been strongly recommended for the purpose, in the wake of feminization of poverty the world-over.

National Policy makers have obviously been playing outstanding role for the development of women while formulating five year plans. An overview can be drawn regarding the emphasis given in each plan period to improve overall status of women as per following sequence.

The concept of women's development in the First Five Year Plan (1951-56) was mainly welfare oriented. The Central Social Welfare Board (CSWB) was set up in 1953, undertook a number of welfare measures through the voluntary sector. In the Second Five Year Plan (1956-1961) women were organized into Mahila Mandals to act as focal points at the grassroots level for the development of women. The Third, Fourth and other interim Plans (1961-1974) accorded high priority to education of women.

Measures to improve maternal and child health services, supplementary feeding for children and nursing and expectant mothers were a shift in the approach for women's development from "welfare to development". The new approach aimed at an integration of welfare with development services. The Sixth Plan (1980-85) was a landmark in the history of women's development as it received recognition as one of the developmental sectors and was included in the Sixth Plan Document as a separate chapter for the first time in the history of developmental planning. The Sixth Plan adopted a multi-disciplinary approach with a three pronged thrust on health, education and employment. In the Seventh Plan (1985-1990), the developmental programmes for women continued with the major objectives of raising their economic and social status and to bring them into the mainstreaming of national development. A significant step in this direction was to promote the *'beneficiary–oriented-programmes'* for women in different developmental sectors which was launched in 1992, promises to ensure that the benefits of development from different sectors do not bypass women and special programmes will be implemented to complement the general development programmes. Therefore, the flow of benefits to women in three core sectors of education, health and employment will be monitored with a greater vigil. Women must be enabled to function as equal partners and participants in the developmental process. The approach to the Eighth Plan marks a further shift from *'developmental'* to *'empowerment'* of women. In order to meet both the increasing and challenging needs of women and children, there has been a progressive increase in the plan outlays over the period of last four developmental decades. The outlay of Rs. 4 crore in the First Plan (1951-1956) has gone up to Rs. 2000 crore in the Eight Plan (1992-1997).

However, 'Empowerment of Women' is considered as an agents of socio-economic change and development became specific objectives of the Ninth Plan (1997-2002). The Plan envisaged primarily to ensure that benefits flow to women from all the general developmental sectors and emphasized on (a) reservation of not less than 1/3rd seats for women in the Parliament and State Legislative Assembly; (b) organizing women self help groups as a major process of empowering women. Some special initiatives were taken during Ninth Plan including launching of an externally aided scheme **Swashakti (1998)** for socio-economic empowerment of women through self-reliant self help group institutions; **Stree Shakti Puraskars (1999)**; adoption of **National Policy for Empowerment of Women (2001)**; celebration of the year 2001 as *Swayamsidha*; launching of **Swadhar (2001)** to extend rehabilitation services for women in difficult circumstances.

Besides that the National Policy on Women 2001, which informed the Tenth Five Year Plan, articulated a service of goals towards women's empowerment. The objectives of the policy include creating an environment through positive economic and social policies for development of women to enable them to realize their full potential, and equal access to participation and decision making of women in social, political and economic life of the nation.

The true empowerment has come with the beginning of Eleventh Plan because it is one of the majestic plans enunciated by the Planning Commission (now it is called NITI AYOG) to empower the poor women. In the Eleventh Plan (2007-12) has focused the many-fold strategies, i.e. (a) economic, social and political empowerment of women with the perspective of globalization; (b) strengthening mechanism for effective implementation of women related legislations; and (c) creating institutional mechanism for gender mainstreaming and strengthening delivery mechanism for effective implementation of women related programmes (Deepali Singh & Nafees A. Ansari, 2008). The Twelfth Five Year Plan (2012-2017) also reiterated the same policies regarding women's emancipation and empowerment.

Various progressive efforts were made in each plan period during last four decades to meet the needs of the women as it has been presented above. There is no denial to state that macro-level planners, policy makers and legislatures have made quite remarkable approaches to empower the women while drafting different plans.

Moreover, the Government of India has ratified several Conventions of the United Nations relating to women's rights. In accordance with prevailing social and economic milieu, India has recorded certain reservations in the course of the ratification of the Convention. Followings are the highlights of different Conventions, Summits, and Conferences organized for women empowerment.

Convention	*Date*	*Special Thrust Areas*
Convention on the Suppression of the Trafficking persons and the exploitation of the prostitution of others.	January 9, 1953	Protection of women from trafficking and from exploitation of any form against them.
Convention on Political Participation of Women.	November 1, 1961	Declaration of rights of women regarding recruitment to, and conditions of services in any of the armed forces of India charged with the maintenance of public order in India.
Women's Information Network for Asia and the Pacific, Japan.	December 1-6, 1986	Emphasis is specially given on information dissemination for the women throughout the country and abroad.
Convention on the Elimination on all forms of discrimination against women.	July 9, 1993	Emphasis was given on elimination of all forms of discrimination against women.

Obviously, all these efforts may claim for a greater implication since adoption of the same at the international level. It is true that many changes have occurred in the traditional conception of the role and status of women through new opportunities for education and employment, emergence of new socio-economic pattern, and privileges of equal legal and political rights. Women in some cases are observed to compete equally with men on an equal footing and have entered into occupations, which were considered as the domain of men.

The Government's continued advocacy for equitable growth opportunities for women is increasingly being reflected in state government policies and plans. These have resulted in:

(a) Increasing participation by women in local government and decision making processes.
(b) An increasing focus of poverty alleviation programmes for women; a mandate to eliminate discrimination

against girl children and adolescents in matter of food, health, education and child labour.

(c) Greater spread of community based organizations, including women's group.

(d) Recognition of the need to sensitize all levels of bureaucracy, legislators and law enforcement agencies to gender issues.

(e) More recently, the promotion of income generation activities, and thrift and credit of Self Help Groups for women.

Concept of Self Help Group (SHG): SHG is a homogeneous group of 10-12 poor women. This group is a voluntary one, formed on areas of common interest so that they can think about recognize and operate for their development. SHGs function on the basis of co-operative principle and provide a forum for members to extend support to each other. It is considered as a means of empowerment. SHGs organize very poor people who do not have access to financial system in the organized sector. In groups, normally transparency and accountability are lacking. However, in a group like SHG, they are ensured through collective action of the members. These help to mobilize the poor people specially women to form groups for mutual benefits. SHGs play a crucial role in improving the savings and credit and also in reducing poverty and social inequalities.

Objectives Behind Forming SHGs

- To encourage their active participation in various developmental progranmes to achieve surest result.
- To train them to book keeping, viz. Resolution Book, Ledger Book and Cash Book.
- To impact capacity building programmes and create capacity strength and stability to undertake various income generation programmes.
- To create awareness about various affairs relating to their socio-economic, health, culture, political and legal rights.
- To encourage women or homogeneous people to form groups to have common platform for sharing their issues or views on their common concern.

- To stand firmly against the malpractice, i.e. child labour, child marriage, dowry, untouchability and other forms of superstitions.
- To promote their ethnic knowledge attaching with modern scientific knowledge to make richer in the field of information, health, culture, environment, economic and societal.
- To inculcate credit and saving habits among the members of the group to create common fund through weekly, fortnight or monthly small savings for their future task.
- To establish harmonious relation among Bank, Panchyat, Block, Zilla Parishad, Police Station and all these resource providing agencies which may help their development.

Characteristics of SHGs

- Decision taken once shall be treated final.
- After inter-loaning the group can apply for loan for their project.
- Documentation and book keeping be done on the day of the meeting after finishing it.
- Members can avail credit facility after regular savings for a period of six months.
- Only one member from one family can register herself as a member of the group.
- Registration of new member shall be possible after repaying gross amount like other members paying.
- Leader's term must be fixed up to 2 years, after that a new leader from the group member must be appointed.
- They should have cooperative and collaborative attitude among themselves.
- They should have similar ideology and common interest.
- Every group is recognized by its name and place of operation.
- Every group member should have clear concept of their group's vision and mission.
- Group must be transparent and each member should be accountable towards group activity.
- Each member should meet with one another with an agenda at least in a week at a common place.

Salient Features of SHGs

The SHGs have special features with **cooperative philosophy** which are discussed below:

Homogeneous membership: As far as possible, the membership of an SHG may comprise people from comparable socio-economic background, same sex and same area.

No discrimination: There should not be any discrimination among members based on caste, religion or political affiliation and education.

Small membership : Ideally, the group size may be between 10-12 so that the members are participative in all activities of SHG. In smaller group the members feel comfortable and get opportunity to speak openly and freely. Too small group means less transaction of money which is not significant to fulfil the objectives of a group and too big means less cohesiveness among the members and ultimately the group will break up.

Attendance: Full and active participation in regular group meeting lends strength to the effectiveness of SHGs. To achieve this SHG should be strong enough to regular attendance of group meeting. If any member willingly does not attend 2 to 3 consecutive meetings then SHG can impose fine on her.

Thrift: The habit of thrift is a fundamental to the SHG and helps in building up a common fund.

Set of Byelaws: Either bank or self help promoting institutions guide SHGs to formulate the byelaws. Even SHGs themselves can formulate set of byelaws. The SHG may discuss and finalize a set of byelaws, indicating rules and regulations, for the SHG's functioning and also roles and responsibilities of members. It is better to have a written set of byelaws.

Transparency in functioning: It is very important that all financial and non-financial transactions must be transparent in an SHG. Maintenance of account books, resolution book, minute's book, attendance registrar etc. is important. These promote trust, cohesiveness, mutual faith and confidence among the members.

Utilizing savings for loaning: Once a group has accumulated sizeable amount in the form of saving for a period of about 6 months, the members may be allowed to avail loan against their own savings (i.e. interlending or interloaning) for emergent consumption and supplements income generation credit needs.

Strategic Model for Effective Functioning of SHGs

Regular savings: Each member saves Rs. 10 to Rs. 20 as monthly savings. Besides, that group can save lumpsum amount during harvesting of crops and vegetables to increase their common fund.

Interlending/Interloaning: After regular savings up to six months, the SHG members can apply for interlending from their common fund to undertake different types of petty trade. The group leader will decide to whom this loan will be given after discussion with group members. For interlending a nominal interest rate has been fixed around 2 per cent to 5 per cent per month to increase their common fund as well as be able to refund the loan with interest in time.

Bank loan: After observing the satisfactory performance of the group members the commercial bank or regional rural bank can offer 4 to 5 times loan against their actual saving, and this loan must be refunded with interest in a stipulated time period after mobilizing it in any profitable income generation activities.

Income generation activities and community development: After receiving loan from the bank the group members can start income generation activities which gives them some confidence of running their individual enterprise or they can start joint venture like collective marketing, paddy purchasing and selling, poultry farming, nursery etc.. After getting security of their own and his family members the SHG members can concentrate on village development programmes like road construction, village cleaning, health camp, sanitation etc.

Promotion of literacy among members: In order to make SHG more effective in functioning there is a need of all members understanding of basic literacy. SHGs operating more or less like bank, so literacy can help in transparency in financial and non-financial activities and make members accountable to achieve the goal.

Proper organization and management of group: In order to improve the organization and management of SHG, there is effective training is needed both for leaders and members of the group. The training must be focused on account maintaining, minutes writing, attendance register maintaining and roles and responsibilities of leader and members of group functioning.

Leadership development: In order to maintain transparency, accountability and confidence there must be needed to rotate leadership roles among potential members. It also helps to share of work and responsibility. So, training to potential leaders must be imparted with focus on developing leadership skills, group dynamics and handling group conflicts.

Regular updated information: Holistic approach of empowerment of women is only possible after incorporating technological interventions. These are social, political, economic, health and hygiene, nutritional, child care and environmental sanitation etc. Effective information would help women to impose their personal and social life.

Social mobilization: The group must show their existence and presence felt by the villagers by taking up some activities that would promote social mobilization and development of their village. For this, taking up some burning issues on health problem (i.e. HIV/AIDS), effective implementation of MGNREGA, prevention of domestic violence, raised a voice against political injustice and social injustice, insure effective utilization of social insurance, social assistance and social security for the poor and marginalized section.

Organizational linkages: In order to develop SHG as a strong platform at village level there is a need of all types of linkages between SHGs and Resource Delivery Agencies. Active and effective linkages would always ensure SHGs to get proper remedy in a shorter time span.

Emerging concept of Microfinance: Before 1990s, credit schemes for women were almost negligible. There are certain misconception about the poor people that they need loans at stabilized rates of interest on short term, they lack skill, capacity to save, credit worthiness and so in India. Financial Institutions have been serving loans to the need of the commercial sector and providing loan to the middle and upper income groups because of the following risks—(i) high transactions and serving cost; (ii) absence of land tenure for financing housing; (iii) lack of tangible proofs for assessment of income; and (iv) unacceptable collateral such as crops, utensils and jewellery. In India, we have multi-agency rural credit delivery structure comprising Commercial Banks, Regional Rural Banks and Cooperative Banks with a large network of more than 1,53,000 retail credit outlets (one for every 4100 population). Yet reaching the poorest whose credit requirement are very small frequent and unpredictable, is still a difficult task and the rural non-formal money lenders continues to be the main agency. Further, the system and lengthy procedure of the banking institution with emphasis on complicated qualifying requirements, tangible collateral etc. also keep them away from these formal agencies.

Banks too experienced certain problems, like poor repayment, lack of supervision and monitoring, high proportion of non-performing assets, and poor repayment. Since the credit requirement of the rural poor cannot be adopted on project lending approach then emerged the need for an informal credit supply through formation of self help groups. In this case group formed by poor people specially women by themselves is the only and foremost option to improve their living standard. And towards these activities certain steps have been taken up like promotion of saving generation to build up the resource of the programme and implementation of a saving led credit programmes to address the various financial requirement of women intermediation is required for:

- Organizing rural poor women,
- Educating them, and
- Imparting training and skill for capacity building.

The informal financial sources generally include funds available from family sources or local money lenders. The local money lender charges exorbitant rates of interest due to their informal behaviour and absence of any other source of credit for non-conventional needs (N. Lalitha, and B.S. Nagarajan; 2002).

In this crucial juncture where commercial bank did not allow poor and disadvantaged people to provide loan for entrepreneurship development whereas Dr. Mohammad Yunus helped the poor and marginalized by providing petty cash for income generation purpose. His noble efforts turn into huge success through creation of Self Help Group. At international level Dr. Yunus of Chittagong University popularized the informal systems of financing by establishing Grameen Bank (GB) in the year 1976. He wanted to encourage landless marginalized women to undertake petty trade with little loan given from his own pocket at the initial stage. This effort was turned into an effort of grand success with its innovative approach to motivate the poor and disadvantaged women to inculcate banking habits through small savings and credit activities, which at present attained a global campaign as "Bangladesh Grameen Bank". The Grameen Bank lending system is simple but effective. To obtain loan, potential borrowers must form a group of five; gather once in a week for loan repayment meeting and to start with learning the bend rules and **'16 Decisions'** which they chant at the start of their weekly meeting session although these are not mandatory. The decisions are:

1. We shall follow and advance the principles of Grameen Bank: Discipline, Unity, Courage and Hard Work in all walks of our lives.
2. Prosperity we shall bring to our family.
3. We shall not live in dilapidated houses. We shall repair our houses and work towards constructing new house at the earliest.
4. We shall grow vegetables all the year round. We shall eat plenty of them and sell the surplus. During the plantation session we shall plant as many seedlings as possible.
5. We shall not practice any child marriage.
6. We shall keep our centre free from the curse of dowry.
7. We shall not inflict any injustice on anyone; neither shall we allow anyone to do so.
8. We shall always keep our children and the environment clean.
9. We shall build and use pit latrines.
10. We shall take part in all social activities collectively.
11. We shall collectively undertake bigger investment for higher incomes.
12. We shall plan to keep our family small. We shall minimize our expenditures. We shall look after our health.
13. We shall drink water from tube well. If it is not available, we shall boil water or use alum.
14. We shall educate our children and ensure that they can earn to pay for their education.
15. We shall not take any dowry on our sons' wedding; neither shall we give any dowry at our daughters' wedding.
16. We shall always be ready to help each other. If anyone is

in difficulty, we shall all help him/her. If we come to know if any breach of discipline in any centre, we shall all go there and help restore discipline.

In Indian context NABARD's pilot scheme, microfinance was launched to bridge the gap between demand and supply of funds in the lower rungs of rural economy. The initiative was taken to develop a supplementary credit delivery mechanism. Microfinance is meant to cure the illness of rural poverty. With this, the concept, viz. self-reliance, self-sufficiency and self-help gained momentum. The Indian microfinance scene is dominated by self help groups and their linkages to banks. The Indian development is unique for its use if formal institutions in providing finance to SHGs, instead of creating parallel non-formal channel of routing finance to poor. Credit delivery through thrift and credit (SHGs) emerging as an alternative to the existing system of credit disbursement by the banks.

We are aware that the Government of India has already been implementing microfinance programme by creating an autonomous body called **"Rastriya Mahila Kosh"** under the Ministry of Women and Child Development. The institution has been formed to promote economic status of women through self help groups.

Micro-credit—The Concept

Micro credit itself is a self-explanatory word that means the extension of very small loan (micro loan) to the unemployed poor entrepreneurs and to others living in poverty that is not bankable. These individuals lack collateral, steady employment and verifiable credit history and so cannot meet even the most minimum qualification to gain access to traditional credit. Micro credits are a part of microfinance, which is the provision of financial services to the very poor, apart from loan, it includes savings, micro insurance and other financial innovations which organized in developing countries where it has successfully enabled improvised people mostly women to work independently and set up projects that allow them to generate an income and in many cases begin to build wealth and exit poverty.

Micro credit has given women in India an opportunity to

become agents of change. Poor women, who are in the forefront of the micro credit movement in the country, use small loan to jumpstart a long chain of economic activity, keeping in view the immense potential inherent in SHGs in saving mobilization and credit multiplication, banks are shedding their age old reluctance to lend the poor and are considering micro credit as one of their important marketing avenues thereby facilitating to create a new market of micro credit. Thus, it has now become a global initiative and is considered as an important agenda of MDG set by the United Nations. The importance of micro credit led the world to announce the year **2005** as the "International Year on Micro Credit" to access and promote the contribution of micro credit towards achieving the MDG (Millennium Development Goal). The overall objective of MDG is to reduce the proportion of the people living in extreme poverty to half of 1990 by 2015 (CGAP Report, 2002).

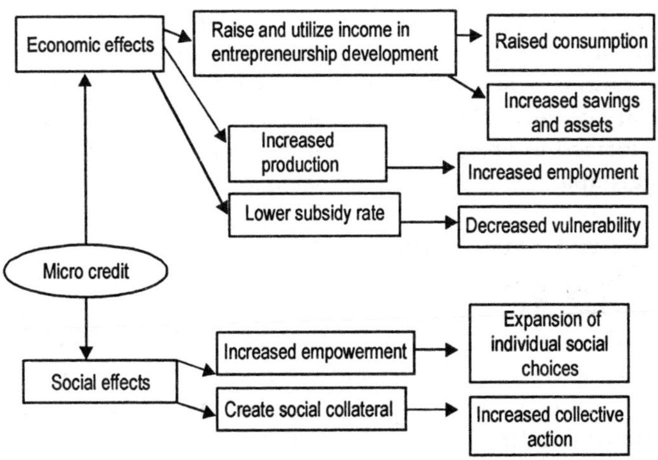

Diagram 1.1: Diagram Showing the Effects of Micro Credit

Micro credit has two types of effects on the members of the SHG, where it gives economic effects in one side and social effects on the other. While the micro credit system is economic in its basic structure, it is not limited to it in its various effects. Its economic aims as described in the figure above are as follows: subsequent to receiving credit, the income is utilized in entrepreneurial well-being and higher income leading to a rise in consumption level, increased savings and assets. More production leads to a better quotient of employment. Besides that it also helps to decrease vulnerability of the SHGs by a lowering of subsidies because it has been noticed that the SHGs tend to become non-functional after they receive subsidies—whereas the SHGs who are not receiving subsidies are not prone to such vulnerabilities.

It is also an evident shown in the figure that social effects go beyond these aims: increased empowerment of the members lead to an expansion of individual social choices (i.e. greater control over commodity bundles and life choices) which may range from a decision to stabilize the number of family members, decision to participate in community affairs. On the other hand social effects also create collateral, viz. respect, trust, we-feeling, active involvement etc. by which SHG members are able to increase collective action.

Emerging Problems, Issues and Gaps

After intensive study of the several research papers on SHG, Microfinance and Women Empowerment, few gaps were identified which need to be addressed for the sake of better understanding of the intended work. The major gap lies in the political manoeuvring with the SHGs which isolate poor women from development process. Large number of SHGs are mushrooming on a daily basis with the consent of panchayat; bank and NGOs are reluctant to clarify the proper cause of forming SHGs. This malpractice is not only providing good business to the bank and NGOs but as the member of SHGs who could be turned into vote. If we go deeper and deeper we will get maximum poor women do not have proper concept of SHG. There is a misconception that SHGs are formulated for getting loan only. The moment they failed to get loan from the bank, the process of dysfunction starts among the members.

It is quite natural phenomenon for NGO field staff to work first with the 'easiest' potential members those who do not need much persuasion. It is evident that the poorest among the poor are 'excluded' from the group or lead to 'self-exclusion', if not excluded by group members or by NGO people, because of financial hardship. Though several developmental schemes and programmes are formulated to mainstreaming the deprived women to bring positive change, but misuse of funds and nepotism prevent the poor women in empowering process which need to be studied carefully.

SHGs seem uniquely placed to support their members on issues of social justice affecting women. Nevertheless, sometimes it is not found that SHGs are dealing regularly with issues of social justice. Nor did many groups report such actions had taken up issues such as domestic and sexual violence, bigamy, and a few cases of dowry death, prevention of child marriage, support for separated women to remarry.

Women in SHGs can work together to address issues that affect not only their own members, but others in the large community. These were all actions by SHG women which represented some degree of agency by women, in terms of decision-making and enhancing women's contribution to community in a way that goes beyond traditional gender roles. Some activities which are not included, such as cleaning the village before village functions—which community leaders increasingly find SHGs useful. Nor have we included general participation in campaigns or rallies—pulse polio, literacy, anti-dowry, for example—for which SHGs are becoming a means of mobilizing women. The mobilization of numbers of women through village or cluster networks, or federations, was a significant feature of effective community action.

Community actions involve a new boldness and confidence for women; often involving putting pressure on the authorities (panchayat, district officers, police) to do their job, whether through petitions or by staging rallies and blockades; and varying degrees of skill in negotiation by SHG leaders.

Put in brief, if we want to have a quick recapitulation then it is possible to proceed in the following itemized way. It is astonishing to note that such an important paradigm as social justice has been neglected as an issue by the SHGs; SHGs are being politicized because they are good platforms for political mobilization; there is very rare instance that SHGs raised that voice against social injustice and SHGs are not accustomed in community mobilization for community development. This could be described as the most basic problem which not yet been addressed by the growing literature on SHGs for women empowerment. The study undertaken tries to address itself to this basic concern. This is also to acknowledge that the other aforesaid problem only could be resolved when these basic questions are answered.

Objectives of the Study

1. To study the formation of SHG and its performance in capacity building among group member to gain self-confidence in the society.
2. To evaluate the impact of small savings and credit facility of micro-finance through SHG.
3. To assess the changes in social, psychological and physical condition in women leading to empowerment due to their association with SHG.
4. To assess the decision making process in domestic, conjugal and social life.
5. To assess the knowledge and awareness level in participation and involvement in rural development activities, politics, capacity building programmes, income generation programmes

Significance and Scope of the Study

Self Help Groups give women a major platform for addressing issues related to income generation activities through microfinance, peace building, and decision making in family matters, social and cultural activities which lead to empowerment. Empowerment helps the women to develop community through full and active participation and mutual relationship in consonance with government and non-government organizations who are trying to bring women to the mainstream of development since long ago. It is seen that women participation in all spheres of life depends on their social, cultural and economic factors. Since women constitute a large section of workforce in the country, so poverty alleviation of women cannot be achieved without full participation of women in all spheres of community development. The Government of India has implemented microfinance programmes in different segments of society, this is because, Microfinance plays a vital role in women empowerment. Microfinance institutions (MYRADA, NABARD) provide small credit to the women for income generation activities.

The major significance of the study is if the study has been able to establish the sustainability of the SHG through microfinance as the most important operational mode—where SHGs are change agents of vast social, psychological and economic aspects of women empowerment, a lot of confusion would be dispelled. Given the fact that lots of organized efforts both from Government and Non-government sectors across the country have been invested over a period of time to promote SHG, Microfinance and Women Empowerment, it is important that the sustainability of SHGs through a significant operational mode among other modes is emphasized. Further studies might deeply inquire into the following questions: why is it that other operational mode (other than micro-finance) have not accrued sustainability to SHGs? Could it be the case that if SHGs do not persist, they do not lead to women's empowerment or led only partially? Such questions have to be explored in a full manner.

The scope of the study could be delimited within the sphere of "Research and Development" in the subject matter of "Self Help Group and Microfinance for Women Empowerment". The study first of all is well inscribed within the social work discourse and the discourse of self-empowerment. The research universe and the domain of population chosen is women and therefore, the study is closely linked to questions of women's issues and will, therefore, purportedly, contribute to women's studies. The study, in its engagement, will touch upon the following aspects: the policies and programmes of government and the ambit of government *vis-à-vis* voluntary self help groups will intrude into the study; the huge discourse of self help voluntarism and the growing literature on self help groups will be included and revised in the study; operational modes including our central concern—microfinance will form our thematic core. Empowerment and empowerment of women will remain our persistent boundary.

The study may help the future investigators to continue further investigation in this area. The findings of the study may influence the Government, NGOs and Stakeholders for formulating policies and programmes aiming at upliftment of women status and their reorganization in the society.

The study may help the members of SHGs to identify their problems and develop a mechanism like identify effective skill development training and exposure visit of the SHG members to nearby active SHG village is needed for development of women SHG members.

The study may prove to be a good and specific review of the status of the SHG members and understand the effectiveness of SHG as an excellent platform towards empowerment.

The findings of the study may fulfil few gaps on self help group, microfinance and women empowerment which are unanswered earlier and help the future researchers to collect valuable information out of it.

2

Feminism

A Tribute to Women Empowerment

Defining Feminism

Imagine you get a new job. On the first day of work, you are getting a tour of the office building, and you notice something strange: only men work here; you wonder where the women are? and you ask your new boss. He looks surprised at the question and says, 'What are you, some kind of feminist?' If this happened to you, what would you think? Would you be offended by the implication that you are feminist? What exactly is feminism, anyway?

First, let's define feminism in general. The global idea of feminism refers to the belief that men and women deserve equality in all opportunities, treatment, respect, and social rights. In general, feminists are people who try to acknowledge social inequality based on gender and stop from continuing. Feminists point out that in most cultures throughout history men have received more opportunities than women.

While this basic idea of feminism simple enough, there are many people who misunderstand what the goal of feminism is. Some people imagine that all feminists are angry, bitter women who only want to subjugate men; of course, this stereotype offends actual feminists. Why is there such a big difference between stereotype and reality when it comes to feminists? One of the reasons for this discrepancy might be because there are, in fact, lots of different, specific types of feminism in the literature.

Types of Feminism

Liberal feminism: This is the variety of feminism that works within the structure of mainstream society to integrate women into the structure. Its roots stretch back to the social contract theory of government instituted by the American Revolution. Abigail Adams and Mary Wollstonecraft were there from the start, proposing equality for women. As is often the case with liberals, they slog along inside the system, getting little done amongst the compromises until some radical movement shows up and pulls those compromises left of centre. This is how it operated in the days of the suffragist movement and again with the emergence of the radical feminists.

Radical feminism: Radical feminism is a movement that believes sexism is so deeply rooted in society that the only cure is to eliminate the concept of gender completely. How this would be possible? Radical feminists suggest changes, such as finding technology that will allow babies to be grown outside of a woman's body, to promote more equality between men and women. This will allow women to avoid missing work for maternity leave, which radical feminists argue is one reason women are not promoted as quickly as men. In fact, radical feminists would argue that the entire traditional family system is sexist. Men are expected to work outside the home while women are expected to care for children and clean the house. Radical feminists note that this traditional dichotomy maintains men as economically in power over women, and therefore, the traditional family structure should be rejected.

Socialist feminism: Socialist feminism calls for an end to capitalism. It is slightly less extreme but still calls for major social change. Socialist feminism is a movement that calls for an end to capitalism through a socialist reformation of country's economy. Basically, socialist feminism argues that capitalism strengthens and supports the sexist *status quo* because men are the ones who currently have power and money. Those men are more willing to share their power and money with other men, which mean that women are continually given fewer opportunities and resources. This keeps women under the control of men.

In short, socialist feminism focuses on economics and politics. They might point out the fact that in the United States women are typically paid only $0.70 for the exact same job that a man would be paid a dollar. Why are women paid less than men for the same work? Socialist feminists point out that this difference is based on a capitalist system.

Cultural feminism: Cultural feminism is a movement that points out how modern society is hurt by encouraging masculine behaviour, but society would benefit by encouraging feminine behaviour instead. Cultural feminism believes in encouraging feminine behaviour rather than masculine behaviour.

Let us think about a couple of examples of this idea. First, we need to identify what traditional masculine might be. These might be traits like being aggressive and competitive. So, how does modern society encourage people to be aggressive and competitive? We can see this in the business world for sure; people who own companies, are CEOs, and are successful in business are certainly likely to be aggressive, competitive people. This is also likely to be true in high-powered politicians, such as senators and presidents. While competition and aggression are useful in certain contexts, cultural feminists point out that by encouraging these behaviours, we are also encouraging the negative aspects of competition and aggression, such as suppression of feelings, crimes like assault and murder, and even social issues, such as domestic violence.

Marxist feminism: It is feminism focused on investigating and explaining the ways in which women are oppressed through systems of capitalism and private property. According to Marxist feminists, women's liberation can only be achieved through a radical restructuring of the current capitalist economy, in which, they contend, much of women's labour in uncompensated.

Theoretical background in Marxism: Influential work by Karl Marx and Engels (1848) in *The Communist Manifesto* and Marx (1859) in *A Contribution to the Critique of Political Economy* laid the foundation for some of the early discourse about the relationship between capitalism and oppression. The theory and method of study developed by Marx (1859), termed *historical materialism,* recognizes the ways in which economic systems structure society as a whole and influence everyday life and experience. Historical materialism places a heavy emphasis on the role of economic and technological factors in determining the base structure of society. The base structure prescribes a range of systems and institutions aimed to advance the interests of those in power, often at the cost of exploiting the working class. Marx (1859) argued that these systems are set by the ruling class in accordance with their need to maintain or increase class conflict in order to remain in power. However, Marx also acknowledged the potential for organization and collective action by the lower classes with the goal of empowering a new ruling class.

In 1884, Engels published *The Origin of the Family, Private Property, and the State*. According to him, the shift from *feudalism* to private ownership of land has had a huge effect on the status of women. In a private ownership system, individuals who do not own land or other *means of production* are in a situation that Engels (1848) compares to enslavement—they must work for the owners of the land in order to be able to live within the system of private ownership. Engels explained that the transition to this type of system resulted in the creation of separate public and private spheres and assigned access to waged labour disproportionately to men.

Engels (1848) argued that women's subordination was not a result of her biological disposition but of social relations, and that men's efforts to achieve their demands for control of women's labour and sexual faculties have gradually become institutionalized in the nuclear family. Through Marxist historical perspective, Engels analyzed the widespread social phenomena associated with female sexual mortality, such as fixation on virginity and sexual purity, incrimination and violent punishment of women who commit adultery, and demands that women be submissive to their husbands. Ultimately, Engels traced these phenomena to the recent development of exclusive control of private property by the patriarchs of the rising slave owner class in the ancient mode of production, and the attendant desire to ensure that their inheritance is passed only to their own offspring: chastity and fidelity are rewarded, says Engels, because they guarantee exclusive access to the sexual and reproductive faculty of women possessed by men from the property-owning class.

As such, gender oppression is closely related to class oppression and the relationship between men and women in society is similar to the relations between *proletariat* and *bourgeoisie*. On this account women's subordination is a function of class oppression, maintained because it serves the interests of capital and the ruling class.; it divides men against women, privileges working class men relatively within the capitalist system in order to secure their support; and legitimates the capitalist class's refusal to pay for the domestic labour assigned, unpaid, to women.

Productive and Reproductive Labour

In the capitalist system two types of labour exist. The first is *productive,* in which the labour results in goods or services that have monetary value in the capitalist system and are thus compensated by the producers in the form of a paid wage. The second form of labour is *reproductive,* which is associated with the private sphere and involves anything that people have to do for themselves that is not for the purpose of receiving a wage (i.e. cleaning, cooking, having children). Both forms of labour are necessary, but people have different access to these forms of labour based on certain aspects of their identity. Women are assigned to the domestic sphere where the labour is reproductive and thus uncompensated and unrecognized in a capitalist system. It is in the best interest of both public and private institutions to exploit the labour of women as an inexpensive method of supporting a work force. For the producers, this means higher profits. For the nuclear family, the power dynamics dictates that domestic work is exclusively to be completed by the woman of the household thus liberating the rest of the members from their own necessary reproductive labour. Marxist feminists argue that the exclusion of women from productive labour leads to male control in both public and private domains.

Accomplishments and Activism

The militant nature of Marxist feminists and their ability to mobilize to promote social change has enabled them to engage in important activism. Though their controversial advocacy often eceives criticism, Marxist feminists challenge capitalism in ways hat facilitate new discourse and shed light on the status of women. hese women throughout history have used a range of approaches n fighting hegemonic capitalism, which reflect their different iews on the optimal method of achieving liberation for women.

Wages for Housework

Focusing on exclusion from productive labour as the most important source of female oppression, some Marxist feminists devoted their activism to fighting for the inclusion of domestic work within the waged capitalist economy. The idea of creating compensated reproductive labour was present in the writing of socialist such as Charlotte Perkins Gilman (1898) who argued that women's oppression stemmed from being forced into private sphere. Gilman proposed that conditions for women would improve when their work was located, recognized and valued in the public sphere.

Perhaps the most influential of the efforts to compensate reproductive labour was the *International Wages for Housework Campaign*, an organization launched in Italy in 1972 by members of the *International Feminist Collective*. Many of these women published a range of sources to promote their message in academic and public domains. Despite the efforts, beginning with a relatively small group of women in Italy, the Wages for Housework Campaign was successful in mobilizing on a international level. A Wages for Housework Group was founded in Brooklyn, New York. As Heidi Hartmann acknowledges (1981), the efforts of these movements, though ultimately successful, generated important discourse regarding the value of housework and its relation to the economy.

Sharing the Responsibility of Reproductive Labour

Another solution proposed by Marxist feminists is to liberate from their forced connection to reproductive labour. In her critique of traditional Marxist feminist movements such as the Wages for Housework Campaign, Hartmann (1981) argues that these efforts take as their question the relationship of women to the economic system, rather than that of women to men, apparently assuming the latter will be explained in their discussion of the former. Hartmann (1981) believes that traditional discourse has ignored the importance of women's oppression as women, and instead focused on women's oppression as members of the capitalist system. Similarly, Gayle Rubin, who has written on a range of subjects including sadomasochism, prostitution, pornography, and lesbian literature as well as anthropological studies and histories of sexual sub-cultures, first rose to prominence through her 1975 essay *The Traffic in Women: Notes on the 'Political Economy of Sex*, in which she coins the phrase "sex/gender system" and criticizes Marxism for what she claims is its incomplete analysis of sexism under capitalism, without dismissing or dismantling Marxist fundamentals in the process.

More recently, many Marxist feminists have shifted their focus to the ways in which women are now potentially in worse conditions after gaining access to productive labour. Nancy Folbre (2010) proposes the feminist movements begin to focus on women's subordinate status to men both in the reproductive (private) sphere, as well as in the workplace (public sphere). In an interview in 2013, Silvia Federici urges feminist movements to consider the fact that many women are now forced into productive and reproductive labour, resulting in "double day". Federici argues that emancipation of women still cannot occur until they are free from their burdens of unwaged labour, which she proposes will involve institutional changes such as closing the wage gap and implementing child care programmes in the workplace. Federici's suggestions are echoed in a similar interview with Selma James (2012) and these issues have been touched upon in many floors.

Intersectionality and Marxist Feminism

With the emergence of Intersectionality as a widely popular theory of current feminism, Marxist feminists are broadening their focus to include persons that would be at an increased risk for exploitation in a capitalist system while also remaining critical of intersectionality theory for relying on bourgeois identity politics. The current organization Radical Women provides a clear example of successful incorporation of goals of Marxist feminism without overlooking identities that are more susceptible to exploitation. They contend that elimination of the capitalist profit-driven economy will remove the motivation for sexism, racism, homophobia, and other forms of oppression.

Feminist Movement in the Western World

Feminism in the West has been divided into three waves by

feminist scholars: first, second and third wave feminism. Recent (early 2010s) research suggests there may be a fourth wave characterized, in part, by new media platforms.

The women's movement became more popular in May 1968 when women began to read again, more widely, the book *'The Second Sex'*, written in 1949 by a defender of women's rights, Simone de Beauvoir, (and translated into English for the first time in 1953; later translation in 2009). Beauvoiur's writing explained why it was difficult for talented women to become successful. The obstacles De Beauvoir enumerates include women's inability to make as much money as men do in the same profession, women's domestic responsibilities, society's lack of support towards talented women, and women's fear that success will lead to an annoyed husband or prevent them from even finding a husband at all. De Beauvoir also argues that women lack ambition because of how they are raised. Girls are told to follow the duties of their mothers, whereas boys are told to exceed the accomplishments of their fathers. Along with other influences, Beauvoir's work helped the feminist movement to erupt, causing the formation of "The Women's Liberation Movement". This determined group of women wanted to turn these ideas into actions. Through actions the women were able to get few equal rights, for example right to education, right to work and right to vote. One of the most important issues that "The Liberation Movement" faced was banning of abortion and contraception. The women saw this banning as a violation of women's rights and were determined to fight it. Thus the women made a declaration known as "Le Manifests de 343" which held signatures from 343 women admitting to having had an illegal abortion. The declaration got published in *Le Nouvel Observateur and Le Monde*, two French newspapers on 5th April, 1971. The group gained support upon the publication. Women received the right to abort with the passing of the *Veil Law* in 1975.

The Women's movement affected change in Western society, including women's suffrage, the right to initiate divorce proceedings and "no fault" divorce, the right of women to make individual decisions regarding pregnancy (including access to contraceptives and abortion), and the right to own property. It has also let to broad employment for women at more equitable wages, and access to university education.

In 1918 Crystal Eastman wrote a article published in the *Birth Control Review*, she contended that birth control is a fundamental right for women and must be available as an alternative if they are to participate in the modern world. "In short, if feminism, conscious and bold and intelligent, leads the demand, it will be supported by the secret eagerness of all women to control the size of their families, and a suffrage state should make short work of repealing these old laws that stand in the way of birth control." She stated "I don't believe there is one woman within the confines of this state who does not believe in birth control."

The *United Nation Development Report 2004* estimated that when both paid employment and unpaid household tasks are accounted for, on average women work more than men. In rural areas of selected developing countries women performed an average of 20 per cent more work than men, or 120 per cent of men's total work, an additional 102 minutes per day. In the OECD countries *(Organization for Economic Co-operation and Development)* surveyed, on average women performed 5 per cent more work than men, or 105 per cent of men's total work, an additional 20 minutes per day. However, men did up to 19 minutes more work per day than women in five out of the 18 OECD countries surveyed: Canada, Denmark, Hungary, Israel and the Netherlands. According to UN women, "Women perform 66 per cent of the world's work, produce 50 per cent of the food, but earn 10 per cent of the income and own one per cent of the property.

The feminist movement's agenda includes acting as a counter to the putatively patriarchal stand in the dominant culture. While differing during the progression of waves, it is a movement that has sought to challenge the political structure, power holders, and cultural beliefs or practices.

Although antecedents to feminism may be found far back before the eighteenth century, the seeds of the modern feminist movement were planned during the last part of that century. Christine de Pizan, a late medieval writer, was possibly the earliest feminist in the Western tradition. She is believed to be the first woman to make a living out of writing. Feminist thought began to take a more substantial shape during the Enlightment with such thinkers as Lady Mary Wortley Montagu and the Marquis de Condorcet championing women's education. The first scientific society for women was founded in Middleburg, a city in the south of the Dutch Republic, in 1785. Journals for women that focused on issues like science became popular during this period as well.

The women who made the first efforts towards women's suffrage came from more stable and privileged backgrounds, and were able to dedicate and energy into making change. Initial developments for women, therefore, mainly benefited white women in the middle and upper classes.

Language

Feminists are sometimes, though not exclusively, proponents of using non-sexist language, using "Ms" to refer to both married and unmarried women, for example, or the ironic use of the term "herstory" instead of "history". Feminists are also often proponents of using gender—inclusive language, such as "humanity" instead of "mankind", or "he or she" in place of "he" where the gender is unknown.

Gender-neutral language is a description of language usages which is aimed at minimizing assumptions regarding the biological sex of human referents. The advocacy of gender-neutral language reflects, at least, two different agendas: one aims to clarify the inclusion of both sexes or genders (gender-inclusive language); the other proposes that gender, as a category, is rarely worth marking in language (gender-neutral language). Gender-neutral language is sometimes described as non-sexist language by advocates and politically correct language by opponents.

Not only has the movement come to change the language into gender neutral but the feminist movement has brought up how people use language. Emily Martin describes the concept of how metaphors are gendered and ingrained into everyday life. Metaphors are used in everyday language and have become a way that people describe the world. Martin explains that these metaphors structure how people think and in regard to science can shape what questions are being asked. If the right questions are not being asked then the answers are not going to be the right either. For example, the aggressive sperm and passive egg is a metaphor that felt 'natural' to people in history but scientists have re-examined this phenomenon they have come up with a new answer. "The sperm tries to pull its gateway act even on the egg itself, but is held down against its struggles by molecules on the surface of the egg that hook together with counterparts on the sperm's surface, fastening the sperm until the egg can absorb it" (Freedman, 1992). This is a goal in feminism to see these gendered metaphors and bring it to the public's attention. The outcome of looking at things in a new perspective can produce new information.

Heterosexual Relationships

The increased entry of women into the workplace beginning in the twentieth century has affected gender role and the division of labour within households. Sociologist Arlie Russell Hochschild (2001, 2003) in the Second Shift and The Time Blind presents evidence that in two career couples, men and women, on average spend about equal amount of time working, but women still spend more time on housework. Feminist writer Cathy Young (2000) responds to Hochschild's assertion by arguing that, in some cases, women may prevent the equal participation of men in housework and parenting. Economist Mark Aguiar and Erik Hurst (2007) calculate that amount of time spent on housework by women since 1960 has dropped considerably. Leisure of both men and women has risen significantly and by about the same amount for both sexes. Jermy Greenwood, Ananth Seshadri and Mehmet Yorukoglu (2005, 2015) argue that the introduction of modern appliances into the home has allowed women to enter the workforce.

Feminist criticism of men's contribution to child care and domestic labour in the Western middle class are typically centred on the idea that it is unfair for women to be expected to perform more than half of a household's domestic work and child care when both members of the relationship perform an equal share of work outside the home. Several studies provide statistical evidence that the financial income of married men does not affect their rate of attending to household duties.

In Dubiuos Conceptions by Kristin Luker (1996) discusses the effect of feminism on teenage women's choices to bear children, both in and out of wedlock. She says that as childbearing out of wedlock has become more socially acceptable, young women, especially poor young women while not bearing children at a higher rate than in the 1950s, now see less of a reason to get married before having a child. Her explanation for this is that the economic prospects for poor men are slim; hence poor women have a long chance of finding a husband who will be able to provide reliable financial support due to the rise of unemployment from more workers on the market, from just men to women and men.

Some studies have suggested that both men and women perceive feminism as being incompatible with romance. However, a recent survey of U.S. undergraduates and older adults found that feminism actually has a positive impact on relationship for women and sexual satisfaction for men, and found no support for negative stereotypes of feminists.

Virginia Satir (2014) said the need for relationship education emerged from shifting gender roles as women gained greater rights and freedoms during the twentieth century.

"As we moved into the twentieth century, we arrived with a very clearly prescribed way the males and females in marriage were to behave with one another. The pattern of the relationship between husband and wife was that of dominant male and submissive female. A new era has since dawned... the climate of relationship had changed, and women were no longer willing to be submissive. The end of the dominant/submissive model in relationships was in sight. However, there was very little that had developed to replace the old pattern; coupes floundered.... Retrospectively, one could have expected that there would be a lot of chaos and a lot of fall out. The change from the dominant/submissive model to one of equality is a monumental shift. We are learning how a relationship based on genuine feelings of equality can operate practically" (Satir, 2014).

Religion

Feminist theology is a movement that reconsiders the traditions, practices, scriptures, and theologies of religions from a feminist perspective. Some of the goals of feminist theology include increasing the role of women among the clergy and religious authorities, reinterpreting male-dominated imagery and language about God, determining the place of women in relation to career and motherhood, and studying images of women in the religion's sacred texts.

The feminist movement has affected religion and theology in profound ways. In liberal branches of Protestant Christianity, women are not allowed to be ordinate as clergy, and in Reform, Conservative and recontructionist Judaism, women are not allowed to be ordinate as rabbis and cantors. In some of these groups, some women are gradually obtaining position of power that were formerly only held by men, and their perspectives are now sought out in developing new statement of beliefs. These trends, however, have been resisted within most sects of Islam, Roman Catholicism, and Orthodox Christianity. Within Roman Catholicism, most women understand that through the dogma of the faith that they are to hold within the family a place of love and focus on the family and the need to rise above that does not necessarily constitute a woman to be considered less than but in fact equal to that of her husband who as well is called to be the Patriarch of the family and provide love and guidance to his family as well.

Christian feminism is a branch of feminist theology which seeks to reinterpret and understand Christianity in the light of the equality of women and men. While there is no standard set of beliefs among Christian feminists, most agree that God does not discriminate on the basis of biologically determined characteristics such as sex.

Early feminist such as Elizabeth Cady Stanton concentrated almost solely on "making women equal to men". However, the Christian feminist movement chooses to concentrate on the language of religion because they viewed the historic gendering of God as male as a result of the pervasive influence of patriarchy. Rosemary Radford Ruether (1983) provided a systematic critique of Christian theology from a feminist and their point of view. Stanton was an agonistic and Reuther is an agnostic who was born to Catholic parents but no longer practices the faith.

Women's Health

Historically there has been a need to study and contribute to the health and well-being of a woman that previously has been lacking. Londa Schiebinger (1999) suggested that the common biomedical model is no longer adequate and there is a need for a broader model to ensure that all aspects of a woman are being cared for.

Schiebinger described six contributions that must occur in order to have success—political movement, academic women studies, affirmative action, health equality act, geo-political forces and professional women not being afraid to talk openly about women issues.

Political movements come from the streets and are what the people as a whole want to see changed. An academic women study is the support from the universities in order to teach a subject that most people have never encountered. Affirmative action enacted is a legal change to acknowledge and do something for the times of neglect people were subjected to. Women's Health Equity Act legally enforces the idea that medicine needs to be tested in suitable standards such as including women in research studies also allocates a set amount of money to research diseases that are specific towards women. Geo-political forces can improve health, when the country is not at a sense of threat in war there is more funding and resources to focus on other needs, such as women's health. Lastly, professional women not being afraid to talk about women's issues moves women from entering into these jobs and preventing them for just acting as men and instead embracing their concerns for the health of women.

Feminist Movement in India

It is a set of movements aimed at defining, establishing, and defending equal political, economic, and social rights and equal opportunities for Indian women. It is the pursuits of women's rights within the society of India. Like their feminist counterparts all over the world, feminists in India seek gender equality: the right to work for equal wages, the right to equal access to health and education, and equal political rights. Indian feminists also have fought against culture-specific issues within India's patriarchal society, such as inheritance laws and the practice of widow immolation known as *Sati*.

The history of feminism in India can be divided into three phases:

1. The *first phase*, beginning in the mid-nineteenth century, initiated when male European colonists began to speak out against the social evils of *Sati*.
2. The *second phase*, from 1915 to Indian Independence, when

Gandhi incorporated women's Movement into the Quit India movement and independent women's organizations began to emerge.

3. The *third phase*, post-Independence, which has focused on fair treatment of women after marriage, in the work force and right to political party.

Despite the progress made by the Indian feminist movements, women living in modern India still face many issues of discrimination. India's patriarchal culture has made the process of gaining land-ownership rights and access to education challenging. In the past two decades, there has also emerged a disturbing trend of sex-selective abortion. To Indian feminists, there are seen as injustices worth struggling against.

As in the West, there has been some criticism of feminist movements in India. They have especially been criticized for focusing too much on women already privileged, and neglecting the needs and representation of poorer or lower caste women. This has led to the creation of caste/specific feminist organizations and movements.

Women's role in Pre-colonial social structures reveals that feminism was theorized differently in India than in the West. In India, women's issues first began to be addressed when the state commissioned a report on the status of women to a group of feminist researchers and activists. The report recognized the fact that in India, women were oppressed under a system of structural hierarchies and injustices. During this period, Indian feminists were influenced by the Western debates being conducted about violence against women. However, due to the difference in the historical and social culture of India, the debate in favour of Indian women had to be conducted creatively and certain Western ideas had to be rejected. Women's issues began to gain an international prominence when the decade of 1975-1985 was declared *the United Nations Decade for Women.*

Historical circumstances and values in India have caused feminists to develop a feminism that differs from Western feminism. For example, the idea of women as "powerful" is accommodated into patriarchal culture through religion, which has retained visibility in all sections of society. This has provide women with traditional "culture space". Furthermore, in the West the notion of "self" rests in competitive individualism where people are described as "born free yet everywhere in chains." In India the individual is usually considered to be just one part of the larger social collective. Survival of the individual is dependent upon cooperation, and self-denial for the greater good is valued.

Indian women negotiate survival through an array of oppressive patriarchal family structures: age, ordinal status, relationship to men through family of origin, marriage and procreation as well as patriarchal attributes. Examples of patriarchal attributes include dowry, desiring sons, kinship, caste, community, village, market and the state. It should however be noted that several communities in India, such as the Nairs of Kerala, Shettys of Mangalore, certain Maratha clans, and Bengali families exhibit matriarchal tendencies. In these communities, the head of the family is the oldest woman rather than the oldest man. Sikh culture is also regarded as relatively gender-neutral.

In India, communities recognized in the National Constitution as Scheduled Tribes, "some are matriarchal and matrilineal" and thus have been known to be more egalitarian. This is because though mothers are in forefront of most of the social activism, the society has always been patriarchal. Their women power is visible because of historical reasons. Manipur was ruled by strong dynasties and the need for expansions of borders, crushing any outsider threats, etc. engaged the men. So, woman had to take charge of home-front.

In Muslim families, women and men are considered equal, but not in the westernized sense. The Quran teaches that the minds of male and females work differently and are generally different biologically. Therefore, Islam grants different rights to the husband and wife. One such right which the wife owes to her husband is being head of the household.

The heterogeneity of the Indian experience reveals that there are multiple patriarchies, contributing to the existence of multiple feminisms. Hence, feminism in India is not a singular theoretical orientation; it has changed over time in relation to historical and cultural realities, levels of consciousness, perceptions and actions of individual women, and women as a group. The widely used definition is an awareness of women's oppression and exploitation in society, at work and within the family, and conscious action by women and men to change this situation. Acknowledging sexism in daily life and attempting to challenge and eliminate it through deconstructing mutually exclusive notions of femininity and masculinity as biologically determined categories opens the way towards equitable society for both men and women.

The male and female dichotomy of polar opposites with the former oppressing the latter at all times is refuted in the Indian context because it was men who initiated social reform movements against various social evils. Patriarchy is just one of the hierarchies. Relational hierarchies between women within the same family are more adverse. Here women are pitted against one another. Not all women are powerless at all times.

There have been intense debates within the Indian women's movements about the relationship between Western and Indian feminisms. Many Indian feminists simultaneously claim a specific "Indian" sensitivity as well as an international feminist solidarity with groups and individuals worldwide. The rise of liberal feminism in the West in the 1970s focused deeply on demands for equal opportunities in education and employment, as well as ending violence against women. To a large extent, the emerging feminist movement in India was influenced by Western ideals. These called for education and equal rights, but also adopted their appeals to local issues and concerns, such as dowry-related violence against women, *Sati*, sex selective abortion and custodial rape. Some Indian feminists have suggested that these issues are not specifically "Indian" in nature but rather a reflection of a wider trend of patriarchal oppression of women.

Unlike the Western feminist movement, India's movement was initiated by men, and later joined by women. The efforts of these men included abolishing *Sati*, which was a widow's death by burning on her husband's funeral pyre, abolishing the custom of child marriage, abolishing the disfiguring of widows, introducing the marriage of upper caste Hindu widows, promoting women's education, obtaining legal rights for women to own property, and requiring the law to acknowledge women's status by granting them basic rights in matters such as adoption.

The Nineteenth century was the period that saw a majority of women's issues came under the spotlight and reforms began to be made. Much of the early reforms for Indian women were conducted by men. However, by the late nineteenth century they were joined in their efforts by their wives, sisters, daughters, protégées and other individuals directly affected by campaigns such as those carried out for women's education. By the late Twentieth century, women gained greater autonomy through the formation of independent women's own organizations. By the late thirties and forties a new narrative began to be constructed regarding "women's activism". This was newly researched and expanded with the vision to create logical and organic links between feminism and Marxism, as well as with anti-communalism and anti-casteism etc. The Constitution of India did guarantee equality between the sexes, which created a relative lull in women's movement until the 1970s.

During the formative years of women's rights movement, the difference between the sexes was more or less taken for granted in their roles, functions, aims and desires were different. As a result, they were not only to be reared differently but treated differently also. Over the course of time, this difference itself became a major reason for initiating women's movement. Early Nineteenth century reformers argued that the difference between men and women was no reason for the subjection of women in society. However, later reformers were of the opinion that indeed it was this particular difference that subjugated women to their roles in society, for example, as mothers. Therefore, there was a need for the proper care of women's rights. With the formation of women's organizations and their own participation in the campaigns, their roles as mothers were again stressed but in a different light: this time the argument was for women's rights to speech, education and emancipation. However, the image of women with the mother as a symbol underwent change over time from an emphasis on family to the creation of a archetypical mother figure, evoking deep, atavistic images.

First phase: 1850-1915: Maharani Jind Kaur, the youngest wife of Maharaja Ranjit Singh, was renowned for her beauty, energy and strength of purpose. But her fame is derived chiefly from the fear she engendered in the British, who described her as *"the Messalina of the Punjab"*, a seductress, too rebellious to be controlled.

The colonial venture into modernity brought concepts of democracy, equality and individual rights. The rise of the concept of nationalism and introspection of discriminatory practices brought about social reform movements related to caste and gender relations. The first phase of feminism in India was initiated by men to uproot the social evils of *Sati*, widow remarriage, to forbid child marriage, and to reduce illiteracy, as well as to regulate the age of consent and to ensure property rights through legal intervention. In addition to this, some upper caste Hindu women rejected constraints they faced under Brahminical traditions. However, efforts for improving the status of women in Indian society were somewhat thwarted by the late Nineteenth century, as nationalist movements emerged in India. These movements resisted colonial interventions in gender relations particularly in the areas of family relations. In the mid of late nineteenth century, there was a national form of resistance to any colonial efforts made to modernize Hindu family. This included the age of Consent controversy that erupted after the government tried to raise the age of marriage for women.

Several Indian sates were ruled by women during British colonial advance including Jhansi (Rani Laxmibai), Kittur (Rani Chennama), Bhopal (Quidisa Begum), Punjab (Jind Kaur) etc.

Second phase: 1915-1947: During this period the struggle against colonial rule intensified. Nationalism became the pre-eminent cause. Claiming Indian superiority became the tool of cultural revivalism resulting in an essentialising model of Indian womanhood similar to that of Victorian womanhood: special yet separated from public space. Gandhi legitimized and expanded Indian women's public activities by initiating them into the non-violent civil disobedience movement against the British Rule. He exalted their feminine roles of caring, self-abnegation, sacrifice and tolerance; and carved a niche for those in the public arena. Peasant women played an important role in the rural *satyagrahas* of Borsad and Bardoli. Women-only organizations like All India Women's Conference (AIWC) and the National Federation of Indian Women (NFIW) emerged. Women were grappling with issues relating to the scope of women's political participation, women's franchise, communal awards, and leadership roles in political parties.

The 1920s was new era for Indian women and as defined as 'feminism' that was responsible for the creation of localized women's associations. These associations emphasized women's education issues, developed livelihood strategies for working/class women, and also organized national level women's associations such as the All India Women's Conference (AIWC). AIWC was closely affiliated with the Indian National Congress. Under the leadership of Mahatma Gandhi, it worked within the nationalist and anti-colonialist freedom movements. This made the mass mobilization of women an integral part of Indian nationalism. Women were, therefore, a very important part of various nationalist and anti-colonial efforts, including the civil disobedience movements in the 1930s.

After independence, the AIWC continued to operate and in 1954 the Indian Communist Party formed its own women's wing known as National Federation of Indian Women. However, feminist agendas and movements became less active right after India's 1947 independence, as the nationalist agendas on nation building took precedence over feminist issues.

Women's participation in the struggle for freedom developed their critical consciousness about their role and rights in independent India. This resulted in the introduction of the franchise and civic rights of women in the Constitution of India. There was provision for women's upliftment through affirmative action, maternal health and child care provision (crèche), equal pay for equal work etc. The state adopted a patronizing role towards women. For example, India's Constitution states that women are a "weaker section" of the population, and therefore, need assistance to function as equals. Thus women in India did not have to struggle for basic rights as did women in the West. The utopia ended soon when the social and cultural ideologies and structures failed to honour the newly acquired concepts of fundamental rights and democracy.

Third phase: Post 1947: Post-Independence feminists began to redefine the extent to which women were allowed to engage in the workforce. Prior to Independence, most feminists accepted the sexual divide within the labour force. However, feminists in the 1970s challenged the inequalities that had been established and fought to preserve them. These inequalities included unequal wages for women, relegation to women to 'unskilled' spheres of work, and restricting women as a reserve army for labour. In other words, the feminists' aim was to abolish the free service of women who were essentially being used as cheap capital. Feminist class-consciousness also came into focus in the 1970s, with feminists recognizing the inequalities not just between men and women but also within power structure such as caste, tribe, language, religion, region, class etc. This also posed as a challenge for feminists while shaping their overreaching campaigns as there had to be a focus within efforts to ensure that fulfilling the demands of one group would not create further inequalities for another. Now, in the early twenty first century, the focus of the Indian feminist movement has gone beyond treating women as useful members of society and a right to parity, but also having the power to decide the course of their personal lives and the right of self-determination.

In 1966 Indira Gandhi became the first female Prime Minister of India. She served as Prime Minister of India for three consecutive terms (1966-77) and a fourth term from 1980 until she was assassinated in 1984.

The state of Kerala is often viewed as the ideal progressive leader in the women's rights movement in India among states. Kerala maintains very high relative levels of female literacy and women's health, as well as greater female inheritance and property rights. For example, a 1998 study conducted by Bina Agarwal found that while only 13 per cent of all women in India with landowning fathers inherited that land as daughters, 24 per cent of such women were able to do so in the state of Kerala. This is important because it has been shown that measures to improve such access to property and economic independence through channels such as education not only directly improve women's well-being and capabilities, but also reduce their risk of exposure to marital or any other sort of domestic violence.

In 2014, an Indian family court in Mumbai ruled a husband objecting to his wife wearing a *kurta* and jeans and forcing her to wear a sari amounts to cruelty inflicted by the husband and can be a ground to seek divorce. The wife was thus granted a divorce on the ground of cruelty as defined under section 27(1)(d) of Special Marriage Act, 1954.

In 2016, a judgement of the Delhi High Court was made public in which it was ruled that the eldest female member of a Hindu Undivided Family can be its *"Karta"*.

3

Reflection on Available Literature

In the course of this work, one has to face new questions on every step that lead towards an end or new findings in a particular area. Thus the "Reflection on available literature" helps the researchers to establish a link between past research and the present work on the subject and also helps to present findings in a systematic and scientific manner. In the process of 'Review of literature' we are able to present an overview of past work, its finding and its relation to the context of the present study. This particular study emphasized on finding out the prospects of the women in the context of self help group and microfinance in Bolpur/Sriniketan Block of Birbhum District. In this study focus is given on how underprivileged women come forward for forming self help group and demanding loan for small entrepreneurship from formal and informal microfinance institution and ultimately empower themselves.

We have made an attempt to glance through the available literature in the sphere of self help group and microfinance for women empowerment in India within the conceptual framework of the study. The concept of women empowerment has been one of the major concerns of the state in the post independence era but the history and development of self help group as a tool towards economic empowerment of the women populace has its root lying experiments made by social scientists and activists over a period of last one decade. In this connection the researchers have tried to conceptualize and highlight the salient features of the trends and practices towards self help group and microfinance for women empowerment. Apart from these, an organized effort has been made by the researchers to have a glimpse on available and accessible literature related to self help group and microfinance for women empowerment. The review collected has been categorized under different heads:

Women Empowerment

Agarwal (1989); Roy and Tisdell (1996) were in the opinion that in both rural and urban areas, poor women relatively to men have limited access to information, about all aspects of paid work. This is mainly due to a lower literacy level, less access to mass media and less social interaction which put together towards projection of low level of empowerment within the household and community. The nature of empowerment can be diverse, depending upon the parameters that denote the lack of power within the institutional framework in operation.

Mohanty (1991) criticizes the underlying assumption of feminists in the Western World that women in the developing world have similar aspirations and empowerment needs. Such an interpretation, he suggests, does not take into account social relations and institutions.

Viswanath (1995) reported that overall empowerment of women in southern states of India when poor women have been organized under self help groups for economic development programme. He tried to bring positive correlation between self help group and microfinance where women empowering themselves with the process of getting loan from the Microfinance Institutions and used it for their development.

Carr *et al.* (2000) reported that few studies find no result in the empowerment level of women even after they are economically employed. Some studies in South Asia find that economic empowerment has been the entry point for overall empowerment of women if they are organized under a common platform. They also reported that SEWA (Self Employed Women Association) realized from their practical experience in the field of union strategy the necessity of undertaking income generation programme for bringing women under a common organization for their struggle in achieving overall social and economic goal.

Besides that A.K. Sen (1990) reported that women's access to appropriate education, which facilitates their empowerment process, is also greatly influenced by the same social customs of gender discrimination, which can be broadly termed as 'ideology of seclusion' or 'classic patriarchy'. Through this process women sometime segregate their offspring by giving extra importance to the male gender in every aspect.

Kabeer (2000), stressed that women's empowerment is about the process by which those who have been denied the ability to make strategic life choices acquire such ability. According to her, it is important to understand empowerment as a process and not an instrumentalist form of advocacy, which requires measurement and quantification of empowerment. Kabeer emphasizes that the ability to exercise choice incorporates three interrelated dimensions/resources (defined broadly to include not only access, but also future claims, to both material and human and social resources); agency (including processes of decision-making, as well as less measurable manifestations of agency such as negotiation, deception and manipulation) and achievements (well-being outcomes).

Kabeer further pointed out that it is resource and agency together that constitute what A.K. Sen (1985) refers to as capabilities: the potential that people have for living the lives they want, of achieving valued ways of 'being and doing' which are valued by people in a given context. 'Functioning' refers to all possible ways of 'being and doing' which are valued by people in a given context and of 'functioning achievements' to refer to the particular ways of being and doing which are realized by different individuals. If the failure to achieve valued ways of 'being and doing' can be traced to laziness, incompetence or individual preferences and priorities, then the issue of power is not relevant. It is only when the failure to achieve one's goals reflects some deep-seated constraint on the ability to choose that it can be taken as a manifestation of disempowerment. Another question that needs examination is whether empowerment is a universal concept irrespective of cultural and geographical location?

In India, women are not the only marginalized section of the society. The Scheduled Castes and Scheduled Tribes are still largely under-privileged in terms of wealth, education and access to basic services, in particular health services. Using the sociological analysis proposed by Andre Beteille (1999), India is the contradiction case of egalitarian political order and is a hierarchical social structure. Thus economic and social inequalities rooted in traditions and cultural norms need to be changed as political measures alone cannot bring empowerment. He points out that empowerment is invoked in the context of economic weakness and insecurity, particularly of marginalized, unorganized and other disadvantaged groups.

In contrast, Nussabaum (2000) refutes the argument from culture, diversity and paternalism to construct a universal framework to assess women's quality of life.

World Bank (2001) report conforms, societies that discriminate on the basis of gender pays the cost of greater poverty, slower economic growth, weaker governance and a lower living standard of their people. The World Bank also identifies four key elements of empowerment to draft institutional reforms: access to information; inclusion and participation; accountability; and local organizational capacity.

Malhotra *et al.* (2002) constructed a list of the most commonly used factors of women's empowerment, drawing from the frameworks developed by various authors in different fields of social sciences. After allowing for overlap, these frameworks suggest that women's empowerment needs to occur along multiple factors including: economic, socio-cultural, familial interpersonal, legal, political, and psychological. Since these factors cover a broad range of areas, women may be empowered within one of these sub-domains. They give the example of 'socio-cultural' factor which covers a range of empowerment sub-domains, from marriage system to norms regarding women's physical mobility, to non-familial social support systems and networks available to women. All these factors together responsible for women empowerment.

World Bank (2003) defines empowerment as "the process of increasing the capacity of individuals or groups to make choices and to transform those choices into desired actions and outcomes. Central to this process is actions which both build individual and collective assets, and improves the efficiency and fairness of the organizational and institutional context which govern the use of these assets."

Empowerment is all about the concepts of strengthening social capital and community driven developmental activities. According to Krishna (2003) empowerment means increasing the capacity of individuals or groups to make effective development and life choices and to transform these choices into desired actions and outcomes. It is by nature a process and/or outcome. Social capital, on the other hand, features social organization such as networks, norms and inter-personal trust that facilitate coordination and cooperation for mutual benefit. It is by nature a stock. And Community Driven Development (CDD) is a methodology of undertaking development enterprises that gives control of decisions and resources to community groups. It is by nature an activity.

Connecting above three dimensions, Grootaert (2003) points out that building social capital facilities empowerment. Social capital and empowerment are supplementary to each other multidimensional concepts and facilitate the link to poverty reduction, whereas CDD is a manifestation of social capital and empowerment.

Summarizing, Krishna (2003) points out that these three concepts need to be pursued separately. For social capital, the emphasis should be on building stronger cognitive structural links among community members, for CDD the emphasis is on making complementary resources and formal authority available to communities. The emphasis should be on improving governance and making individuals and communities' better agents of their own development.

Dr. Indrabhusan Singh and Dr. Usha Kumari (2008) stressed that true sense of empowerment comes when women inherit property (movable and immovable), get education, obtain credit, earn income through working inside or outside home, control their fertility. But unfortunately they still lack these rights in many countries. They are still widely underrepresented in decision making at the household or social level. Empowerment by means of modest generation project is clearly insufficient to ameliorate the prospects for a high quality of life for women.

Beside that Shashi Bhushan Kumar (2010) pointed out in his article that for sake of empowerment of women they should not be confined only in grassroots level representation in panchayat and municipalities through 73rd and 74th amendment in 1992 but their representation in Lok Sabha and State Assemblies also need to be felt. That's why the Bill was passes by the Rajya Sabha on March 9, 2010 with clear majority. It is proposed that 33 per cent reservation for women in Parliament and the Legislative Assemblies through the 108th Constitution Amendment Bill (Women Reservation Bill, 2008). If so happened it would be a giant leap of women for the direction of empowerment.

SHG and Women Empowerment

The origin of formal kind of SHGs is the creation of Grameen Bank of Bangladesh, which was founded by Mohammed Yunus in 1975. In India National Bank for Agriculture and Rural Development (NABARD) has taken initiative in SHG formulation and nurturing in the year 1986-87. But the real effort was taken after 1991-92 form the linkage of SHGs with the banks. We reviewed the important research papers and documents related to Self Help Group, Microfinance and Women Empowerment which enhance the capability of the researchers to contribute something new and different in this intended study. SHGs have consistently been visualized as tools for women empowerment. The reasons are various as proposed by different authors: in the past few decades where large numbers of schemes did not have much impact on women's life, self help programme is such programme where large number of deprived women gets a meaningful life out of it.

Katz (1965) observed that in the fields on physical handicap, mental illness, mental retardation and drug addiction, the self help organizations formed by parents, ex-parents and their relatives assumed prominent roles in providing social services, education, group aid and support to research and have significantly influenced public awareness and policy in these field. These practical developments often occurred without much professional aid or understanding.

NABARD (1992) stated that the primary purpose for formation of self help groups was to undertake social and other developmental activities. Thrift, credit and incomer generating activities were taken up later. Access to timely and adequate credit, transparency with simple procedures, and elimination of middleman and group empowerment has been the other motivating factors for group formation.

NABARD (1995) defined—"A self help organization denotes an institutional framework for individual or households who have agreed to cooperate on a continuing basis to pursue one or more objectives. A self-help organization is a membership organization, which implies that its risks, costs and benefits are shared among its members on an equitable basis and that its leadership and for manager for their deed."

NABARD (1995) while documenting the best practices of banking with the poor, commented on the characteristics of SHGs. It was stated that SHG members should be residents of the same area, homogeneous and numbering at least five persons, should hold regular meetings and the leaders should be elected by the members with group functionaries or positions being rotated among the members. Regarding banks, it stated that the poor were capable of meeting commercial loan obligations without seeking any concession or subsidies. Hence, banks should take significant initiatives to reach the poor. They could do this by providing credit in quantities both significant and sitting overtime for productive and income generating activities of the poor.

NABARD (1998) while analyzing on SHG bank linkages programme, commented on common fund through regular savings, supplemented by outside borrowing, loan for traditional and non-traditional production and consumption activities, terms of credit decided by consensus in group meetings. Collateral consists of mutual confidence and trust, simple documentation, peer pressure and group dynamics to ensure repayments.

Moreover N. Lalitha (1998) visualized SHG as a group process and the basic principles of the SHGs are group approach, mutual trust, organization of small and manageable groups, group cohesiveness, sprit of thrift, demand based lending, collateral free, women friendly loan, peer group pressure in repayment, skills training, capacity building and empowerment which are required to bring sustainable development among the SHG members.

Tyagi (1999) quoting the concept of self help promotion explained that its promotion as a development approach believes that even poor people have the inherent capacity to organize themselves and improve their lot. It tries to build upon this existing self help potential of the poor and assist them as producers and in the identification of occupations and activities, which provide a higher net return on invested labour and capital. Thus, it attempts to raise the level of voice of majority of the poor in the economic system by the building up of an institutional framework that is tuned to their capacities of self-administration and better geared towards serving their needs. People organize themselves into self help groups/organizations (SHGs/SHOs) and through these groups; people with few resources start to change their conditions of production and consumption at a micro level. It may steer the development of a village economy in a different direction by enlarging the scope for village level enterprises. Usually it starts with economic activities, but need not necessarily be limited to that and it may well be extended to social, political and cultural activities.

Murugan and Dharmalingam (2000) reiterated that the concept of SHG serves to underline the principle "for the people, by the people and of the people". This was exclusively established for the poor. Self help group is a small economically homogeneous and affinity group of rural poor, which voluntarily agrees to contribute to a common fund to be lent to its members as per group decision, which works for group solidarity, self and group awareness, social and economic empowerment in the way of democratic functioning.

Jayesh Ranjan *et al.* (2002) envisaged that the concept of SHG has been found very crucial for sustainable development of human resource as well as livelihood. Besides many other advantages, it provides a unique opportunity to replace subsidy-oriented development with revolving fund oriented development. At present, various types of agencies are organizing SHGs-government departments, NGOs, international agencies and innovative members of the community. It is interesting to observe that more than 95 per cent of the existing SHGs are promoted and then assisted with revolving fund to take up income generating activities. Other programmes like NABARDS's SHG linkage, Rashtriya Mohila Kosh (RMK) and Integrated Child Development Services also focus on organizing women into SHGs. In the same way, a number of NGOs are also organizing women into SHGs and attempting to help them.

The important Self Help Promoting Institutions (SHIPs) are doing better jobs and side by side developing the social capital. among such institutes ASSIST, BAIF, CEAD, DPIP, GVK, PRADAN, ISPWDK, KAWAD, KWDP, MYRADA, OUTREACH, PRAWARDA, SERP, VIP, WCUSS, GVT are noteworthy. This has particularly been observed in those areas where women's SHGs are functioning well. Some steps of the government towards upliftment of women are appreciable. The National Commission on Self Employment of Women has focused on the tremendous contribution that the women of different sectors make to the national economy, which led to specific programmes like STEP (Support to Training for Employment Programme), DWCRA (Development of Women and Children in Rural Areas), and RMK (Rashtriya Mahila Kosh). Women Development Corporations set up in different states are also making concerted efforts towards improving the condition of women by upgrading their skills through training programmes and offering greater employment opportunities to them through schemes like public distribution, dairy development, food preservation, social forestry, rural marketing etc. which are related to them in traditional occupations like agriculture, animal husbandry, fishery and others. However, priority to agriculture and rural development, generating productive employment and eradication of poverty, ensuring food and nutritional security for the women and children are some of the objectives of the Common Minimum Needs Programme of the government, which would definitely result in the development and empowerment of women.

Beside that V.M. Rao (2003) has some opinion like Abhaskumar Jha (2004) where he emphasized that economic upliftment is very much possible if members aspired to change their economic status. He stressed out that SHGs have been recognized as useful tool to help the underprivileged and as an alternative mechanism to meet the imperative credit needs of underprivileged through thrift. He also emphasized that women are encouraged to form SHGs because women are in advantageous position in saving than men. The underlying principle of SHGs is that due to cooperative in nature, women come forward to help each other in the matter of social, economical and psychological aspects. It has been seen that women are the best performer in the field of savings. They are really champion of managing their savings and credit than anyone else. The inherent quality helps to overcome many catastrophic situations. It has also been seen that women are the best investor in their development. They invest money in the field of constructing or repairing house, children's education, daughter's marriage, assets building etc.

S. Rajamohan (2003) supplemented that SHG is the best media

for empowerment. It encourages women for saving and credit which led to holistic development. Holistic development in the sense of all-round development where women can use their full potential to earn empowerment and empowerment will come through good practices of regular meeting, regular savings and social mobilization process. The above mentioned phenomena help to nourish and cherish the latent talent of women which is very much visible in the rural side, need to re-shape and encouragement to act against the maladies to achieve their goal for fulfilment of their life in the long run.

On the other hand Ritu Jain (2003) has little contradiction of the impact of SHGs on women empowerment. She argued that until and unless SHGs are vowed to make a difference in their daily life by enhancing their status through equal participation, decision-making and beneficiaries in the democratic, economic, social and cultural spheres of life, the meaning of empowerment will remain unachievable. It is absolutely true that empowerment can not be imposed, it can be achieved. When women become greedy to social, economical, political, cultural and psychological aspect then they want change in their present status.

In this regard Abhaskumar Jha (2004) had a tremendous experience on SHG. He viewed self help group as a best alternative for poverty alleviation. He recommended that the rural poor who are experiencing extreme poverty should formulate self help group collectively to get rid of this problem. He also mentioned that savings and credit helps them to develop confidence of thrift and meet members' emergency needs and to provide collateral free loans decided by the group to overcome the problem of money lenders. Besides giving economic independence SHGs also help social and psychological upbringing in women. This particular study helps to give us a synoptic view about SHGs which is ultimate strategy for alleviating poverty. Presently it becomes an established form of mechanism for development. Undoubtedly, it seems to be modern techniques of change. Above all the dynamism of SHGs is a participatory in nature for change. Henceforth, Central and State Governments used it as platform of poverty alleviation.

According to India-2005 Reference Manual, many development programmes in India are being implemented on the basis of self help groups. Accordingly, the Union Minister of Rural

Development launched a restructured poverty alleviation programme, Swarnajayanthi Gram Swarozgar Yojana (SGSY) with effect from 1st April, 1999, which has replaced IRDP and its allied schemes, viz. Training of Rural Youth for Self Employment (TRYSEM), DWCRA, Supply of Improved Toolkits to Rural Artisans (SITRA), Ganga Kalyan Yojana (GKY) and Million Wells Schemes (MWS).

SGSY is a holistic programme covering all the aspects of self-employment such as organizing of poor into self-help groups, training, credit, technology, infrastructure and marketing. The scheme is funded on 75 : 22 basis by Centre and State and is implemented by DRDAs through Panchayat Samitis.

Beside that Dr. P. Loganathan and Asokan (2006) visualized SHGs as a viable and vibrant media towards the change. They emphasized that micro credit act as a catalyst to bring change. They analyzed that inter-regional performance of SHGs depends on in terms of their total number, level of credit and per capita credit per SHG. The study revealed that SHGs have provided access to credit to their members, promoted savings, reduced dependence on money lenders and above all empowered rural women.

In the same time Dr. M. Soundarapandian (2006) evaluated SHGs based on qualitative and quantitative aspects of change. He analyzed that the growth of SHGs and the role of microfinance in developing the rural entrepreneurship which suggest that though there is positive growth rate of SHGs in the State but in terms of the growth of SHGs there is a wide variation among states. Linkages of Banks with SHGs are found impossible for this variation.

The concept of SHGs is catching up as the most viable means in recent years to empower women, especially at the grassroots level. Women have shown extraordinary dynamism in organizing themselves in group activities for income generation, better bargaining power and improvement in the quality of life. Membership in a group provides women a legitimate forum beyond the private domestic sphere and inputs to which they previously lacked access. It permits a gradual building of her capacity to interact effectively and redistribute economic opportunity. It is against this backdrop that the SHGs have emerged as an alternate structure to cater to the needs of the women. The equality of women with men remains a myth till women become economically self-reliant. Women need to be viewed as productive members of the society, sharing equal authorities and responsibilities. The status of women is, thus closely connected with the economic position, which in turn, depends upon the access to productive resources of the country.

Micro-Credit and Women Empowerment

Hashemi, Schuler and Riley (2012) explored the impact of credit on a number of indicators of empowerment: (i) the reported magnitude of women's economic contribution; (ii) their mobility in the public domain; (iii) their ability to make large and small purchases; (iv) their ownership of productive assets, including house or homestead land and cash savings; (v) involvement in major decision making, such as purchasing land, rickshaw or livestock for income earning purposes; (vi) freedom from facing domination, including the ability to make choices concerning how their money was used, the ability to visit their natal home when desired and a stay in decision relating to the sale of their jewellery or land or to taking up outside work; (vii) political awareness such as knowledge of key national and political figures and the law on inheritance and participation in political action of various kinds; and (viii) a composite of all these indicators. They found that women's access to credit was a significant determinant of the magnitude of economic contributions reported by women; an increase in assets holding in their own homes; an increase in their purchasing power; their political and legal awareness and their composite empowerment index. BRAC (Bangladesh Rural Advancement Committee) was established in 1972 and started working in the field of micro-credit from 1974. Loanees reported significantly higher level of mobility and political participation. Grameen members reported higher involvement in 'major decision making'. The study also found that access to credit was associated with an overall reduction of the incident of violence against women; women's participation in the expanded set of social relationships as a result of membership of credit organizations rather than increases in their productivity *per se* were responsible for reductions in domestic violence.

Goetz and Sen Gupta (2013) viewed micro credit as an

empowering device for rural women has in recent years come under close and in some instances off-putting scrutiny. It gives women enormous opportunity to fight against the poverty. They are able to manage their handful resources with meaningful ways. Critics have argued that micro credit accessed by women often misused by their husbands or by themselves without knowing the consequences and often been leaving women burdened with the responsibility of repayment of default with interest.

Grameen Bank of Bangladesh has great impact on deprived women of that area. Todd. H. (2009) conducted a comparative study of the members of Bangladesh Grameen Bank and non-members of Grameen Bank about the impact of a decade of Grameen Bank membership on the lives of forty poor women who live in remote villages without basic amenities. Where he found it has tremendous impact on women members who are members of Grameen Bank. The report said that (a) ten years membership had worked a fundamental change in the family relationships of most of the members; (b) twenty seven women played an active role in all the aspects of household management and budgeting. Their husbands discussed their economic activities with them; including cultivation of land; and (c) some of the women typified the mix of traditional power and the new kind of power which was the power to refuse. This kind of power was the product of a process over a decade of loan use.

Kabeer, N. (1998) reported that the effectiveness of credit in addressing the needs and priorities of the underprivileged and women's empowerment through using evaluation data of the Small Enterprise Development Project (SEDP) to standardize other methods to see the comparative result. Report and baseline findings of a two stage study on the impact of participation in micro enterprise services of the SEWA Bank, an institution of the Self Employed Women's Association shown positive impact. It provides preliminary indications of the nature and magnitude of benefits resulting from participation in this programme. Results suggest positive programme impacts at the household, enterprise, and individual levels.

Scoggins, A. (2005) reported that rural bank have taken pivotal role to promote micro credit to the poor people and disadvantaged women. The report recommended that (a) provision of skill upgradation training programme for new and appropriate enterprises to be created; (b) financial and technical assistance to be provided to organize the saving and credit organizations into cooperatives; (c) provision to be created for insurance and identification for livestock; and (d) interventions to be made to reduce women's workload. The above mentioned points are very important to reduce the risk of availing credit from the formal and non formal credit institutions for income generation, ultimately which helps them to be self-confidence.

Chen Martha Alter, Donald S. (2012) reported that micro credit has been minutely utilized by the women folk for their all-round development through the lending of the Micro Credit Project for Women. It was found that: (a) involvement in a credit programme does have enough potential to empower women; (b) micro credit has gradually become successful in reaching out to poor women; (c) through contact with savings and credit group members, women developed self-identity and status; (d) income generation activities raise women's decision making power in the household and community; (e) women still consult with men, who claim to confer with their wives on important issues; (f) loans have been mainly used for livestock raising, poultry, small shops and fertilizers with little fungibility; and (g) in most cases the responsibility for loan repayment was also felt by husbands and defaulting was rare. The author concluded by saying that provision of credit is not enough, orientation and training should be given for procedures of access loan utilization, interest payment and instalments in order to provide informed use of services.

On the other hand Zaman (2001); Simanowitz and Walker (2002) reported that self help groups and micro credit are a part and parcel to each other. He stressed out that in India, SHGs intermittent by micro credit are shown to have optimistic effects on women and poor section of the society, with some of these impacts being ripple effects to one geographical area to other. They have played important roles in reducing the vulnerability of the poor, through asset creation, income and consumption, provision of emergency assistance, and empowering and emboldening women by giving them control over assets and increased self-esteem and knowledge. Several recent studies have also shown positive impacts of micro credit on self help groups. Studies done on women self help groups dealing with income generation activities lead to empowerment have noted positive profit levels.

Perhaps Lalitha and Nagarajan (2009) had given interesting representation on loan for women to trickle down the poverty. They reflected that women are the better credit manager than men. They reported that in India, micro credit studies done on women self help groups dealing with income generation activities lead to empowerment have noted positive profit levels and short repayment periods for loans. Livelihood from such entrepreneurship has been influential in increasing the physical well-being of the household.

K.K. Tripathy (2006) reported that micro credit which includes micro savings is gradually emerging as one of the most effective strategies to alleviate poverty particularly women's poverty. He added that it can effectively generate employment and sustain the income of the households by giving them opportunities of work. Although Micro Credit Institutions are effective weapons in the war against poverty still they alone cannot reduce the effect of non-physical symptoms of poverty which deprive the poor of a full social existence. Positive effects and ripple effects are needed to improve and strengthen microfinance to set a burning example in the deprived section of the community to fight against poverty.

Harford, Tim (2008) wrote about a recent controversy within the Micro Credit world where Muhammad Yunus opposed microfinance lenders such as Comparators "as indistinguishable from the moneylenders". But it is clear that the increasing commercialization of Micro Credit, the polarization of Micro Credit agencies, the coercive nature of extraction are all an obvious outcome of the process itself and the dynamics of the logic of capital. And in the same process Grameen Bank itself gave birth to highly profitable business enterprise. Yunus turned into one of the world's leading businessmen, and became an advocate for foreign corporate investment in Bangladesh. The number of the poor and vulnerable has increased.

On the other hand author like Anu Muhammad (2013) has different view on Grameen Bank's micro credit programme. She criticized its style of functioning as it only looking at profit and concentring on refund back its loan with high rate of interest, forgetting its main motto of "poverty eradication". Though Grameen Bank's micro credit programme has been recognized internationally as a successful model. This model has become an integral part of development thinking and had earned global attention as new form of banking, but the findings from inside and outside Bangladesh contradict the current myth around the model. The model created a good opportunity for expanding the market for finance capital, thereby ensuring Grameen Bank's spectacular success. However, it failed as a tool for poverty alleviation and empowerment of women.

Microfinance and Women Empowerment

On the contrary Hashemi *et al.* (2000) reported that women's access to savings and credit system has hardly any impact on their lives. Their results shown that women's access to savings and credit system contributes notably to the degree of the economic contributions reported by women, to the likelihood of an increase in asset holdings in their own names to an increase in their exercise of purchasing power, and in their political and legal awareness as well as in composite empowerment index. They also found that access to credit was also associated with higher levels of mobility, political participation and involvement in 'major decision making' for particular credit organizations.

Microfinance programmes target disadvantaged women with the overt goal of empowering them. There are different arguments varying underlying motivations for pursuing women empowerment. Some argue that women are amongst the poorest and the most vulnerable of the underprivileged and thus helping them should be a priority. Whereas, other believe that investing in women's capabilities empowers them to make a choice which is the goal in itself but it also contributes to greater economic growth and development. It has been well documented that an increase in women's status through different resources results in well-being of the family, especially children (Mayoux, 1997; Kabeer, 2001; Hulme and Mosley, 1996). Besides that a more feminist approach stresses that an increased access to financial services represents an opening opportunity for greater empowerment through new avenues of income generation. Such organizations explicitly perceive microfinance as a tool for the women's rights and independence. Moreover, keeping up with objective of financial viability, an increasing number of microfinance institutions prefer women members as they believe that they are better and more reliable borrowers who can use their money in appropriate project for their overall development and can refund money in time.

The aspect of microfinance has something long term effect on women empowerment. Sometimes, it may be positive as well as negative. That's why Mayoux (1997) argues that the impact of microfinance programme on women is not always positive. Women that have set up enterprises benefit not only from small increases in income at the cost of heavier workloads and repayment pressures. Sometimes, their loans are used by men in the family to set up enterprises, or sometimes women end up being employed as unpaid family workers with little benefit. She further points out that in some cases women's increased autonomy has been temporary and has led to the withdrawal of male support. It has also been observed that small increases in women's income are also leading to a decrease in male contribution to certain types of household expenditure.

Mayoux (1997) further discusses that the impact of entrepreneurship developed by the self help group members by using credit given by bank varies from woman to woman. These differences arise due to the difference in productive activities or different background. Sometimes, programmes mainly benefited the women who are already better off, whereas the poor women are either neglected by the programmes or are least able to benefit because of their low resource base, lack of skills and market contacts. However, poorer women can also be more free and motivated to use credit for production.

Some realistic features are given by Rahaman (2014) about the proper usage of loan by the members of the group to their development which is practically bases on the basis of anthropological approach with in-depth interviews, participant observations, case studies and a household survey in a village. On proper usage of loan by women self help group and reached the conclusion that between 40 per cent to 70 per cent of the loans disbursed to the women group are used by the husband and that create tensions among the husband-wife and group members within the household increases which later turned to democratic violence.

On the other hand Mayoux (2001) also reported that about the intrinsic dangers in excessive use of social capital to cut costs in the context of other policies for financial sustainability. It is observable that the reliance on peer pressure rather than individual incentives and penalties may create disincentives and corruption within groups. Reliance on social capital of women clients along with increasing emphasis on ideals on strict economic accounting at the programme level require increases voluntary contribution by the members in terms of time and effect. It has been noted that those putting in voluntary contributions also expect to be repaid in the form of leadership of the group etc.

Though much resource invested on women through microfinance, it is hardly seen any changes of women's traditional roles instead of promoting gender equality. A woman's practical needs are closely linked to the traditional gender roles, responsibilities, and social structures, which contribute to a tension between meeting women's practical needs in the short-term and promoting long-term strategic change. By helping women meet their practical needs and increase in their efficacy in their traditional roles, microfinance can help women to gain respect and achieve more in their traditional roles, which in turn can lead to increased esteem and self-confidence. Although increased esteem does not automatically lead to empowerment, it does contribute decisively to a woman's ability and willingness to challenge the social injustice and discriminatory systems that they face (Cheston and Kuhn, 2015).

Holvoet (2005) reported that in direct bank-borrowing system does not give women an opportunity to gain self-confidence and therefore, they do not reach much in terms of decision making patterns. Eventually women must come through a process called forming self help group. However, when loans are channeled through women's groups and are combined with more investment in social intermediation, substantial shifts in decision-making patterns is observed. This involves a remarkable shift in norm-following and male decision making to more bargaining and sole female decision making. Effects are even more striking when women have been members of a group for a longer period and especially when greater emphasis has been laid on genuine social intermediation. Social group intermediation had further gradually transformed groups into actors of local institutional change.

Renu Verma (2012) emphasized that woman empowerment had been split into different components and measured separately in order to understand the underlying factors and their relationships with them. The microfinance helped poor women by providing independent sources of income outside the home, which reduces the independency on the husband's income, by increasing the assertiveness of women and providing independent source of income with exposure to new set of ides, values and social supports had brought rapid economic development in the situation of women by creating confidence, assertiveness, intelligence, self-reliance, and consciousness of their rights.

Savita Shankar and Mukul G. Asher (2013) advocating the microfinance, which helps to enable the country to leverage this interest and use it to progress towards the goal of financial inclusion. But it is important to develop a bureaucratic regulatory structure for the sector, for a number of reasons. First, regulation is needed to enable microfinance institutions to offer saving services, the lack of which is a major shortcoming of the sector. Second, with the entry of commercially oriented participants, the need for supervision and consumer protection is even more pressing. Third, with IMF (International Monetary Fund) broadening their range of services to include services such as insurance and pension products, coordinated regulation of the sector is required. Finally, given the diversity of legal forms of IMF, a regulatory frame work would enable a level playing field and prevent regulatory arbitrage.

Neil MacFarquhar (2011) argued that in recent year IMF making money out of the poor people. The phenomenon is very astonishing and has grown up so popular that some of its biggest proponents are now wringing their hands over the direction it has taken. Drawn by the prospect of hefty profits from even the smallest of loans, a raft of banks and financial institutions now dominate the field, with some charging interest of 100 per cent or more from their impoverished customers. Micro credit has been created to fight the loan sharks; but not to encourage new loan sharks. Yunus (2016) said at a gathering of financial officials at the United Nations; "Microcredit should be seen as an opportunity to help people get out of poverty in business way, but not as an opportunity to make money out of the poor people."

Income Generation and Women Empowerment

McCormack *et al.* (1986) reported that bargaining power of women coming from regular meeting with their group members about the income generation activities which they opt for. Minute details of the activity helps them to negotiate with the other SHGs, entrepreneurs, bank official, service provider etc. It provides a woman an opportunity to earn more which is representing empowerment.

Kandiyoti (2000) and Buvinic (2001) reported that development practitioners have been debating over the years to find the best way by which they can increase the empowerment level of women. Income generation through self help group is the best option for them because they work on the project very sincerely. It helps to enhance their self-confidence. Some studies argue that income generation activities of poor women help them to raise their overall status in a family and society. It is obvious that economic development programme could automatically increase the economic status of women and thereby their status in community and family.

Smith (1995) reported that the participatory element embodied in the development strategy might not always enhance the economic benefit of women beneficiaries under self help group through an economic development programme because of faulty selection of the members. Until and unless they see their group as a viable media for empowerment they do not bother for change their attitude. So, at the initial stage of formation of group, women should be collected from same socio-economic condition of the members to make the women of the SHG empowered.

Carr *et al.* (2000) and Viswanath (1995) emphasized on the income generation activities through women's group helps to achieve ultimate empowerment. They also emphasized that the selection of income generation activities replicate their major decision making in their life since all the other ingredient related to empowerment automatically come into force. So, women should be very careful while select the income generation activities.

Basu (2005) reflected the idea of good linkages with women SHGs and service delivery agencies which are very important to gain self-confidence. Mobility outside the boundary of the home and interaction with outside people including service delivery agencies helps to negotiate for availing better services. The economic development programmes for income generation of the SHGs have significant impact on their mobility outside home.

Kabeer (2000) reported that income generation from home based work is often irregular and low due to the low skill requirement of much of the work, high competition of the work and family intervention in decision making about the amount of work done. Sometimes, women select their income generating activities getting influenced by their husbands or male members of their families. As a result women hardly concentrate on their selected jobs since it is looked after by their husbands or male members. The drawback is that women could not be able to acquire or at least acquaint with knowhow of the project which leads to unnecessary dependence on the male members of the family or society.

An appraisal of the above literature on Self Help Group and Microfinance for Women Empowerment leads us to believe that women empowerment by micro finance has itself been a split component and has been extensively disputed. The opinion of Hashemi *et al.* (1996) and Mayoux *et al.* are a testimony to the above. Nevertheless, the relation between microfinance and women empowerment through SHGs has not been disputed by any thinker and that this relation could be productively and positively fostered is in no doubt too. Dr. Renu Verma's (2008) endorsement of this view in the last section is an important rejoinder. It is important to realize that empowerment is a process which is clear from the different interpretations; the need for empowerment of women in order to promote gender equality to make women an agent of change in society and to increase their capacity to enjoy life to the full extent. Using the World Bank's definition of empowerment along with Kabeer's rational analysis of women empowerment argues for a more harsh interpretation of women empowerment. It is interpreted as the process in which a woman challenges the existing norms and culture to effectively improve her well-being. Looking at development as freedom and women's issues from the angle of increasing their capabilities are better than concentrating on women's well-being. An evaluation of the above commentaries provokes us to remark that economic empowerment programmes are now solidly grounded in overall development programmes and the major target here is, to upgrade women's social status and opportunity going beyond economic development aims more so because mere income generation—even participatory grounded ones—does not lead to expansion of women's social choices. Taking the case of home based work of as an explanatory sample, it is learnt from the above authors that the empowerment equity for such work is low and its affinity to unpaid household labour is another similarity that needs to be interrogated. Therefore, mobility to the boundary of home and an intense social interaction acts as an incentive to building up the confidence geared to improvement and empowerment. Thereby suggestions of the author like N. Lalitha and Anhaskumar Jha that to 'organize the women under a common group or forum' may be more practical in this regard. 'A new entrepreneurial culture' may come to our rescue while we think of self help groups. These studies focus on how women group can be uplifted through SHGs. It provides an opportunity to improve their financial, social and political status by their involvement as a team. SHGs promotes the quality of life by motivating female on humane potential. In addition the studies quoted above emphasis that if women were encouraged actively involved in SHGs they would exhibit better roles and responsibilities as an entrepreneurs, wife, mother etc. SHGs is agreed to be one of the effective means of empowerment of women. Nevertheless the role of microfinance has taken pivotal role for women empowerment. Thus micro financing through SHGs could help in a big way in eradicating poverty which have shown optimistic effects on women and poor section of the society, with some of these impacts being ripple effects to one geographical area to other. They have played important roles in reducing the vulnerability of the poor, through asset creation, income and consumption, provision emergency assistance, and empowering and emboldening women by giving them control over assets and increased self-esteem and knowledge. But credit itself is not enough to mitigate their abject poverty until and unless credit is available as a package which covers underlying risks to avoid unprecedented incidents. Credit is such a facility which needs to be handled very carefully. However, what is a real change in the community's attitude to leave the traditional approach of highly subsidized support to the promotion of Self Help Group. This is a time consuming process by regular follow up and guidance are sure to bring about substantial improvement.

4

Methodology

Here, we have made an attempt to highlight and discuss intensively the various components of methodology which have been adopted by us to carry out the study. Methodology denotes a systematic approach or line of action through which the investigation is to be completed. It helps to explore new knowledge or to reach a new conclusion. It consists of following parts:

- Universe of the study,
- Research design,
- Selection of samples and sampling techniques,
- Statistical techniques used,
- Tools of data collection,
- Pilot study, and
- Data processing and analysis.

Universe of the study—The term universe means aggregates of units/elements of the population in the geographical area or the setting where the study is being conducted. In this particular study the members of Self Help Groups residing in villages of Birbhum district were the universe. To know the universe better one should know the geographical area of Birbhum. The area (1757 sq miles i.e. 4550 sq. km) comprises two district regions. To the west lies undulating, generally barren upland, art of the eastern fringe of Chota Nagpur Platueau, rising to 3000ft (900 metres); to the east is a densely populated alluvial plain of Gangetic Delta. The Ajay, Mor, Mayurakshi provides irrigation for about 600000 acres (240000 ha) and 2000 kW of electricity. Rice, legumes, wheat, maize, and mangoes are the chief crops in the east, coal china clay, and iron ore deposits are found in the west. The district's principal industries include cotton and silk weaving, rice and oilseed milling, and metal wire and pottery manufacture. Suri is the district headquarters. Few important statistics of Birbhum district are given below:

Area	Square km	4545.00
Forest	Square km	158.22
Net sown area	Square km	3246.87
Net irrigated area	Square km	2409.57
Population	Census 2011	3502387
Male	–	1791017
Female	–	1711370
Urban	In thousand	229.56
Rural	In thousand	2326.10
Population growth (pa)	In per cent	2.01
Population density	Persons/sq.km	771
Relative Index of Development	–	68
Urbanization	In per cent	8.98
Literacy	Census 2011 (%)	70.90
Male		77.42
Female		64.07
Workers as of total population	In per cent	33.15
Workers as per cent of main workers		
Agriculture and allied activities	In per cent	73.28
Mining and Quarrying	In per cent	0.95
Mfg, (non-household) industries	In per cent	4.60
Household industries	In per cent	3.60
Construction	In per cent	0.96
Services	In per cent	16.61
Mjor Rivers	–	Ajoy, Kopai, Mayurakshi, Bakreswar
Forest area as of reporting area	In per cent	3.50
Gross integrated area as of cropped area	In per cent	54.20
Fertilizer consumption per ha	Kg.	127
Per capita food grain production	Kg.	306
Road length per sq.km	Km.	47.74
Railway route length per 100 sq. km	Km.	4.80
Post offices per 100000 persons	Number	17.65
Per capita bank deposit	Number	910
Per capita bank credit	Number	401
Per capita bank credit to SSIs	Rs.	40
Per capita Bank credit to industries	Rs.	72
Telegraph offices per 100000 persons	Number	3.65
Bank branches per 100000 persons	Number	6.77

Major Crops

Crops	Quantity (tonnes)	Value as % of District Total
Rice	729773	77.75
Potatoes	193850	8.30
Rapessed	35923	7.60
Wheat	46786	3.38
Sugacane	80613	0.84
Gram	4170	0.70
Sesame	1889	0.46

Minerals

Minerals	Quantity in tonnes	Value in Rs. (Millions)
Coal	243000	60.50
Kaolin	108377	15.48
Fireclay	35465	1.68

This district is not so agriculturally developed because majority of the agricultural land is mono cropping due to its soil pattern and natural landscape and therefore, employment opportunities for the women population in other than rainy season are very meagre.

The researchers belong to the district of Birbhum. Henceforth the researchers are quite well acquainted with the district and its surrounding villages. It gave them lots of insight to the researchers about the said district and the villages selected for the study. The researcher's belongingness to the same district where the study was conducted as well as the objectives of this study lead the researchers to elect the district purposively (*see* Figs. 4.1 and 4.2).

Research Design: The research design or designing of research is one of the important aspects of social science research. The term design means a plan that guides the line of action of any activity. The design in research work help the researchers to formulate the line of action through which the study would be carried out. Therefore, a research design is logical and systematic plan prepare for directing a research study. It specifies the objectives of the study, the methodology and techniques to be adopted for achieving the objectives. It constitutes the blueprint for collation, measurement and analysis of data. It is the plan,

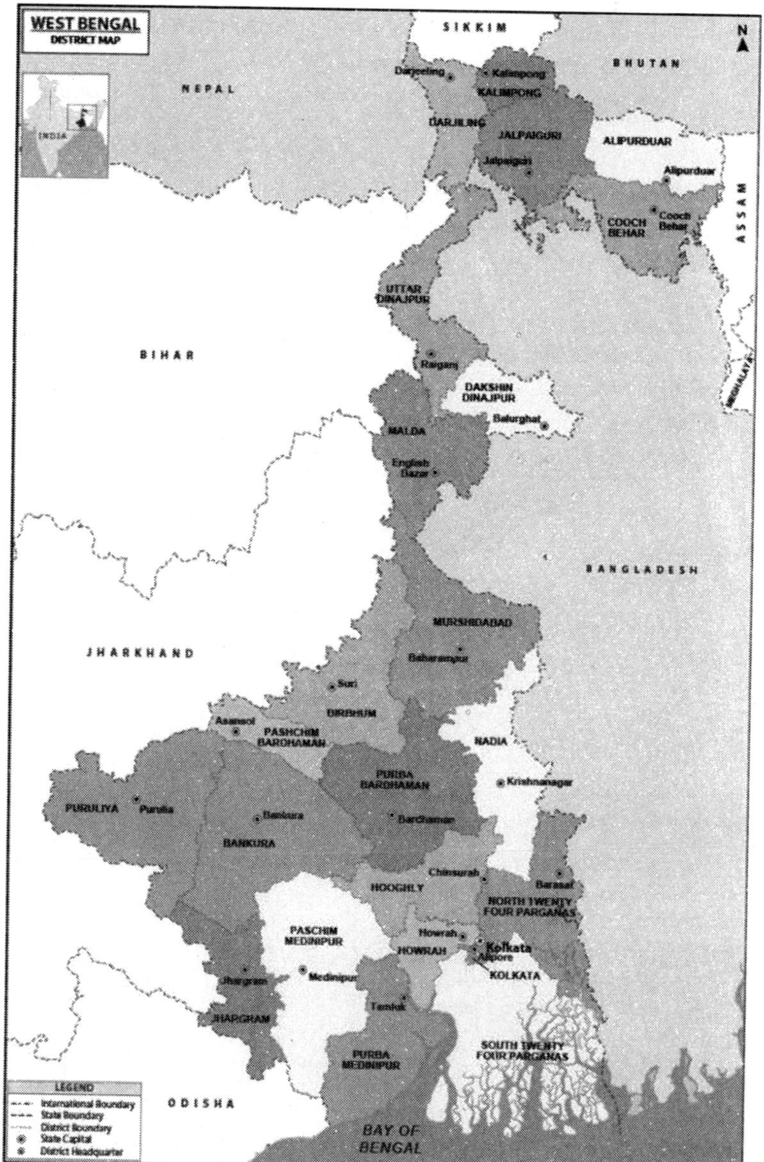

Map not to Scale

Fig. 4.1: Map of West Bengal

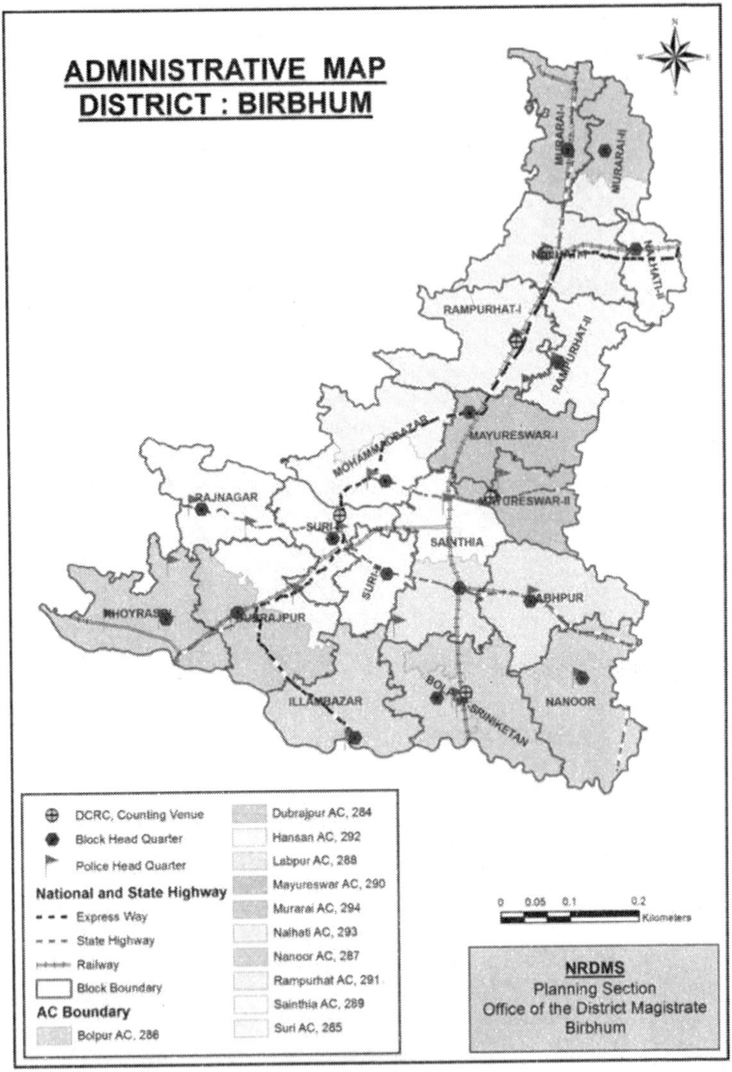

Map not to Scale

Fig. 4.2: Map of Birbhum District

structure and strategy of investigation conceived so as to obtain answers to research questions.

The researchers adopted exploratory study design for the

study. The main purpose of such study is that of formulating a problem for more precise investigation. The exploratory study design tries to demonstrate the problem more comprehensively and in greater depth by having a concrete and reasonable understanding of it and subsequently establish priority for further research work.

This particular study helps to find out the scope of social work intervention by acquiring the perception of the SHG members, SHG leaders and villagers as a whole. The researchers have made their best effort to find out the problematic areas in the SHG, microfinance and women empowerment where the profession of social work could intervene as well as open the door for future research by examining the view obtained accurately for the inhabitants of these villages.

Sample and Sampling Techniques

Selection of Block: The Bolpur Sriniketan Community Development Block has been chosen purposively because of the easy accessibility and experience of working with the SHGs. The Bolpur Sriniketan Community Development Block of Birbhum District consists of nine Gram Panchayatas and Bolpur Municipality area, which is recognized as the business centre of this Block, The Gram Panchayats under Bolpur Sriniketan Community Development Block of Birbhum District are:

- Rupur Gram Panchayat
- Sattore Gram Panchayat
- Kasba Gram Panchayat
- Singhee Gram Panchayat
- Bahiri Panchsowa Gram Panchayat
- Kanalitala Gram Panchayat
- Raipur-Supur Gram Panchayat
- Sian-Muluk Gram Panchayat
- Sarpalehana-Albndha Gram Panchayat

Purposive sampling comes under non-probability sampling method in which the researchers deliberately and purposively select the sample units because of its unique characteristics which are deemed important for the research and this sample can bring most desired result. This is also known as judgement sampling. This involves selection of cases which we judge as the most appropriate ones for the given study. It is based on the judgement of the researchers or some experts. In purposive sampling, the investigators have some belief that the sample villages being selected is very good representative of the population. This method ensures that those villages will be included in the *sample* that is relevant to the *research design*.

Selection of Gram Panchayts: The study was conducted under Singhee Gram Panchyat, Raipur-Supur Gram Panchyat, Bahiri-Panchsowa Gram Panchyat and Kankalital Gram Panchayat at Bolpur-Sriniketan Community Development Block of Birbhum District in West Bengal where large number of Scheduled Caste and Scheduled Tribe and minority people are living. The Gram Pnchayatas were selected randomly from nine Gram Panchayats because of the characteristics of probability, homogeneity and every element has equal chance of being selected.

Selection of the villages: 12 villages from one Gram Panchayata were selected randomly. Total 50 villages from four Gram Panchayats were selected by the researchers mainly for three reasons, firstly, availability of women self help groups in the village; secondly, for its easy accessibility and thirdly, for good amount of researchers' exposure of working with these self help groups previously.

Selection of SHGs: One SHG from each village operating minimum one year had been chosen randomly. Total 50 SHGs were taken for the study.

Selection of respondents: From each SHG, three members were considered randomly for the study. The criteria followed were: (1) they should be existing office bearer and members of the SHG; (2) out of three members, two were ordinary members and other was office bearer; (3) total 150 respondents (100 general members and 50 leaders) were chosen as sample size.

Tools of data collection: Exploring the empowerment level of Scheduled Caste, Scheduled Tribe and mainly dominated women Self Help Group is the essence of the study; so interview schedule obviously would play a pivotal role in collecting primary data. The researchers did assessment of the situational background while formulating interview schedule. Relevant review was also examined in order to develop questions on socio-economic conditions of the respondents. As per the objectives of the study, the researchers had formulated specialized interview schedule for general members and leaders separately. Questions on the status of the respondents as self help group members were given utmost priority. Semi-structured interview schedule was developed at par with the need of the study. The schedule has been divided into three parts: (a) identifying personal and socio-cultural information; (b) particulars about the SHGs; and (c) general questions related with study. Close-ended questions were used in maximum possible number using different scales for coding the responses developed by social scientists to present the collected data through tables and graphs. The variable selected for the statistical tests were also selected after careful examination.

Pilot study: Before conducting the actual study, a pilot study was carried out by the researchers with the non-samples to understand the basic situational background and understanding the level about the impact of Self Help Group and Microfinance among the respondents. During this period and comprehensive list of SHG members were developed within the block with help of the Local Self Government, Local Bank, Block Development Office, Agriculture Development Office, Rural Extension Centre of Visva-Bharati University and NABARD. Beside Government agencies the researchers had taken help of Faith Based Organization (FBO) and Community Based Organization (NGO and Club). This study had helped the researchers to some extent to make necessary addition and alteration in the interview schedule as well as selection and identification of proper tools and techniques as for need of the study.

Data processing and analysis–Data was collected through interview schedule and then it was coded on the code sheet and transferred into the code book developed for this purpose. Data was processed with the help of computer using SPSS software. Various tabular and graphical representations tests were also employed to test the variables at different significant levels to establish the relationship among them.

Limitations of the study: All researches must have some limitations. The Self Help Group is a natural phenomenon scattered all over India empowering huge number of women. To conduct this particular study, it was quite impossible to cover all the population of different region across India. So, like other studies, this study too has certain constraints.

- The particular study is restricted to the Birbhum District of West Bengal and the Bolpur Sriniketan Block.
- The selection of sample has been limited to three numbers (two general members and a leader) from one SHG group.
- The sample size of the respondents is limited to 150 (100 general members and 50 leaders).
- The study has been conducted exclusively in rural areas.
- This study was conducted in SHGs formulated by NABARD's guideline, not SGSY, a scheme of Government of India.
- The opinions of the social activists, NGO personnel, local administration and local leaders of the political parties have not been considered to avoid manipulation and biasness.

5

Results, Discussions and Analysis

This chapter contains both tabular and graphical presentation of collected data. The tables and graphs are based on frequency distribution method. The result, discussion and analysis of collected data are based on the responses of one hundred (100) general members and fifty (50) leader respondents from fifty (50) self help groups. Data are collected from fifty (50) villages under the Bolpur-Sriniketan Block of Birbhum district in West Bengal. The Frequency distribution tables as well as graphs are prepared on the basis of selected close-ended questions from a structured interview schedule. Apart from interview schedule, discussions with the respondents have also been carried out to get the in-depth information from the self help group members. Table 5.1 to Table 5.31 show the comparison between leaders and general members about their opinion regarding self help group, microfinance and women empowerment. Tables 5.32 to 5.36 show the general members' view regarding self help group, microfinance and women empowerment. Tables 5.37 to 5.46 also depict the leaders' view with in respect of self help group, microfinance and women empowerment.

Questions for Both the General Member and Leader respondents

Table 5.1 shows the distribution of the respondents in accordance with their age groups. The Table reflects that the majority of the general member respondents 57 (57%) belong to 26-35 age group. The next higher percentage 22 (22%) and 15 (15%) respondents

Table 5.1: Age of the respondents

Types of respondent	*Age groups*						*Total (%)*
	14-18 yrs	*19-25 yrs*	*26-35 yrs*	*36-45 yrs*	*46-50 yrs*	*50+ yrs*	
General Member	1 (1%)	15 (15%)	57 (57%)	22 (22%)	3 (3%)	2 (2%)	100 (100%)
Leader	0 (0%)	9 (18%)	29 (58%)	11 (22%)	0 (0%)	1 (2%)	50 (100%)

Source: Field Survey.

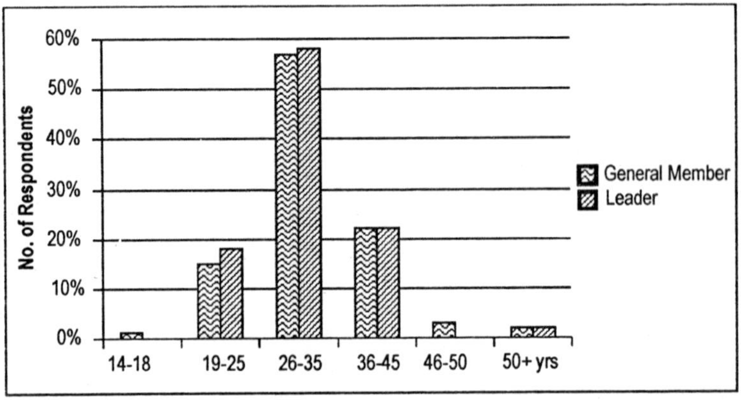

Chart 5.1: Age of the Respondents

belong to 36-45 and 19-25 years age groups respectively, followed by 3 (3%), 2 (2%) and 1 (1%) respondents belong to 46-50 years, 50+ years and 14-18 years age group.

In the case of leader the majority of the respondents 29 (58%) belong to 26-35 years age group, followed by 11 (22%), 9 (18%) and 1 (2%) respondents belong to 36-45 years, 19-25 years and 50+ age groups respectively. No single respondent was found from 14-18 years and 46-50 years age groups.

The trend clearly suggests that majority of the respondents of the self help group from both the categories (leader and general member) belong to 26-35 years age groups and leader respondents have clear majority 29 (58%) as compare to general member 57 (57%). It is because of predominance of middle aged women might be seen in large number in the society. They have enough free time and being more responsible citizen than their younger counterpart towards their children, family and community at large. This age group is recognized as the most productive where the women put in their best to perform any task. They are very much frantic and target oriented and they are motivated in such a way to change their social and economic status through cooperative and collaborative attitude. It is also important to notice from the above table that in this age women always strives to secure themselves from probable threat of economic and health insecurity. They try to accumulate fund as much as possible which might provide them safety from impending danger. It had also been observed that the age gap between wife and husband, lack of potentiality of husband to earn at growing stage, sickness of husband, number of children increased in the middle age and per head per capita income decreased were some of the reasons where large number of middle aged women represent in SHG. Older women are discouraged due to poor health and lack of stamina.

The figure (bar diagram) number 5.1 also support the tabular presentation where tallest bar of the diagram, i.e. 58 per cent leader respondents and 57 per cent general member respondents belong to age group of 26-35.

It is revealed from Table 5.2 that majority of the general member respondents 81 (81%) were married, followed by 8 (8%) were widowed. The next higher percentage 5 (5%) were single and 3 (3%) each were abandoned by husband/family and separation respectively. No single respondent had been found from divorced or any other category.

In Chart 5.2 bar diagram also supports the tabular value where tallest bar of the diagram where 88 per cent leader respondents and 81 per cent general member respondents were married.

In the case of leader the majority of the respondents 44 (88%) were married, 4 (8%) were widowed, 1 (2%) each were abandoned by husband/family and separation respectively. No single respondent had been found from single, divorced or any other category.

It is amazing to see that the majority of the respondents of the self help group from both the categories (leader and general member) were married and leader respondents had clear majority 44 (88%) as compare to general member 81 (81%). On the other hand it is also significant that only 5 (5%) general member

Table 5.2: Marital Status of the Respondents

Types of respondent	Marital status							Total %
	Single	Married	Widow	Divorced	Abandoned by husband/ family	separation	Any other	
General member	5 (5%)	81 (81%)	8 (8%)	0 (0%)	3 (3%)	3 (3%)	0 (0%)	100 (100%)
Leader	0 (0%)	44 (88%)	4 (8%)	0 (0%)	1 (2%)	1 (2%)	0 (0%)	50 (100%)

Source: Field Survey.

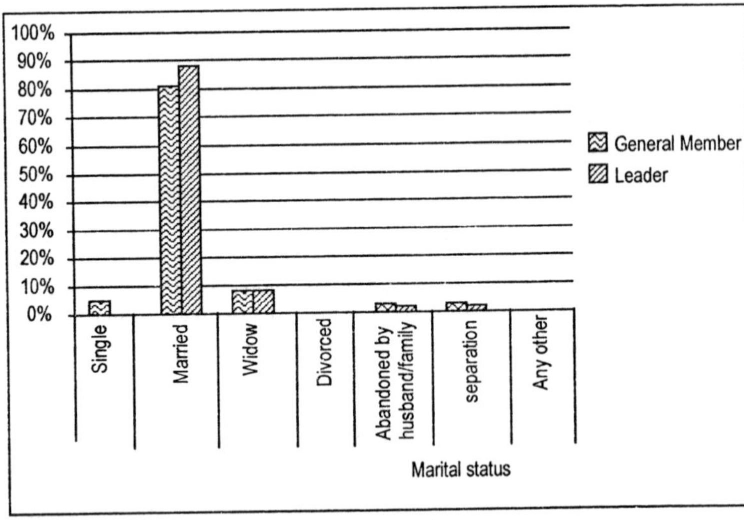

Chart 5.2: Marital Status of the Respondents

respondents were single as compare to 0 (0%) leader respondents. It was because of socio-economic and cultural practices of our society where girls are compelled to marry at tender age and had to look after their family members. When their husbands' income becomes insufficient to manage their family they need to come out from the family and put their best effort to earn money through small activities. SHGs had given them an opportunity to manage their family members. That is why large number of married woman had joined SHGs to run their family smoothly.

It has also been seen that before marriage girls spend their most of the time in study, playing with their friends and help their parents in domestic work without having any pressure of maintaining family members. Once they got married they might loose all sorts of privileges and engaged in all sorts of unpaid familial activities. Their labour was not recognized and mostly considered as voluntary work. Women remain idle without having proper income generating activities. That is why it was quite clear from the above table that maximum number of married women are participating in SHGs to overcome economic insecurity and in that way they want to strive for their economic upliftment as well as community development. It had also been seen that women hardly have any monetary support to fulfil their personal need. They place first priority to fulfil family needs than their need. The peculiarity of the patriarchal society was that women all the time have to depend on husband or father to fulfil their basic need. The subordination and secondary citizenship makes women voiceless and powerless. Women have to play different role in different sphere of life. Before marriage women have to play the role of daughter. After marriage women have to play the role of daughter in law and mother and mother in law and they need to look after their husband, children and family members at large. But their economic as well as social status never been change either in parent's house or in-laws house.

Table 5.3: Caste of the Respondents

Types of respondent	*Category of caste*				*Total (%)*
	General	*OBC*	*SC*	*ST*	
General Member	33 (33%)	4 (4%)	54 (54%)	9 (9%)	100 (100%)
Leader	18 (36%)	1 (2%)	28 (56%)	3 (6%)	50 (100%)

Source: Field Survey.

It is obvious from the above table that the Birbhum district of West Bengal is largely dominated by the Scheduled Caste (SC) and the area is backward in terms of resources and facilities. The table denotes that the majority of the general members respondents 54 (54%) belong to SC category and the next higher percentage 33 (33%) belong to General category. The next higher

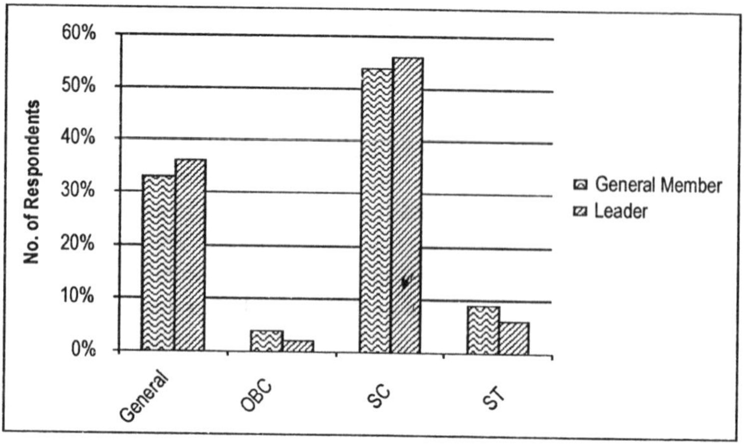

Chart 5.3: Caste of the Respondents

percentage 9 (9%) belong to ST category and remaining 4 (4%) belong to OBC category.

On the other hand the majority of the leader respondents 28 (56%) belong to SC category. The next higher percentage 18 (36%) belong to General Category. The next higher percentage 3 (6%) belong to ST category and remaining 1 (2%) respondents belong to OBC category.

It is clearly reflects that the majority of the respondents 54 per cent each from leader and general members belong to SC caste. It is also significant that only 4 (4%) general member respondents belong to OBC as compare to 1 (2%) leader respondent.

It has been seen that SC, ST and OBC belong to socially and economically disadvantaged class and their participation in the existing self help group is quite good except OBC. The SC and ST caste came under reserved category before OBC in the reservation policy. Both the SC and ST enjoy lots of provisions for their development due to reservation policy. That is why both the castes are little in advantageous position than OBC. That is why OBCs' participation in existing SHGs is absolutely low. Apart from that predominance of SC and ST population was quite high in compare to the OBC in the district of Birbhum. Caste is such factor which disintegrates national integrity and put India behind to achieve its goal of equity with justice.

In Indian context lower castes are not allowed to take part of any kind of social, cultural, ritual and even developmental activity because they are considered as an untouchable. Though untouchability is prohibited under the law still some part of India it is widely practiced. It compels the SC/ST to split them from national development. Casteism compels lower caste to adopt the caste based lower jobs, i.e. scavenging, sweeping or other low graded jobs which modern society never think of. In the name of casteism the so called higher caste exploits them by forcefully engaging them as a bonded labour or confined them in low graded jobs. Perhaps it would be one of the major reasons to make India under-developed. Until and unless the people of India irrespective of castes, creed, sex, race and religion takes active participation in nation building India could not achieve full-fledged development. The Constitution of India has framed several enactments to safeguard the lower caste but it will not work until and unless people of India realize the fraternity and solidarity and work for them. But SHGs are considered as a panacea of all and try to make them united irrespective of all the diversity. Through SHGs all members are getting chance to know each other and empathize of other's problem and unanimously decided to work for their development and national development at large.

In Chart 5.3 bar diagram also supports the same where tallest bar of the diagram 54 per cent leader respondents and 54 per cent general member respondents belong to SC castes.

Table 5.4: Literacy Rate of the Respondents

Types of respondent	*Literacy rate*		*Total (%)*
	Literate	*Illiterate*	
General Member	87 (87%)	13 (13%)	100 (100%)
Leader	100 (100%)	0 (0%)	50 (100%)

Source: Field Survey.

In Table 5.4 the majority of the general member respondents 87 (87%) were literate followed by 13 (13%) general member respondents were illiterate. On the other hand the majority of the leader respondents 100 (100%) were literate and none of the respondents found illiterate.

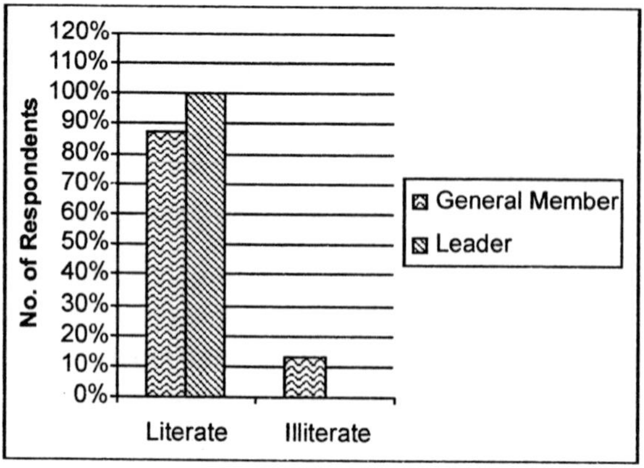

Chart 5.4: Literacy Rate of the Respondents

It is clear from the Table 5.4 that the majority of the leader respondents 100 (100%) were literate than general member respondents 83 (83%). Perhaps leaders were provided the opportunity to enroll themselves in the formal education where they can learn, play and acquire life skill to become all-rounder in their life. But few general members were not so much lucky like the leaders. It has also been observed that their parents decide their daughter's education. Girls' education is largely influenced by the socio-economic, religious, cultural factors of the society. Though women account 50 per cent of total Indian population still they do not have access to education. Women are considered secondary citizen and associate with two major roles, i.e. reproductive role and housekeeping. Child marriage and dowry also plays significant role to undermine girls' education. Apart from that casteism; untouchability, caste based jobs, language barrier, distance of school from home are the crucial factors of determining girls' education. It is happening throughout the country that a girl when she should have been studying, playing, learning and acquiring skills for earning a livelihood is taught with looking after a new generation. In the process of child marriage we have deprived the young girl to be educated and a capable citizen and also deprived a new generation of children from getting proper care by a well informed and healthy mother. Until and unless girls are educated we cannot build a healthy nation. To make the dream reality the Government of India has come up with majestic bill that is free and compulsory education for all the children ranging from 6-14 years age group. On 1st April, 2010 India joins a group of few countries in the world with a historic law making education a fundamental right of every child coming into force. Making elementary education an entitlement for children in the 6-14 age group, the Right of Children to Free and Compulsory Education Act, 2009 will directly benefit close to one crore children who do not go to the school at present. The students, who had either dropped out of schools or never been to any educational institution due to whatsoever the reason, will get elementary education as it will be binding on the part of the local and State governments to ensure that all children in the 6-14 age group get schooling. This act helps to make progressive nation.

Table 5.5: Educational Status of Respondents

Types of respondent	*Level of education*									*Total (%)*
	Illite-rate	Can read and write	Can read only	Class I-IV	Class V-VIII	Class IX-X	H.S	Gra-duate	P.G	
General Members	13 (13%)	30 (30%)	26 (26%)	21 (21%)	8 (8%)	2 (2%)	0 (0%)	0 (0%)	0 (0%)	100 (100%)
Leader	0 (0%)	0 (0%)	0 (0%)	26 (52%)	15 (30%)	6 (12%)	3 (6%)	0 (0%)	0 (0%)	50 (100%)

Source: Field Survey.

A complete opposite scenario has been found in respect to educational status is concern. It could be seen from the above table that the majority of the general member respondents 30 (30%) comes under 'can read and write' category followed by 26 (26%) comes under 'can read only'. Subsequently 21 (21%), 13 (13%), 8 (8%) and 2 (2%) respondents come under 'class I–IV', 'Illiterate', 'class V–VIII' and 'class IX–X' respectively. There is no single respondent had been found in 'Higher Secondary', 'Graduation' and 'Post Graduation' level.

On the other hand 26 (52%) leader respondents belong to 'class I–IV', followed by 15 (30%) belong to 'class V–VIII'. The next higher percentage 6 (12%) and 3 (6%) respectively belong to 'class IX–X' and 'H.S.' None of respondents has been found in 'Graduation' and 'Post Graduation' level. The Table also reflects that 100 per

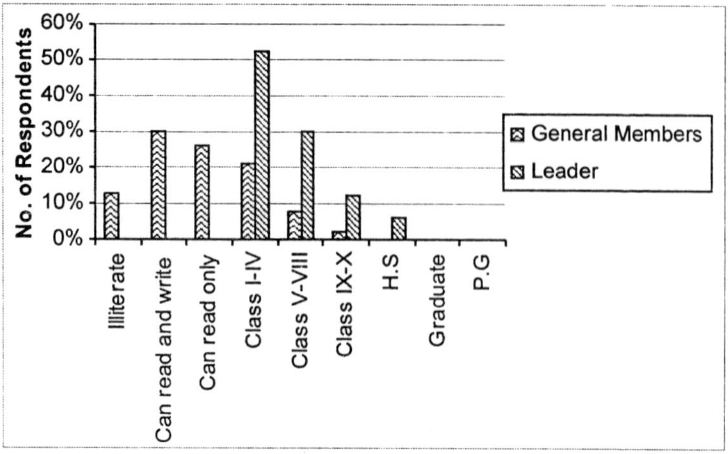

Chart 5.5: Educational Status of Respondents

cent leader respondents had attained their primary schooling whereas nearly 70 per cent general member respondents did not attain their primary schooling.

It was obvious from the above trend that majority of the respondents of the self help group from both the categories (leader and general member) belong to class I–IV and leader respondents have clear majority 26 (52%) as compare to general member 21 (21%). On the other hand it was also significant that 13 (13%) general member respondents were illiterate whereas no leader respondent had been found illiterate.

A wide range of factors, which are deeply embedded in the gendered nature of culture and society, prevent women from participating in formal education. As a result they are on unequal terms with men in employment and self-employment. As a cost benefit analysis investing in the education of the female has the highest rate of return of any possible type of investment. Girls begin helping out at an early age with the household chores that burden women with fetching fuel, water, preparing food, childcare and working in the field. And these responsibilities increase as they grow older, resulting in a decline in participation in education with increasing age. A combination of mutually reinforcing customs and attitudes place greater value on males than females in many societies. Preferences within families are often for boys to advance their education since social and cultural perception confine girls to two roles that are reproductive and care giver. Henceforth, it is thought that girls require little education or no education to perform these tasks. The poor family is less likely to send their girls to the school because their labour is required at home and in the field.

Regarding education is concerned it is one of the important indicators for growth and development of any country. Education of a person is also considered the most important variable in the behavioural outlook of an individual. It is perhaps the single most important instrument through which the human resources can be fully developed. It also enables people to acquire basic skills and indicated abilities, which are helpful in raising the social and economic status of the person.

Table 5.6: Types of Family of the Respondents

Types of respondent	*Family types*		*Total (%)*
	Nuclear	*Joint*	
General Member	76 (76%)	24 (24%)	100 (100%)
Leader	39 (78%)	11 (22%)	50 (100%)

Source: Field Survey.

The researcher also placed a question before the respondents about the types of family they belong. It was found from the above table that the majority of the general member respondents 76 (76%) belong to the nuclear families followed by 24 (24%) respondents belong to joint family. On the other hand the majority

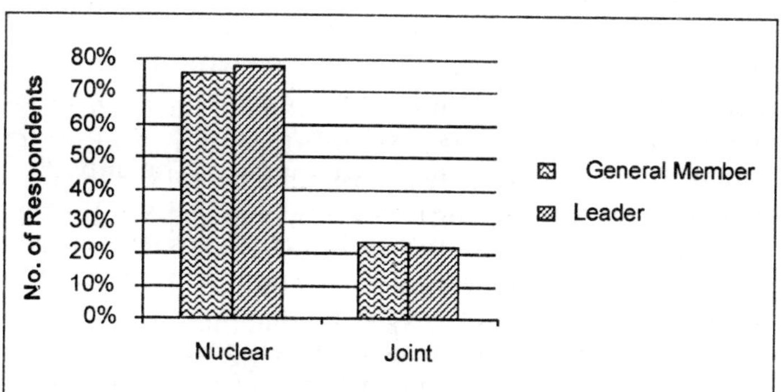

Chart 5.6: Types of Family of the Respondents

of the leader respondents 39 (78%) belong to nuclear family followed by 11 (22%) belong to joint family.

It could be articulated from the above trend that the majority of the respondents of the self help group from both the categories (leader and general member) belong to the nuclear family and leader respondents had clear majority 39 (78%) as compare to general member 76 (76%). On the other hand it was also significant that 11 (22%) leader respondents belong to joint family whereas 24 (24%) general member respondents belong to joint family as well.

This was really a new phenomenon for the rural families to live in nuclear family. India is a place of joint and extended family, which ensure security to the old and infirm. After new economic policy of 1991 which allow foreign traders to invest directly in Indian market which has brought desirable and undesirable social change in many sphere of life. Attitudes, customs, socialization process, pattern of living, livelihood etc. are largely affected by this policy. On the other hand industrialization and urbanization has been speeding up. Thus inter-state and intra-state migration has been taking place. People largely influxes from the village to the industrial places to get job and bound to live in surrounding of the work place. Henceforth slums are mushrooming at nearby of the workplace without the basic amenities. This leads to breaking up the joint and extended family and sometime women and children remain home without their male bread earner.

Due to new economic policy a nation has to open up their market for foreign traders for direct investment which helps the consumers to avail the product with best affordable price. It has good and bad effect too. Good thing is that it has given option to the consumers to bargain with the product and can choose the different varieties of product with comparatively low price. Bad thing is that it has left thousands of population underemployment, displaced and migrated. The impact of new economic policy is deeply penetrated in rural economy and destroyed all sorts of cottage industry, artisanship and the product which are produced by the joint and extended family earlier. Due to these factors maximum family became idle and lost their traditional jobs which they suppose to perform. Many institutions perform this role on behalf of the family and charge exorbitantly. For example, earlier elder suppose to provide education to the juniors but now this role has large been taken by the coaching centre. Due to emergence of nuclear family we are very much dependent on other service providers and thus living cost becomes very high today.

The bar diagram is also supporting the Table where tallest bar of the diagram, i.e. 78 per cent leader respondents and subsequently taller bar diagram 76 per cent general member respondents belong to nuclear family.

Table 5.7: Family Size of the Respondents

Types of respondent	*Family Size*		*Total (%)*
	Less than 5	More than 5	
General Member	34 (34%)	66 (66%)	100 (100%)
Leader	35 (70%)	15 (30%)	50 (100%)

Source: Field Survey.

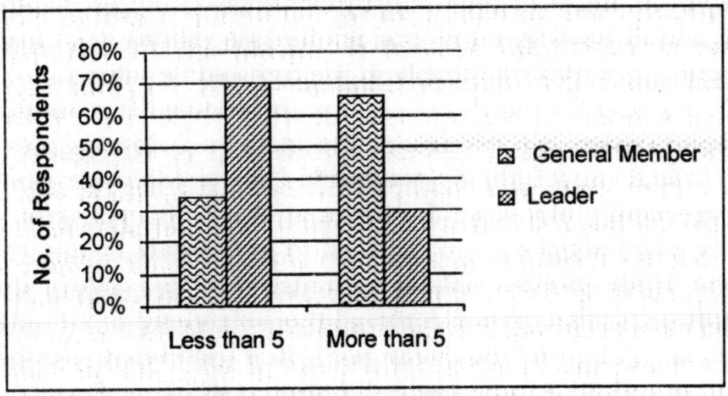

Chart 5.7: Family Size of the Respondents

Table 5.7 depicts that the distribution of the respondents for both general members and leaders of SHGs according to their family size in terms of number of family members. It shows that the majority of the general members and leader respondents had completely different scenario in case of family size. It shows that the general members 34 (34%) had less than 5 members in the family where as leader respondents 35 (70%) had less than 5 members in the family. On the other hand general members 66 (66%) had more than 5 members in the family and leader respondents 15 (30%) had more than 5 members in the family. It was clear from the above table that leader preferred small family norm than general members.

It was quite interesting to see that the leader respondents 35 (70%), i.e. majority of them preferred small family size as compare to general member 34 (34%). It is also significant that 66 (66%) general member respondents preferred big family size as compared to the 15 (30%) leader respondents.

We are somewhat influenced and controlled by the experiences and past experience and had taught us that attempts to control the member of the children through behavioural changes in men and women have failed because families do not see the benefit of fewer children. Children especially boys are viewed as extra hands that can provide income and help with family chores. The poorer the family the more children they seek. Hence it is evident that the economic status of the family plays a major role in family planning. Birth control and reproductive health of women are behavioural issues affected mostly by economic, access to health care, and education. Until this reality is accepted, the desired changes may not be attainable in the foreseeable future.

Regarding the number of children is concern it has been seen that population explosion was the major problem in present context and henceforth it was decided to curve the population through family planning. Therefore, in third fifth year plan the family planning was incorporated to give stress in two child norms. Through family planning material or IEC (Information, Education, and Communication) the behaviour of expectant parents likely to be changed. But behaviour change communication can not be achieved until and unless an economic aspect is addressed properly.

The bar diagram 5.7 reflects completely opposite scenario in regard to family size. The tallest bar of the diagram, i.e. 70 per cent leader respondents had less than five members in the family whereas 66 per cent general member respondents had more than five members in the family.

Again a completely opposite scenario had been found in respect of primary occupation is concern. Table 5.8 depicts that the majority of the general members respondents 55 (55%) were getting their livelihood through daily labour followed by 27 (27%) engaged in agriculture and allied activities as their occupation.

Table 5.8: Occupation of the Respondents

Types of respondent	Types of Occupation								Total (%)
	Agriculture & Allied activity	Full time Service on monthly wage	Daily labour	Contractual Labour	Rural Artisan	Small independent business	House wife	Anything	
General Member	27 (27%)	0 (0%)	55 (55%)	1 (1%)	6 (6%)	6 (6%)	5 (5%)	0 (0%)	100 (100%)
Leader	27 (54%)	2 (4%)	7 (14%)	0 (0%)	5 (10%)	4 (8%)	5 (10%)	0 (0%)	50 (100%)

Source: Field Survey.

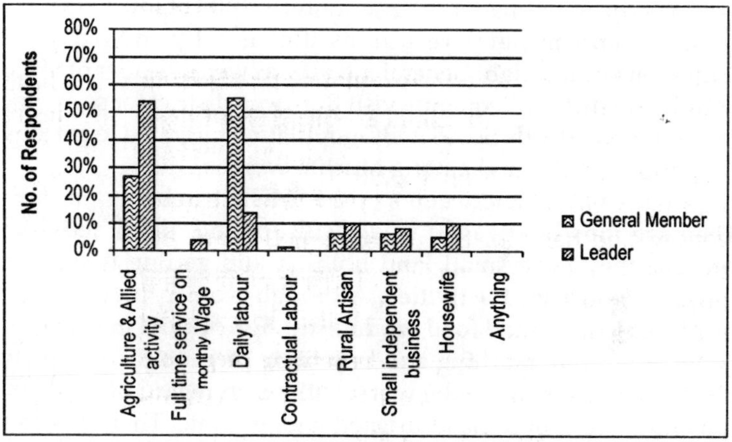

Chart 5.8: Occupation of the Respondents

The next higher respondents 6 (6%) each was employed as rural artisan and small and independent business respectively and 5 (5%) respondents were house wives and do not have any occupations. Remaining 1 (1%) is engaged in contractual labour.

On the other hand the majority of the leader respondents 27 (54%) had their primary occupation as agriculture and allied activities followed by 7 (14%) engaged as daily labour. The next higher respondents 5 (10%) and 4 (8%) had their prime occupation as rural artisan and small and independent business. Only 5 (10%) respondents were house wives and do not have any livelihood option. Remaining 2 (4%) were engaged in full time service on monthly wage.

The trend clearly reflects that the majority of the general member respondent 55 (55%) were engaged in agricultural daily labour whereas the majority of the leader respondents 27 (54%) were engaged in agriculture and allied activities. It is also significant that 5 per cent and 10 per cent respondents from general member and leaders were housewives and belonged to Muslim community without much movement from home for earning livelihood.

The occupation chosen by the SHG members depends on the availability of skills, demand for the product in the market and availability of resources. Since Birbhum district is one of the backward districts of West Bengal announced by the Planning Commission in the matter of agriculture, fertility of soil, irrigation, industry and mineral resources that is why inter-district migration is quite high. General member as well as leader of SHGs of Birbhum district frequently visit Burdwan district for searching of livelihood. Mostly SC/ST/OBC population migrated to get jobs. Migration is not found among Muslim women.

On the other hand leaders of the SHG are in better position. They are mostly engaged in agriculture and allied activities because they have small land holding and getting livelihood through land based activities. Although women play a major role in agriculture and food production. Agricultural information is not effectively reaching and benefiting them to food security. Most of the women are the worst sufferer in regard of food and nutrition and found malnourished and anaemic. There is wide-spread reorganization of the need to improve both agricultural education and extension work with the help of rural women. Women from minority section were very much busy in *kantha* stitching, tailoring or happy to play only the role of housewife since their religion does not allow them to go outside of home in searching of jobs.

Regarding the occupation is concern the bar diagram (5.8) reflects completely opposite scenario. The tallest bar of the diagram 55 per cent general member respondents were engaged in agricultural daily labour whereas bar diagram of 54 per cent leader respondents were engaged in agriculture and allied activity.

Table 5.9: Annual Income of the Respondents (Before being SHG Member)

Types of respondent	*Level of income*						*Total (%)*
	<Rs. 2000	*Rs. 2001-6000*	*Rs. 6001-8000*	*Rs. 8001-10000*	*Rs. 10001-30000*	*>Rs. 30000*	
General Member	5 (5%)	14 (14%)	73 (73%)	8 (8%)	0 (0%)	0 (0%)	100 (100%)
Leader	5 (10%)	15 (30%)	19 (38%)	11 (22%)	0 (0%)	0 (0%)	50 (100%)

Source: Field Survey.

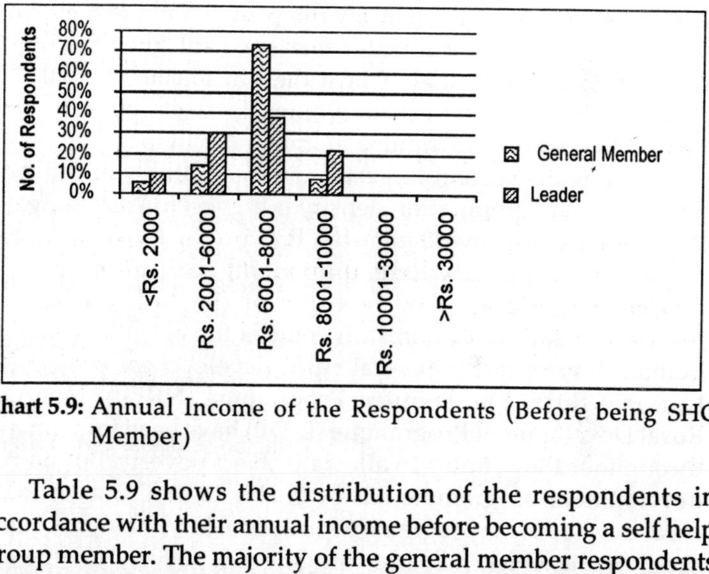

Chart 5.9: Annual Income of the Respondents (Before being SHG Member)

Table 5.9 shows the distribution of the respondents in accordance with their annual income before becoming a self help group member. The majority of the general member respondents 73 (73%) had annual income in the range of Rs. 6001-8000. The next higher percentage 14 (14%) had annual income in the range of Rs. 2001-6000, followed by 8 (8%) whose annual income was in the range of Rs. 8001-10000. Only 5 (5%) respondents had annual ncome less than Rs. 2000.

In the case of leader 19 (38%) respondents said their annual ncome was in the range of Rs. 6001-8000 followed by 15 (30%), 1 (22%), and 5 (10%) whose annual income were in the range of s. 2001-6000, Rs. 8001-10000 and less than Rs. 2000.

The trend clearly depicts that the majority of the general member respondents 73 (73%) and leader respondents 19 (38%) had annual income between Rs. 6001 and Rs. 8000. It was also significant that no respondent from general member and leaders had annual income of Rs 10001-30000. It is because no woman was associated with Self Help Group which gives them extra money from different income generation activities beside their daily occupation.

The majority of women getting livelihood mainly from agriculture and allied activities and agricultural daily labour. Beside that women also earn livelihood from contractual labour, rural artisan and small independent business. Through these occupations it is very hard to get sufficient amount of money to run their family. Though women perform better than men still they are unpaid, under paid and less paid against their male counterpart. These kinds of discrimination push women to abject poverty which endangered women to indulge in immoral activities.

India is the second largest populous country in the world after China and population density is highest in West Bengal. So it is not easy to provide gain-full and productive employment to all. Abject poverty, unemployment, corruption, political power struggle are few features of the India; which are responsible for youth unrest. Income is the essential criteria of human development. Several rural development projects, i.e. National Rural Employment Programme (NREP), Integrated Rural Development Programme (IRDP) have been implemented throughout the country to alleviate abject poverty. But no rural development programme has been able to eradicate. All these rural development programmes are some kind of inputs supply programme which helps to mitigate the poverty for the time being but could not address or solve the problem of unemployment permanently. Though Mahatma Gandhi National Rural Employment Guarantee Act, 2010 (MGNREGA) has been articulated to address poverty through demand based jobs; still it is a question the way jobs are provided and assets are being created. Beside rural development project, self help programmes are also important to alleviate chronic poverty. Self help group is very famous among the women. It empowers the women to fight against the poverty, discrimination and disparity.

Income generation activities (IGA) are one of the parts of SHG through which they are able to generate income. It is evident that many SHGs have enhanced their economic status through IGA and increase their annual income. Collective action, democratic outlook, and joint venture helps the SHGs to earn profit and reduction the risk and hazards to become prey in the society. Though, few programmes address the needy properly but corruption, nepotism, favouritism let down the programme. The poor become poorer due to the inflation, over population, lack of technical education etc.

Regarding annual income (before being the SHG members) is concern bar diagram 5.7 reflects that the tallest bar of the diagram

Table 5.10: Annual Income of the Respondents (After being SHG Member)

Types of respondent	*Level of income*						*Total (%)*
	<Rs. 2000	*Rs 2001-6000*	*Rs. 6001-8000*	*Rs. 8001-10000*	*Rs. 10001 - 30000*	*>Rs. 30000*	
General Member	1 (1%)	2 (2%)	11 (11%)	78 (78%)	8 (8%)	0 (0%)	100 (100%)
Leader	0 (0%)	0 (0%)	13 (26%)	23 (46%)	14 (28%)	0 (0%)	50 (100%)

Source: Field Survey.

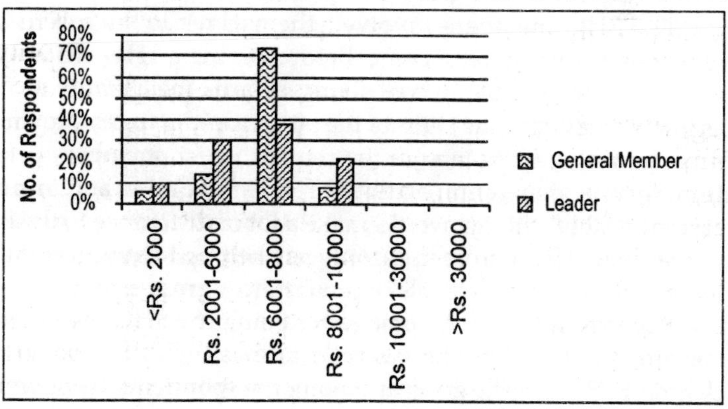

Chart 5.10: Annual Income of the Respondents (After being SHG Member)

73 per cent general member respondents had annual income in the range of Rs. 6001-8000 and subsequently taller bar diagram 38 per cent had annual income in the range of Rs. 6001-8000 which is supportive evidence of table.

Table 5.10 shows the distribution of respondents in accordance with their annual income after becoming the members of Self Help Group (SHG). The majority of the general member respondents 78 (78%) have highest annual income of Rs. 8001-10000 followed by 11 (11%) whose annual income was Rs. 6001-8000. Remaining 8 (8%), 2 (2%) and 1 (1%) have their annual income of Rs. 10001-30000, Rs, 2001-6000 and less then Rs. 2000.

In the case of leader the majority of respondents 23 (46%) have highest income between Rs. 8001-10000, followed by 14 (28%), 13 (26%) respondents whose annual income were in between Rs. 10001-30000 and Rs. 6001-8000.

It is evident from the above table that majority of the respondents 78 (78%) and 23 (46%) from both categories (leader and general member) have annual income between Rs. 8001-10000 after association with the SHGs. It is also significant that no leader respondent has annual income of Rs. 2001-6000 except 2 (2%) general member whose annual income was Rs. 2001-6000. If we compare Table 5.7 and Table 5.8 then it is quite clear that nearly 70 per cent of women enhance their annual income and it is happened because women are associated with Self Help Group which help them to earn money from different income generation activities beside their daily occupation.

The SHG members involved themselves in such activities which give them good income. Before joining a SHG; majority of women were not able to contribute towards their family income as they do not have the skills or the opportunities for employment. After joining a SHG though the returns which members getting from income generation activities remain irregular and in many cases unstable still this would make a lot of difference to the lives of the poor. The increased income has helped to supplement the income to reduce the levels of poverty to a great extent.

Regarding annual income (after being the SHG members) is concern the bar diagram 5.8 reflects that the tallest bar of the diagram 78 per cent general member respondents have annual income in the range of Rs. 8001-10000 and subsequently taller bar diagram 46 per cent have annual income in the range of Rs. 8001-10000 which is supportive evidence of the table.

Table 5.11: Opinion of the Respondents of being SHG Members

Types of respondent	Reasons of being SHG members							Total (%)
	Poverty	Ignorance by family	Self-survival	Survival of the children	Self-reliance	Better future	Any other	
General Member	56 (56%)	12 (12%)	1 (1%)	3 (3%)	6 (6%)	22 (22%)	0 (0%)	100 (100%)
Leader	9 (18%)	5 (10%)	2 (4%)	4 (8%)	2 (4%)	28 (56%)	0 (0%)	50 (100%)

Source: Field Survey.

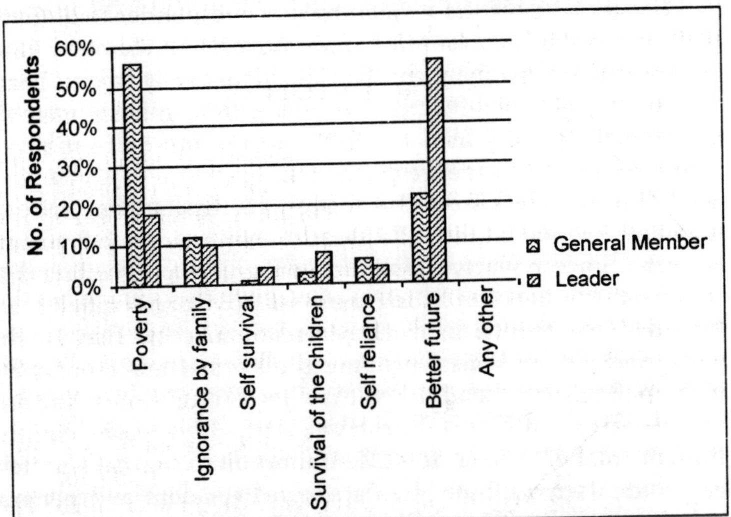

Chart 5.11: Opinion of the Respondents of being SHG Members

When the researcher has asked the respondents regarding the reason of being SHG members the above table shows completely opposite scenario in this case. The majority of the general member respondents 56 (56%) have joined the SHG because the members want to eradicate poverty through this. The next higher percentage 22 (22%) have joined the SHG for better future, followed by 12 (12%), have joined the SHG since the women were very much ignored by the family member. Perhaps this helps members to make other feel their presence in the family. 6 (6%) women have joined SHGs because they thought that their labour is not recognized by the family members and women all the time have to depend on their male for any kind of financial assistance. That is why they joined SHGs to become self-reliance. Subsequently 3 (3%) and 1 (1%) women have joined SHGs for survival of the children and self survival respectively since no body is there in the family to provide food, shelter, cloth and security.

On the other hand 23 (56%) leader respondents have joined the SHG for securing better future followed by 9 (18%), 5 (10%), 4 (8%) have joined SHG because the member want to eradicate poverty, reduce the ignorance committed by the family and survival of the children respectively. Remaining 2 (4%) each have joined the group because of self-survival, and self-reliance.

The majority of the general member respondents 28 (56%) have joined the SHG for eradicating poverty on the other hand majority of leader respondents had joined the SHG to secure better future. It is also significant that only 6 (6%) general member respondents have joined the SHGs to become self-reliant as compare to 2 (4%) leader respondents.

It is quite clear from the above table that the majority of members had joined the SHG because they wanted to eradicate poverty. Since poverty alleviation programme have failed to achieve the target of uplifting the poor from poverty; Self Help Groups have proven its track record of success. That is why Government of India also encourages lots of self help programme to help woman to lead a healthy life through joint venture, cooperative and collaborative attitude which are the fundamental of success. It is also important to see that very few respondents from both the categories (leaders and general members) responded that they wanted to become self-reliant. It is because women habituated to be controlled and guided by their husband or father. Since patriarchy plays the crucial role of women socialization and their empowerment right from her birth to death; henceforth women think themselves inferior as against the male counterpart in the matter of decision making of certain issues.

The bar diagram 5.11 reflects that the tallest bar of the diagram 56 per cent general member respondents and leader respondents have joined the SHGs to eradicate poverty and to secure better future in the society.

Table 5.12: Opinion of the Respondents regarding the Sources of Information about SHGs

Types of respon-dent	Sources of information about SHGs									Total (%)
	Neighbour	Panchayat members	Other SHG member	NGO/CBO worker	Local Bank	Political member	Peer group	Social worker	Any others	
General Member	37 (37%)	24 (24%)	15 (15%)	22 (22%)	2 (2%)	0 (0%)	0 (0%)	0 (0%)	0 (0%)	100 (100%)
Leader	7 (14%)	22 (44%)	0 (0%)	5 (10%)	16 (32%)	0 (0%)	0 (0%)	0 (0%)	0 (0%)	50 (100%)

Source: Field Survey.

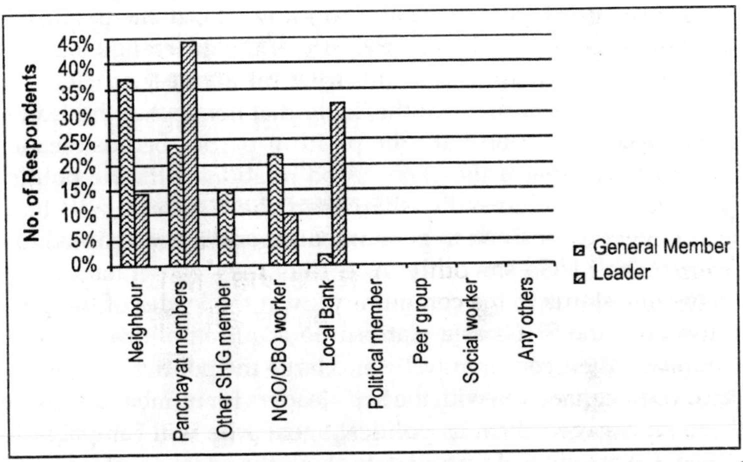

Chart 5.12: Opinion of the Respondents Regarding the Sources of Information about SHG

Table 5.12 regarding the sources of information about Self Help Group is concern gives us an odd reflection. The Table shows that the majority of the general member respondents 37 (37%) came to know about the self help group from neighbour. The next higher percentage 24 (24%) respondents came to know about the Self Help Group from panchayat member. The next higher percentage 22 (22%) came to know about the SHG from NGO/CBO worker, followed by 15 (15%) and 2 (2%) respondents came to know about the SHG from other SHG members and local bank respectively. The frequencies of the Table show that the panchayat, local bank and NGO/CBO worker played the crucial role as Self-Help Promoting Institute (SHPI). Role of SHPI is very essential for forming, developing and promoting SHGs through imparting skill training for adopting and promoting income generation activities, entrepreneurship development, exposure visit, disbursing financial assistance to the SHGs, providing productive equipments at subsidized price etc.

In the case of leader 22 (44%) respondents are usually getting the information from panchayat member and 16 (32%) of the respondents came to know about the self help group from local bank. The next higher percentage 7 (14%) leader respondents came to know about the SHG from neighbour. Only 5 (10%) leader respondents came to know about the SHG from NGO/CBO worker.

The trend clearly suggests that majority of the leader respondents 44 per cent came to know about the SHG from panchayat member whereas majority of the general members 37 per cent who likely to get information about the SHG from neighbour. It is clear from the Table that somewhat the leaders had good connection with the political parties because leaders had fair idea that if they keep good relations with the political parties or Panchayat Pradhan then their groups will be in advantageous position to get immediate and uninterrupted loan to run the SHGs smoothly. And thus they can enhance their economic status in the community. Even the leader of the SHGs might use the SHGs as a platform to acquire political power to represent their community. By and large the political parties had also good connection with the SHG leaders for number of reasons, viz., (i) engaged them as political agent who will campaign for them, (ii) provide all sorts of data about the latest development in the village, (iii) convert the SHG members into the vote bank, (iv) collect party fund by curtailing few percentage of loan through extending help to negotiate with the bank manager to avail bank loan easily and uninterruptedly. An unhealthy competition is going on among the political parties to attract the SHGs through their political manifesto to increase their vote bank. That is why all the parties try to capture maximum SHGs by giving false promises of helping them to get bank loan with subsidized rate. Even the political parties sometimes assured them to abate bank loan of the SHGs. Sometimes it has also been observed that panchayat officials and members of political parties are the leader of SHGs who influenced the other member regarding distributing bank loan. Sometimes a great political nexus has been found among SHG leaders, panchayat members and bank officials in the matter of opening bank account, getting loan, loan disbursement and loan repayment.

The bar diagram 5.12 reflects that the tallest bar of the diagram represent the majority of the leader respondents 44 per cent came to know about the SHG from panchayat and next bar of the diagram represent the majority of the general member respondents 46 per cent came to know about the SHG from neighbour.

Table 5.13: Resistance from Family to Become SHG Member

Types of respondent	*Resistance from family*			*Total (%)*
	Yes	*No*	*To some extent*	
General Member	11 (11%)	62 (62%)	27 (27%)	100 (100%)
Leader	6 (12%)	29 (58%)	15 (30%)	50 (100%)

Source: Field Survey.

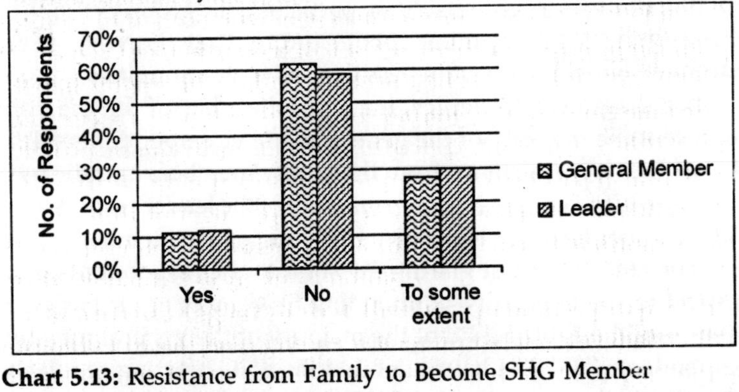

Chart 5.13: Resistance from Family to Become SHG Member

Through the above Table the researcher is willing to have response from the members regarding member had faced any resistance from family member. The Table depicts that the majority of the general member respondents 62 (62%) do not face any resistance from the family member followed by 27 (27%) have to face resistance from the family members to some extent and remaining 11 (11%) general member respondents have experienced absolute resistance from family members.

On the other hand 29 (58%) leader respondents do not face any resistance from family members. The next higher percentage 15 (30%) have to face resistance from the family members to some extent and remaining 6 (12%) have faced absolute resistance from the family members because of stereo type cultural attitude towards the women.

The trend clearly suggests that the majority of general member 62 (62%) and leader respondents 29 (58%) do not face resistance from their family members. It is because West Bengal took the pivotal role in major social reform movement much ahead than today. The catalyst role of West Bengal helped to persuade others to take active role in social movement, freedom movement or land reform movement. People of West Bengal are culturally very rich, and women were not left untouched about this matter. Those faced the resistance from family members is because of socio-cultural and religious practices of the community. Especially Muslim women were facing absolute resistance from the family members. Orthodox and submissive behaviour of the Muslim women are also responsible for their own adversity. Muslim women generally are not allowed to go outside or participate in group activity or community development programme that is why their participation in SHG is quite less than other communities.

Bar diagram 5.13 depicts that the tallest bar of the diagram represent the majority of the general member respondents (62%) do not face any resistance from the family members and the next bar of the diagram represent the majority of the leader respondents (58%) do not face any resistance from the family members.

The researcher put glaring question to the respondents with respect to the regularity of attending SHG meeting. It has been seen from the Table 5.14 that the majority of the general member respondents 73 (73%) have attended the SHG meeting regularly. The next higher percentage 17 (17%) respondents have attended the SHG meeting to some extent and remaining 10 (10%) respondents do not attend the SHG meeting at all.

On the other hand leader respondents 35 (70%) have attended the SHG meeting regularly followed by 9 (18%) of the leader respondents never attended the SHG meeting and remaining 6 (12%) respondents have attended a few SHG meeting.

Table 5.14: Opinion of Respondents regarding Regularity of Attending SHG Meeting

Types of respondent	*Regularity of attending SHG meeting*			*Total*
	Yes	*No*	*To some extent*	
General Members	73 (73%)	10 (10%)	17 (17%)	100 (100%)
Leader	35 (70%)	9 (18%)	6 (12%)	50 (100%)

Source: Field Survey.

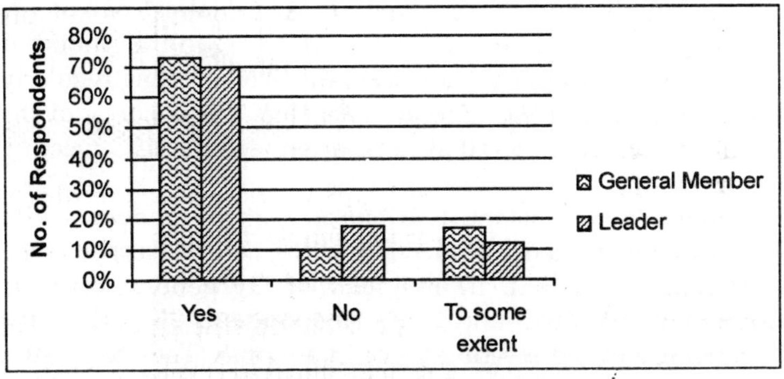

Chart 5.14: Opinion of Respondents Regarding Regularity of Attending SHG Meeting

The trend clearly suggests that the majority of the general member 73 (73%) and leader respondents 35 (70%) have attended the SHG meeting regularly and it was also significant to see that very low respondents 10 (10%) general members and 9 (18%) leader respondents not at all attend the SHG meeting. Meeting is an integral part of SHG where women share their emotion, problem, achievement and failure among the group members. It also helps women to mitigate the grievance of SHG members. It also helps to bring amicable solution of certain problems. It is hypothecated that more the members of SHG attend the meeting the more members of the SHG achieved empowerment. It has also been seen that minimum one meeting in a month is indispensable to perform administrative activities, managerial function and account keeping. To make the group most vibrant, member should meet twice or thrice a month to redress the grievance of the members beside maintaining book of accounts, meeting resolution, income generation activities, and participation in community development. It has also been observed that the members who never attend the meeting or attending the meeting in casual manner, never been achieving the empowerment. Total participation in regular group meetings lends the group strength, stability and prestige in the community and henceforth the SHGs become effective one to address all sorts of problem of the community. To achieve this, the SHGs should place strong emphasis on regular attendance in the group meetings.

The bar diagram 5.14 reflects that the tallest bar of the diagram represent the majority of the general member respondents 73 (73%) have attended the SHG meeting regularly and the next bar of the diagram represent the majority of the leader respondents 35 (70%) have attended the SHG meeting regularly.

Table 5.15 explains the distribution of the respondents with respect to the frequency of group meeting held. It has been seen from Table 5.13, that the majority of the general member respondents 66 (66%) and leader respondents 25 (50%) have attended the group meeting twice in a month. The next higher percentage 22 (22%) general member respondents and 15 (30%) leader respondents have attended the meeting once in a month followed by 10 (10%) general member respondents and 9 (18%) leader respondents never attended the meeting. Significantly low respondents, i.e. 2 (2%) general member respondents and 1 (2%) leader respondents had attended the meeting thrice in a month.

Table 5.15: Opinion of the Respondents about Number of SHG Meetings Attended

Types of respondent	*Number of SHG meetings attended*					*Total (0%)*
	Once in a month	*Twice in a month*	*Thrice in a month*	*Four times in a month*	*Never met*	
General member	22 (22%)	66 (66%)	2 (2%)	0 (0%)	10 (10%)	100 (100%)
Leader	15 (30%)	25 (50%)	1 (2%)	0 (0%)	9 (18%)	50 (100%)

Source: Field Survey.

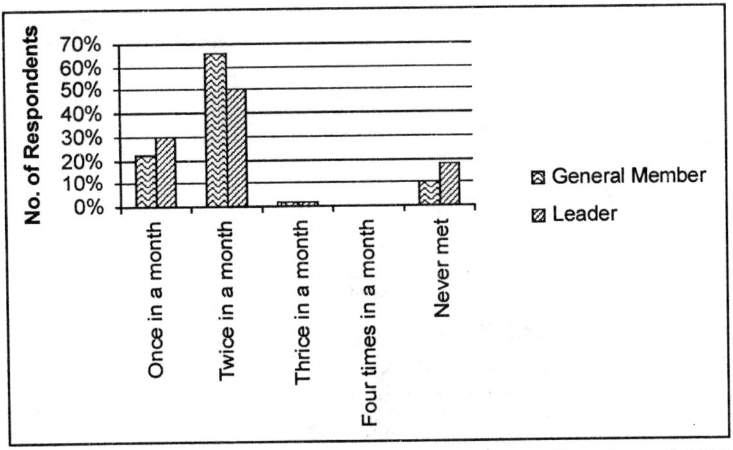

Chart 5.15: Opinion of the Respondents About Number of SHG Meetings Attended

From the above trend it could clearly be found that the majority of the general member respondents 66 (66%) have attended the meeting twice in a month and the majority of the leader respondents 25 (50%) have attended the meeting twice in a month. There is really a great benefit of attending meeting more than once. One meeting is not sufficient to address the need of the women. In one meeting group is busy to collect subscription of membership from the member and tallying the account part of the individual member. In second meeting members get chance to discuss their personal problem as well group related problem. Number of meetings decides the quality of the SHG and its success. It is also noteworthy that significantly low respondents from general members 10 (10%) and leaders 9 (18%) never attended the meeting. Those who never attended the meetings definitely they do not have the attachment with the SHG or they become member by chance without knowing the philosophy or importance of group in socio-economic development.

Regarding the number of meetings is concern bar diagram (5.15) reflects that the tallest bar of the diagram represent the majority of the general member respondents 66 (66%) have attended the meeting twice and the next bar of the diagram represents the majority of the leader respondents 25 (50%) have attended the meeting twice.

Table 5.16: Opinion of the Respondents regarding the Types of Training Received in SHGs

Types of respondent	*Types of training received*								*Total (%)*
	Youth Leadership & SHG Mgt. Training	Domestication of small ruminant/animal husbandry	Poultry management	Tailoring/Kantha stitch & Batik Printing	Kitchen gardening small firm	Food processing	Craftsmanship/artisan	Any other	
General member	10 (10%)	38 (38%)	17 (17%)	23 (23%)	12 (12%)	0 (0%)	0 (0%)	0 (0%)	100 (100%)
Leader	7 (14%)	16 (32%)	2 (4%)	20 (40%)	5 (10%)	0 (0%)	0 (0%)	0 (0%)	50 (100%)

Source: Field Survey.

Training is very important part of the SHGs through which members of the SHGs are enabled to perform the task in better manner. It helps to capacitate the SHG members to upgrade their skills to achieve the task smoothly. Henceforth, the majority of the general member respondents 38 (38%) have received training on domestication of small ruminants/animal husbandry followed by 23 (23%), 17 (17%), 12 (12%) and 10 (10%) general members have received training in tailoring/kantha stitch and batik printing, poultry management, kitchen gardening, small firm, and youth leadership and SHG management training respectively.

On the other hand the majority of leader respondents 20 (40%) have received training in tailoring/kantha stitch and batik printing followed by 16 (32%), 9 (18%), 3 (6%) and 2 (4%) leader respondents have received training on domestication of small ruminants/animal husbandry, youth leadership and SHG management training, kitchen gardening and small firm, and poultry management respectively.

It has been clearly articulated from the above trend that the majority of the general member respondents 38 (38%) have received training on domestication of small ruminants/animal husbandry and the majority of the leader respondents 20 (40%) have chosen to get training on tailoring/kantha stitch and batik

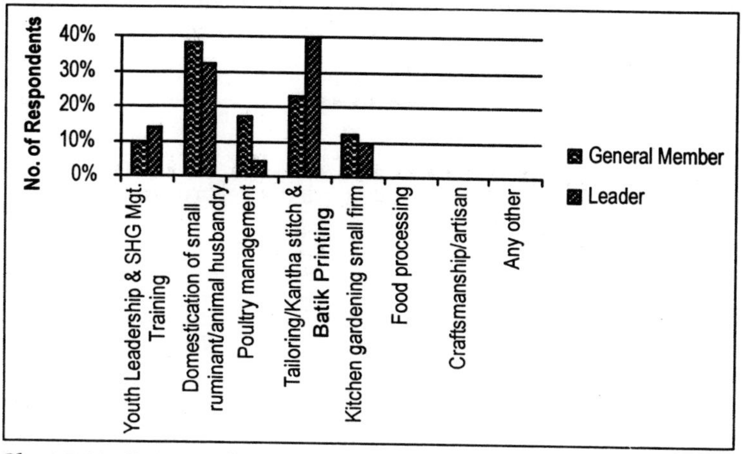

Chart 5.16: Opinion of the Respondents regarding the Types of Training Received in SHGs

printing. Most of the land of Birbhum district is dry and fallow and there is no dearth of land for grazing their cattle and ruminants. That is why most of the general members of the SHGs preferred to get training on domestication of small ruminants/ animal husbandry. Though the input cost of local breed is high but women get output (i.e. a local breed can give birth twice in a year) two times in a year and the demand of the local breed is quite high in the local market. Women do not have to invest extra cost to manage their birds and animals. It was also significant to see that low respondents i.e. 17 (17%) general members and 2 (4%) leaders chose to get training on poultry management because death rate of poultry is quite high. In recent past bird flu has created panic among the poultry owners. It is a contagious disease which spread from birds to human. Apart from that women do not show the interest because managing poultry farm is a laborious work. To manage a poultry firm women must have proper training on poultry shed, its food and vaccinate the birds in regular interval. It also requires thorough cleaning and maintaining hygiene in the poultry shed which is very much time consuming. That is why members are not enthusiastic about poultry management in the district of Birbhum.

Regarding types of training is concern bar diagram (5.16) reflects that the tallest bar of the diagram represents the majority of the general member respondents 38 (38%) have received training on domestication of small ruminants/animal husbandry and the taller bar of the diagram represents the majority of the leader respondents 20 (40%) had received training in tailoring/kantha stitch and batik printing.

Table 5.17: Opinion of the Respondents regarding the Training Organized by the Agencies

Types of respondent	*Training organized by the agencies*						*Total (%)*
	Pan-chayat	*Block office*	*DRDA*	*Local Bank*	*Local NGO*	*Any other Agency*	
General Member	8 (8%)	4 (4%)	1 (1%)	15 (15%)	66 (66%)	6 (6%)	100 (100%)
Leader	12 (24%)	7 (14%)	3 (6%)	2 (4%)	26 (52%)	0 (0%)	50 (100%)

Source: Field Survey.

The above table indicates that the agencies both government organization and non-government organization imparted training to the respondents both, SHG members and SHG leaders. It is quite clear from the table that the majority of the general member respondents 66 (66%) had received training from local

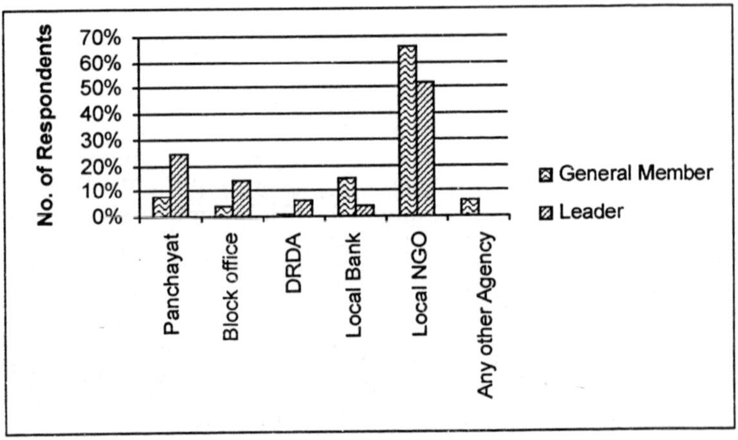

Chart 5.17: Opinion of the Respondents regarding the Training Organized by the Agencies

NGOs. The next higher percentage 15 (15%) have received training from local banks followed by 8 (8%), 6 (6%), 4 (4%) and 1 (1%) general member respondents have received training from panchayat, other Institutions (like Bandhan Microfinance Institution), Block and DRDA respectively.

On the other hand the majority of the leader respondents 26 (52%) have received training from local NGOs followed by 12 (24) have received training from panchayat. Subsequently 7 (14%), 3 (6%), 2 (4%) respondents have received training from Block, DRDA and local bank.

It is quite clear from the above trend that the majority of the general member respondents 66 (66%) and the leader respondents 26 (52%) have received training from local NGOs. There are two types of SHG, i.e. SGSY, a subsidized scheme of Government of India. It is formulated by the panchayat and nurtured, maintained and financed by DRDA, Government of India and other is non-subsidized SHG formulate and nurtured by Self Help Promoting Institute (SHPI), i.e. NGOs financed by NABARD. Since local NGOs are responsible for imparting maximum training to the members of the SHGs and NABARD supposed to reimburse all the programme cost of the SHGs. It is, because NABARD does not impart any kind of training to the SHG members that is why they need support from Self Help Promoting Institute (i.e. NGOs) to organize training progrmme and NABARD incurs all sorts of expenses. The objective behind giving responsibility to SHPI is that they (local NGOs) find easy to assess the needs of the SHGs and accordingly identify the resources and facilitate the members of the SHGs to market their product to the local area. Using these principles local NGOs articulate such training programme for the SHG members which is based on the local demand. It is also important to see that DRDA had imparted training to the SHG members significantly low because NABARD model of SHG is not directly linked to the DRDA. DRDA directly deals with SGSY.

The bar diagram 5.17 reflects that the tallest bar of the diagram represent the majority of the general member respondents 66 (66%) have received training from local NGOs and the next taller bar of the diagram represents the majority of the leader respondents 25 (50%) have received training from local NGOs.

Table 5.18: Opinion of the Respondents regarding the Level of Knowledge about the Functioning of SHGs

Types of respondent	*Level of knowledge about the functioning of SHGs*			*Total (%)*
	High	*Moderate*	*Low*	
General Member	16 (16%)	83 (83%)	1 (1%)	100 (100%)
Leader	29 (58%)	21 (42%)	0 (0%)	50 (100%)

Source: Field Survey.

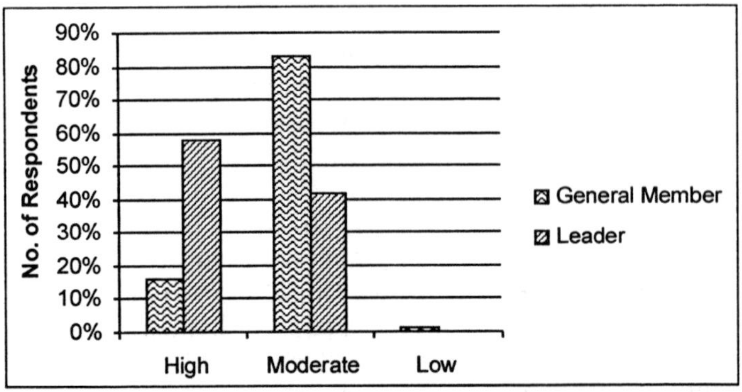

Chart 5.18: Opinion of the Respondents regarding the Level of Knowledge about the Functioning of SHGs

Table 5.18 reflects that the distribution of the respondents with respect to their level of knowledge about functioning of the SHG. It depicts that the majority of the general member respondents 83 (83%) have moderate knowledge of functioning of SHG and the next higher percentage 16 (16%) have high knowledge of functioning of the SHG. Only negligible 1 (1%) has low knowledge of functioning of the SHG.

On the other hand 29 (58%) leader respondents have high knowledge of functioning of the SHG and remaining 21 (42%) have moderate knowledge of functioning of the SHG. There was no single leader respondent found who had low knowledge in functioning of the SHG.

A clearly opposite picture has been found in respect of level of knowledge about functioning of the SHGs. It is quite clear from the above Table 5.18 that the majority of the general member respondents 83 (83%) have moderate knowledge about functioning of the SHGs whereas leader respondents 29 (58%) have high knowledge about functioning of the SHGs. It is because leaders directly lead the group and have to face lots of challenges everyday. Generally they are more qualified than general members and more responsible and accountable to the SHGs. Beside that they have good contact with the NGOs, panchayat, DRDA and other service provider which help them to accumulate lots of information. High knowledge about functioning of the SHG helps the leader to run the SHGs smoothly. A SHG having highly knowledgeable leader helps to perform uninterrupted group affairs in savings and credit, income generation activities, community participation etc. Only 1 (1%) general member respondent in comparison to 0 (0%) leader respondent have low level of knowledge about the functioning of the SHG and it might have several reasons, viz. (i) the member does not have any attachment with the SHG; (ii) member could not arrange monthly subscription fee which she supposed to deposit in the common fund; (iii) members never attended the meeting of the SHGs; (iv) political compulsion to become member of the SHGs; (v) disparity among the group members regarding individual savings, loan disbursement, loan repayment, decision making, educational status, caste, religion etc.

Regarding the level of knowledge about functioning of the SHGs the bar diagram 5.18 reflects that the tallest bar of the diagram represent the majority of the general member respondents 83 (83%) have moderate knowledge regarding functioning of the SHGs and the next taller bar of the diagram represent the majority of the leader respondents 29 (58%) possessed high knowledge regarding functioning of the SHGs.

Table 5.19: Members failed to Deposit their Savings in the Group

Types of respondent	*Members fail to deposit their savings*			*Total (%)*
	Yes	No	To some extent	
General Member	21 (21%)	65 (65%)	14 (14%)	100 (100%)
Leader	8 (16%)	30 (60%)	12 (24%)	50 (100%)

Source: Field Survey.

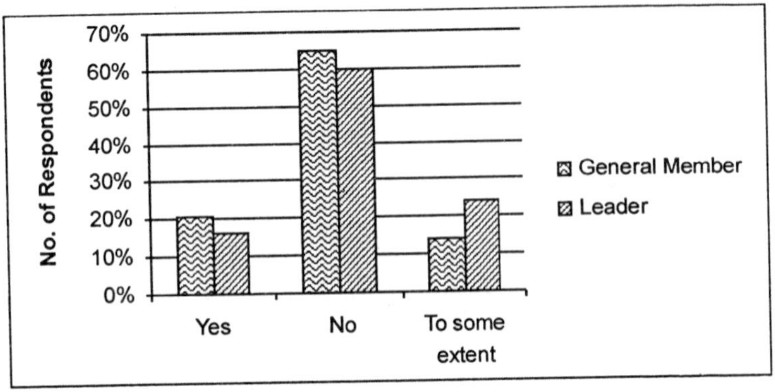

Chart 5.19: Members failed to deposit their savings in the group

Savings and credit is the principal aspect of success for any SHG. SHGs allow women for thrive which is the ultimate empowerment. To investigate regarding members fail to deposit their savings, the majority of the general member respondents 65 (65%) do not fail to deposit their savings in the group. The next higher percentage 21 (21%) respondents said they have failed to deposit their savings in the group. Remaining 14 (14%) general member respondents said they have failed to deposit their savings to some extent.

On the other hand the majority of the leader respondents 30 (60%) do not fail to deposit their savings in the group. The next higher percentage 12 (24%) respondents said they have failed to deposit savings to some extent and remaining 8 (16%) respondents never fail to deposit their savings in the group.

It is quite clear from above trend that the majority of the general members respondents 65 (65%) and leaders respondents 30 (60%) have deposited their saving regularly and timely. Development of saving habit is the major benefit received by the SHG members. Saving habit tends to increase income, better status and decision making power, access to various promotional assistance, access to larger quantum of resources, and window for better technology. It is also important to see that significantly low percentage of general member 21 (21%) and leader respondents 8 (16%) have failed to deposit their savings due to several reasons. The major reason of failing to deposit their savings was poor economic condition. Their husbands neither bother to contribute to their savings nor encourage them to save in the SHG's fund. Women have to manage their own savings by curtailing expenses from different allotment.

The bar diagram 5.19 reflects that the tallest bar of the diagram represent the majority of the general member respondents 65 (65%) do not fail to deposit their savings and the next taller bar of the diagram represent the majority of the leader respondents 30 (60%) also not failed to deposit their saving.

Table 5.20: Opinion of the Respondents regarding Receiving Bank Loan

Types of respondent	*SHGs received bank loan*		*Total (%)*
	Yes	*No*	
General Member	78 (78%)	22 (22%)	100 (100%)
Leader	39 (78%)	11 (22%)	50 (100%)

Source: Field Survey.

The bank loan is also considered one of the important impetuses for success of any SHG. However, honesty should play imperative role in the SHG. The bank loan motives the member for opting entrepreneurial activities and it has been observed that the majority of the general member respondents 78 (78%) have received bank loan followed by 22 (22%) do not receive bank loan.

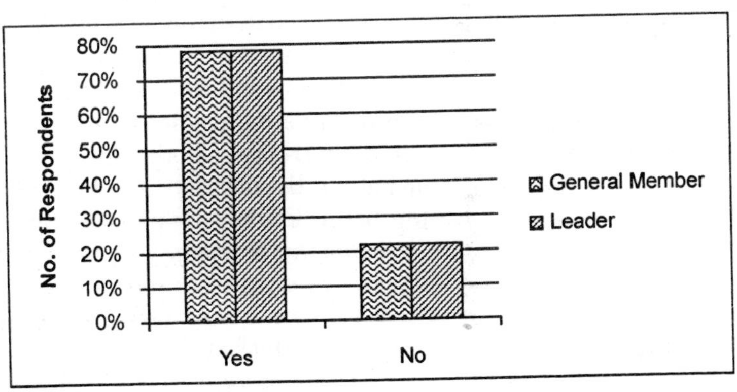

Chart 5.20: Opinion of the Respondents regarding Receiving Bank Loan

On the other hand the majority of the leader respondents 36 (78%) have received bank loan and only 11 (22%) do not receive bank loan for income generation activity.

Once the SHG has accumulated sizeable amount in the form of savings up to the period of 6 to12 months, the members may be allowed to go for inter-loaning against their own savings for emergent consumption and supplementary income generation credit needs. After satisfactory using and refunding of their own loan they may avail bank loan.

The trend clearly suggests that the majority of the general members 78 (78%) and leader 39 (78%) have taken bank loan and they used it to different income generation activities beside consumption in health and education. Bank loan is given to those SHGs who are matured and confident enough to use bank loan for earning profit. It is a procedure of the bank to provide loan to those SHGs who have experience of doing income generation activity with their own savings through inter-lending process. Inter-lending is a preparatory stage of getting bank loan. It had also been observed that significantly low, i.e. 22 (22%) general member respondents and 11 (22%) leader respondents not yet received bank loan because they might not be matured enough to handle bank loan or they do not have the experience of inter-loaning. There might be other reasons too for not receiving bank loan; these are: (i) their loan possibly used by the husband; (ii) tendency to become defaulter; (iii) faulty selection of income generation activity; (iv) lack of investment capacity; (v) risk of loss in entrepreneurial activities etc. Bank is leveraging collaterals free loan to the SHG members for entrepreneurship and in so doing the members become economically empower. The members used to refund the loan with interest after certain period. Nevertheless, it becomes win-win situation for both the SHGs who follows the philosophy of SHG and the banks. On the other hand bank loan becomes burden to the SHGs who are not following the philosophy of the SHGs and the members become more disempowered. So, it would be better for the members to introspect and retrospect themselves about their position to receive bank loan and use it to appropriate venture. It is highly desirable that members must have ready proposal on income generation activity before getting bank loan. They should not waste their valuable time of selecting their venture. Otherwise it will increase the vulnerability rather decreasing it.

It has also been observed that though bank has given loan to a group, not any individual, still members divided the loan among the group members for the income generation activities. Through this practice each individual chooses separate income generation activities on which they have the mastery. And each individual refunds their bank loan with interest to the group and subsequently group also refunds bank loan. It helps them not only to avoid unnecessary chaos of doing common income generation activities but also to stay away from clashes of refunding loan with interest. It is just opposite of the group activity and violating the basic principle of Self Help Group.

The bar diagram 5.20 reflects that the tallest bar of the diagram represent the majority of the general member respondents 78 (78%) and the majority of the leaders respondent 39 (78%) have applied for bank loan for income generation activities.

Table 5.21: Opinion of the Respondents About Income Generation Activities (IGA)

Types of respondent	*SHG doing Income Generation Activities (IGA)*		*Total (%)*
	Yes	*No*	
General Member	78 (78%)	22 (22%)	100 (100%)
Leader	39 (78%)	11 (22%)	50 (100%)

Source: Field Survey.

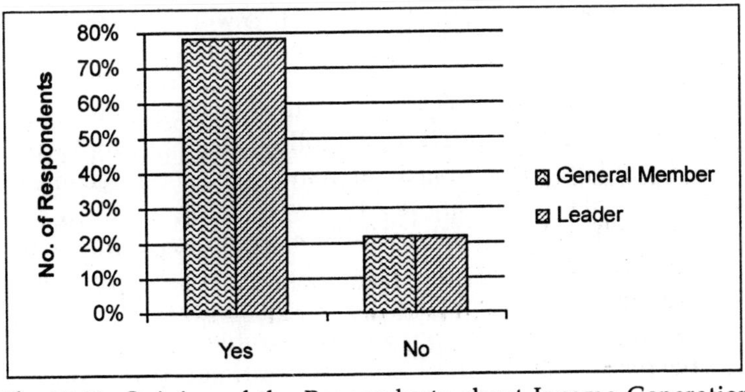

Chart 5.21: Opinion of the Respondents about Income Generation Activities (IGA)

The distribution of respondents has been given in Table 5.21, which shows in accordance with the SHGs doing income generation activity. The Table reflects that the majority of the general member respondents 78 (78%) have engaged in different income generation activity, whereas only 22 (22%) general member respondents do not have any kind of income generation activity.

On the other hand in the case of leader respondents the majority of the respondents 39 (78%) are doing different income generation activity and only 11 (22%) respondents said they are not doing any kind of income generation activity.

It is quite clear from above trend that the majority of the general member respondents 78 (78%) and leader respondents 39 (78%) are engaged in different income generation activities. Micro-Finance Institutions (MFI) helps the SHGs in providing loans and also guides them in choosing appropriate income generation activities. The members of the SHGs are taking up numbers of activities like animal husbandry, poultry farming, kantha stitch, and different micro enterprises etc. The activities of the SHGs are not limited. There are many activities which are taken up by the SHGs. As SHGs have many advantages like micro-finance as their core competency, sustained and significant investments by small amounts in various activities, low or no transaction costs, low or no default rate, value added services etc. helps Indian policy maker to think and take SHG as poverty alleviating tool.

As we all know that the feminization of poverty in India has been well documented, demonstrating the rising levels and differential gender impact of poverty on women. Liberalization of the economy has led to a paradigm shift in country's economy towards technology dominated sectors rendering women dominated sectors like agriculture, unviable and without any security cover. Liberalization has increased wage differentials, jobs vulnerability and unpaid work burden for women which lowering their social safety nets, unequal access for women to schooling, land, credit facilities, alternate employment, skill training and technology also undermines their prospects for poverty reduction. To avoid all those consequences the Self Help Groups might become a panacea to all.

The bar diagram reflects that the tallest bar of the diagram represents the majority of the general member respondents 78

(78%) and the majority of the leaders respondent 39 (78%) are doing income generation activities.

Table 5.22: Opinion of the Respondents regarding types of Income Generation Activities (IGA)

Types of respon-dent	*Income Generation Activities (IGA)*								
	Tailoring/Kantha stitch/Batik Fabric	*Kitchen gardening/small farming*	*Food processing/Making pickles*	*Craftsmanship/ Artisanship*	*Domestication of small ruminants/ animal husbandry*	*Poultry Management*	*Purchase & sale of paddy or puffed rice*	*Any other*	*Total (%)*
General Member	27 (27%)	18 (18%)	0 (0%)	3 (3%)	17 (17%)	0 (0%)	13 (13%)	0 (0%)	78
Leader	20 (40%)	6 (12%)	1 (2%)	0 (0%)	6 (12%)	4 (8%)	2 (4%)	0 (0%)	39

Source: Field Survey.

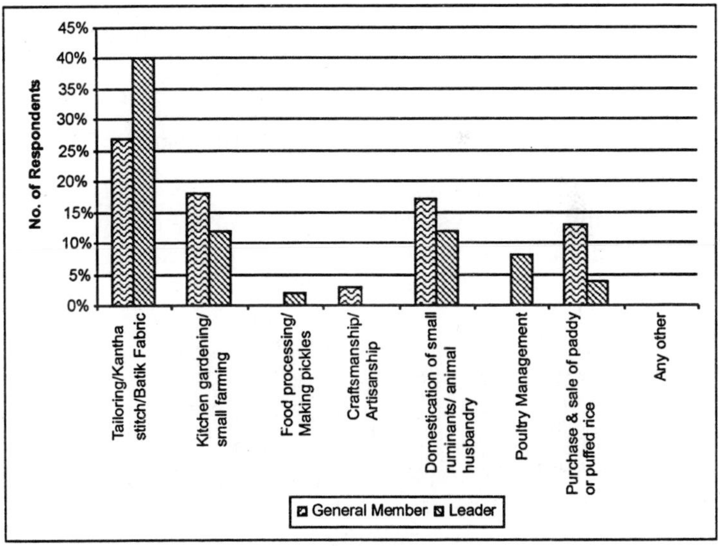

Chart 5.22: Opinion of the Respondents regarding types of Income Generation Activities (IGA)

Table 5.22 reveals that the wide range of activities undertaken by the SHG members and leaders. The members and leaders of

SHGs took up a number of income generation activities due to the credit and savings provided by their respective SHGs. The Table shows the distribution of respondents in accordance with the income generation activity adopted by the SHGs. The Table depicts that the majority of the general member respondents 27 (27%) are doing tailoring/kantha stitch/batik fabric as income generation activity. The next higher percentage 18 (18%) respondents were doing kitchen gardening/small farming as income generation activity. The next higher percentage 17 (17%) respondents said they are domesticating small ruminants/animal husbandry, followed by 13 (13%) respondents said they purchased and sale of paddy or puffed rice as income generation activity. Only 3 (3%) respondents said they preferred craftsmanship/artisanship as income generation activity.

On the other hand in the case of leader respondents the majority of the respondents 20 (40%) are doing tailoring/kantha stitch/batik fabric as income generation activity. The next higher percentage 6 (12%) are doing kitchen gardening/small farming and domestication of small ruminants/animal husbandry respectively as income generation activity. The next higher percentage 4 (8%) respondents are doing poultry management followed by 2 (4%) and 1 (2%) are doing purchase and sale of paddy or puffed rice and food processing/making pickles as income generation activities.

The trend clearly suggests that majority of general member 27 (27%) and leader respondents 20 (40%) are doing tailoring/kantha stitch/batik fabric as income generation activities because of huge demand of these products. The district of Birbhum becomes very much famous for Kabiguru Rabindranath Tagore, the first Nobel laureate of Asia and his famous Sriniketan Experiment and Visva-Bharati University. Apart from these, famous temple at Tarapith, Kankalitola, and eco-tourism at Bolpur-Santiniketan also are main attractions of the tourists and pilgrims which creates huge demand of kantha stitch and batik fabric. To purchase raw materials it requires huge amount of money since the input cost is quite high. It is quite impossible for the SHG members to arrange the said amount. That is why the bank loan becomes great help for the SHG members. Still they find difficulties to fulfil the demand of the market. However, the SHGs usually are taking help from the middleman or businessman to fulfil the immediate demand of the product. Otherwise they may face lots of challenges from the other competitors. Though the making charges provided by the middle man is quite less still they considered it profitable because they are getting jobs regularly and uninterrupted consignment throughout the year besides their regular venture. To prepare these products they must have patience, creativity and innovativeness. The large number of SHG members are doing this because they do not want to bear any risk of loss. On the other hand significantly very low respondents 2 (2%) leader and no single respondent from general member had taken IGA in food processing and pickle making because of several reasons—(i) input cost is very high; (ii) there is no cold storage facility available for the SHGs to preserve their product; and (iii) there is not so much demand of locally processed food and pickle in the local market where big private players, like Kishan, MPS group etc., are giving tough competition to each other.

Though women in rural areas are exposed to some of the enterprises but it is not sufficient for them to establish in that venture. It is imperative to lay stress that a woman must be guided and helped in choosing which enterprise she can take up. Also it must be ensured that SHG members are helped thoroughly to have knowledge on the process of establishing an enterprise, management and marketing. If these inputs are not supported strongly then women are least likely to succeed in taking up any income generation activity on sustainable basis even after having a desire and need.

Table 5.23: Opinion of the Respondents regarding repayment of Bank Loan

Types of respondent	*Members fail to repay bank loan*		*Total (%)*
	Yes	*No*	
General Member	14 (14%)	86 (86%)	100 (100%)
Leader	11 (22%)	39 (78%)	50 (100%)

Source: Field Survey.

The opinion in Table 5.23 reflects that the majority of the general member respondents 86 (86%) said they never failed to repay the bank loan followed by 14 (14%) said they failed to repay the bank loan. On the other hand the majority of the leader respondents 39 (78%) said they never failed to repay the bank loan, followed by 11 (22%) said they have failed to repay the bank loan.

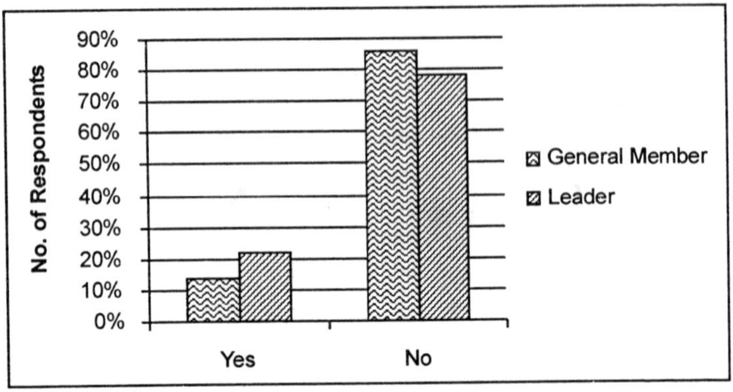

Chart 5.23: Opinion of the Respondents regarding Repayment of Bank Loan

It is quite clear from Table 5.23 that the majority of the general members 86 (86%) and leader respondents 39 (78%) never failed to repay bank loan. It is because of peer pressure, willing to enhance economic status, democratic attitude, regular meetings, and active participation in community development activities leads the members of the SHGs to repay the bank loan. They knew that without the help of bank they never been able to succeed in income generation activities. Even they also knew that once the loan is repaid they could apply for another loan with bigger amount for their venture. On the other hand significantly low number of respondents 11 (22%) and 14 (14%) from both leader and general member respondents have failed to repay loan and it is because of irregular meeting, lack of peer pressure, lack of awareness on legal harassment of loan default and unwilling to improve themselves.

Moreover members of the SHGs may well acquaint with themselves in the pace of development through utilizing bank loan in proper IGA which gives them stable income. They have seen and experienced that SHGs could transform the attitude of the SHG members and bring all-round development. Perhaps SHGs utilize the democratic decentralization, cooperative and collaborative attitude and synchronization of work, healthy environment to grow were the imperative factors to help the members to repay bank loan. Members might understand the advantages of collective work in accumulation of fund, inter-loaning, utilization of bank loan in IGA, refund of loan and decision making in all spheres of development. Thus, SHGs not only bring desired changes in the attitude and behavioural outlook but also bring desired result in health, education, economy, housing etc. Bank loan is essential for economic development that is why bank loan must be refunded within timeframe so that another loan could be availed later on.

The bar diagram reflects that the tallest bar of the diagram represent the majority of the general member respondents 86 (86%) do not fail to repay bank loan and the next taller bar of the diagram represent the majority of the leader respondents 39 (78%) not failed to repay bank loan.

Table 5.24: Opinion of the Respondents regarding Preference for Different Credit Sources for IGA

Types of respondent	*Different credit sources for IGA*		*Total (%)*
	Formal credit sources	*Informal credit sources*	
General member	89 (89%)	11 (11%)	100 (100%)
Leader	44 (88%)	6 (12%)	50 (100%)

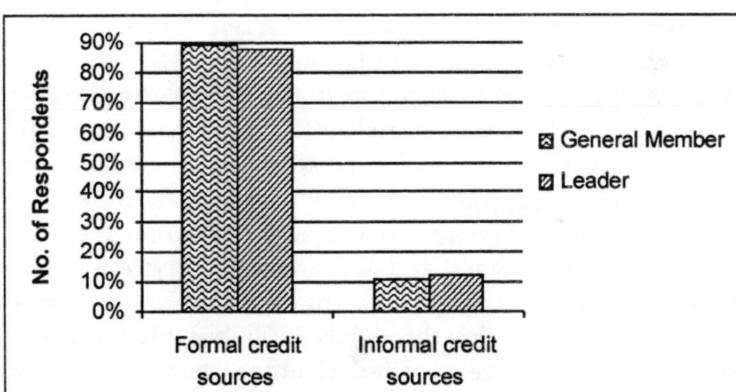

Chart 5.24: Opinion of the Respondents regarding Preference for Different Credit Sources for IGA

Source: Field Survey.

Through the above Table the responses regarding preferences of different credit sources for Income Generation Activities (IGA) has been reflected properly. The majority of the general members 89 (89%) preferred formal credit sources followed by 11 (11%) preferred informal credit sources. On the other hand the majority of leader respondents 44 (88%) preferred formal credit sources followed by 6 (12%) preferred informal credit sources.

It is quite clear from above trend that the majority of the general members 89 (89%) and leader 44 (88%) preferred formal credit sources. Formal credit source means government commercial bank, regional rural bank, government cooperatives and post office providing credit to the SHG members. They preferred formal credit source because of low rate of interest, enough time to repay the loan, no security deposit, cooperative behaviour of the staff members and transparency in work. Members of the SHGs relay on government bank and institutions hope to secure their scarce amount to the safe custody of government bank. And it has been observed that maximum urban population have bank account than rural population, but it has also been observed that maximum women population does not have bank account irrespective of rural and urban. To mitigate this disparity, Government of India has brought an innovative plan of financial inclusion where every citizen of India has the right to open his bank account to nearby bank without any harassment. According to this plan at least one bank must be set up to an area covering 2000 population within 2012.

The major thrust of financial inclusion comes after National Rural Employment Guarantee Act (NREGA). According to this act every productive citizen who wish to offer their labour for unskilled or semi-skill manual work will get job for at least 100 days in a year. Through financial inclusion, Government of India tries to bring transparency and accountability in the matter of wage repayment. Though government of India has given major thrust in financial inclusion through NREGA but it has long term implications where citizens of India getting chance of opening bank account to their regional area which will help them to save their money in time without wasting much time and could avail other provisions provided by the government. It has other objective too. It tries to minimize the role of moneylenders and other private players who spread their market in the rural areas and exploit the farmers, artisans, SHG and community at large. Since rural population needs credit immediately for agricultural work, handicrafts, education, housing, marriage and health purposes so they find moneylender and other private microfinance institutions are best option for them. Even private players do not take any collateral security for giving loan to the rural poor. They have experienced and realized that government bank does not provide such type of opportunity to avail loan immediately for emergency purposes. That is why financial inclusion through Self Help Group is one of the major answers of all those questions. SHGs and microfinance helps to curtail the role of moneylenders who leverages loan to the poor persons and charge exorbitant rate of interest.

It is also significant that very low respondents 11 (11%) from general members and 6 (12%) leaders preferred informal credit sources. Informal credit source means government does not have any direct control over their business, viz. moneylenders, traders, NGOs (Bandhan Microfinance Institution, Ujjiban Microfinance Institution etc.) and relatives. They preferred informal credit sources because of no security deposit, more flexible credit policy, enough time to repay the loan, less time consuming, interest rate of credit can be negotiated, credit can be accessed on good faith and reliability and more credit can be accessed as per requirement. It has been observed that there is no significant difference between government bank and private microfinance institutions in the matter of interest rate but private microfinance institutions charges nearly Rs. 200 per individual in the group as Loan a Processing Fees (LPF) which is not seen in the government banks. Henceforth if any SHG having fifteen members in a group then Rs. 3000 become loan processing fees. Even the rate of interest also varying among the SHGs and informal MFIs (Microfinance Institution).

The bar diagram reflects that the tallest bar of the diagram represent the majority of the general member respondents 89 (89%) had preferred different credit sources for IGA and the next taller bar diagram represents the majority of the leader respondents 44 (88%) had preferred different credit sources for IGA.

Table 5.25 reflects the respondents in accordance with their preferences of formal credit sources. The majority of the general

Table 5.25: Opinion of the Respondents regarding Preference in Formal Credit Sources

Types of respondents	*Preferences in different formal credit sources*							*Total (%)*
	Rural Bank	Nationalized Bank	NABARD	Post Office	Block & District Authorities	Co-operative Bank	Any other	
General member	72 (72%)	16 (16%)	0 (0%)	1 (1%)	0 (0%)	0 (0%)	0 (0%)	89 (89%)
Leader	35 (70%)	7 (14%)	0 (0%)	2 (4%)	0 (0%)	0 (0%)	0 (0%)	44 (88%)

Source: Field Survey.

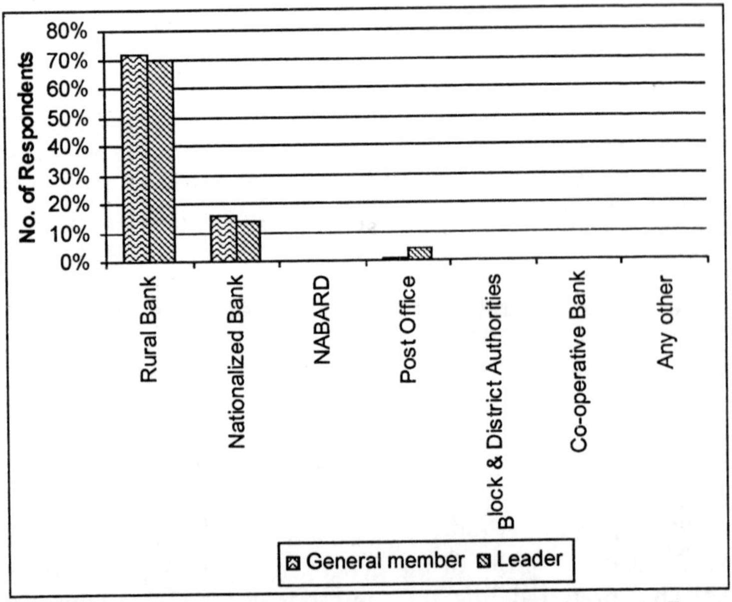

Chart 5.25: Opinion of the Respondents regarding Preference in Formal Credit Sources

member respondents 72 (72%) preferred to have savings and credit facility from rural bank followed by 16 (16%) preferred to have savings and credit facility from nationalized bank. Remaining

1 (1%) respondents have preferred to have savings and credit facility from post office. No respondent has been found to have savings and credit facility from NABARD, Block and district authorities, cooperative bank and any other service providers.

On the other hand majority of leader respondents 38 (76%) preferred to have savings and credit facilities from rural bank followed by 7 (14%) preferred to have savings and credit from nationalized bank. Remaining 2 (4%) respondents have preferred savings and credit from the post office. No single respondent has been found to have savings and credit from NABARD, Block and district authorities, and any other service providers.

The trend clearly suggests that the majority of general members 72 (72%) and leader 38 (76%) preferred to have savings and credit facility from regional rural bank because SHG is very much popular in rural area than urban area. Rural women find no difficulty to face the rural bank officials since banks are situated to their locality or nearby locality. The environment of the rural bank is not so much sophisticated like commercial bank. Even official of rural bank frequently visit the villages to make people understand about the importance of SHGs in enhancement of women status. It is also important to see that significantly low respondents 16 (16%) general members and 7 (14%) leader preferred to have savings and credit facility from nationalized bank There are several reasons behind low turnout in the nationalized bank—(i) bank is situated generally in urban areas; (ii) complex behaviour of the bank staff; (iii) very much time consuming; (iv) very much sophisticated environment of the bank etc.

Table 5.26 shows the distribution of respondents in accordance with the preferences of informal credit sources. The majority of the general member respondents 6 (6%) preferred Non-Government Organizations (NGOs) (Bandhan microfinance, Ujjiban microfinance, Arohan microfinance, SKS Village microfinance, L & T microfinance etc.) for getting credit followed by 3 (3%) general members preferred to get credit from moneylender followed by 1 (1%) preferred to get credit from friends and relatives respectively. None of the respondents have been found to have credit from Faith Based Organization (FBO), traders, shopkeeper and any other respectively.

Table 5.26: Opinion of the Responden**ts** regarding Preferences of Informal Credit Source

Types of respondents	*Preferences in different informal credit source*								*Total (%)*
	Money lenders	NGO (Private Microfinance Institution)	FBO	Trader	Friends	Relative	Shopkeepers	Any other	
General member	3 (3%)	6 (6%)	0 (0%)	0 (0%)	1 (1%)	1 (1%)	0 (0%)	0 (0%)	11 (11%)
Leader	2 (4%)	4 (8%)	0 (0%)	0 (0%)	0 (0%)	0 (0%)	0 (0%)	0 (0%)	6 (12)%

Source: Field Survey.

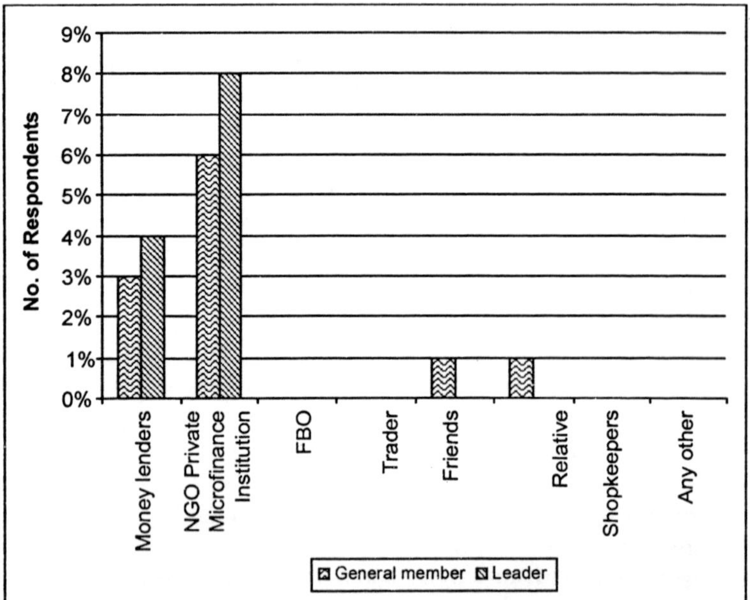

Chart 5.26: Opinion of the Respondents regarding Preferences of Informal Credit Source

On the other hand the majority of leader respondents 4 (8%) preferred NGOs (Bandhan microfinance Ujjiban microfinance, Arohan microfinance, SKS Village microfinance, L&T microfinance etc.) to get credit followed by 2 (4%) preferred to get credit from moneylenders. No respondents have been found to have credit from FBO traders, friend, relatives, shopkeeper and any other respectively.

The trend clearly suggests that the majority of general member 6 (6%) and leader respondents 4 (8%) preferred to get credit from NGOs (Bandhan microfinance, Ujjiban microfinance, Arohan microfinance, SKS Village microfinance, L&T microfinance etc.) for income generation activities because the organization is bound to help the poor women as per instruction of NABARD. The workers of NGOs are extending their cooperation to the rural poor and makes them understand about the benefit of the SHGs and microfinance. They also help the poor to develop the proposal of suitable IGA based on the availability of local needs and local resources and also make the members of the SHG understand about the probable risks lie with the IGA. Many a time exposure visit on the principle of "seeing is believing and doing is learning" may help the member to motivate of doing profit making income generation activity.

Since NGO's viability depends on the loan processing fees and high rate of interest charged by the NGOs while disbursing loan to the SHGs. Still members of the SHG never mind of giving extra charges if they are guided properly. Members of the SHG need guidance in the matter of choosing right income generation activities which have low or no risk of loss. That is why the staff of the NGO always encourages women to use the credit in low or no loss joint venture following the fundamental principle of availability of local resources and local market.

Credit is one of the important inputs in the development process. Development in the sense of economic, social and political empowerment and is incomplete without developing the women who constitute about 50 per cent of the total population. There are many problems in the field of rural credit for poor. The problem becomes much more aggravated and it is related not only to rural poor but also to the rural women because women bear the brunt of multiple forms of exploitation that originate from class, caste, culture and patriarchal system. The inability of the credit institutions to deal with the credit requirements of the poor particularly poor women in rural areas effectively has led to the emergence of the microfinance and micro credit system for the poor. In rural India it can be seen that poor sections of the society and destitute cannot avail the credit from banks and other formal financial institution due to their inability to deposit collateral security and mortgage property. The government sponsored poverty alleviation programme are involved centrally and planned without participation of the local people and therefore, often fail to address the needy and requirements of the poor. Lack of participation in planning and execution of these programme results in complete failure to improve social and economic conditions of the poor masses for which they were involved. At this point microfinance is looked upon as an instrument that can be considered as the golden stick for poverty alleviation *vis-à-vis* rural development.

The significantly low respondents, i.e. 3 (3%) general members and 2 (4%) leaders preferred to get credit from moneylenders. It is evident that before forming SHGs, maximum women preferred to get credit from moneylenders, because it is the easiest way to get credit. But the exorbitant amount of interest charged by moneylenders which made the SHG member poor to poorer and discouraged potential borrowers to have credit from the moneylenders. After privatization, liberalization and globalization government had to open up their economy and allow the private player to do their business which helped the SHG members to take credit with low interest. Even competition among the private players also helped the SHG to take the credit with lower interest rate. After forming SHGs, women hardly take any credit from moneylenders because the members get loans from their savings (Table 5.26 and Chart 5.26).

The researcher willing to see the involvement level of the SHG members in the matter of rural and community development. It is evident that women have been leading many communities in the matter of community mobilization and community building. Without the active participation of women in community development, prosperity will not be achieved. It is saying that if a woman of the family learns then all the family members will learn. Henceforth, Table 5.27 indicates that the majority of the general member respondents 40 (40%) never participate in rural and community development activities followed by 33 (33%) and 27 (27%) respondents have actively participated and participated to some extent respectively in rural and community development activities.

Table 5.27: Opinion of the Respondents regarding Involvement in Rural/Community Development Activities

Types of respondent	Involvement in rural/community development activities			Total (%)
	Yes	No	To some extent	
General member	33 (33%)	40 (40%)	27 (27%)	100 (100%)
Leader	30 (60%)	11 (22%)	9 (18%)	50 (100%)

Source: Field Survey.

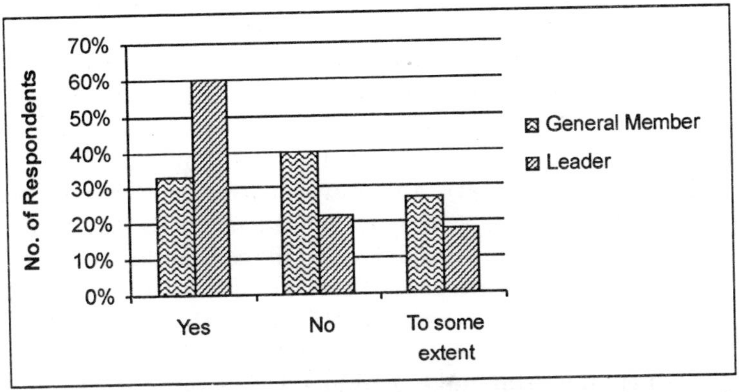

Chart 5.27: Opinion of the Respondents regarding Involvement in Rural/Community Development Activities

On the other hand majority of the leader respondents 30 (60%) have participated in rural and community development activities followed by 11 (22%) and 9 (18%) never participated and participated to some extent respectively in rural and community development activities.

Table 5.27 clearly gives opposite representation in respect of participation of SHG members in community development activities are concern. The majority of leader respondents 30 (60%) have participated in community development activities whereas the majority of the general member respondents 40 (40%) not at all participated in community development activities. It is because leaders have shown extra responsibility in managing SHGs and society at large besides their family. The leaders have accumulated much experience through exposure visit and congregation with other SHGs. Leaders of the SHGs have to visit or attend many training programmes and come across different SHG leaders who have better experience in this regards. Leaders have the experience and opportunity of exposure visit where they meet SHGs who are doing activities for betterment of the society.

Leaders are actively involved in community development because they understand the essentiality of SHGs in regard of rural development. Leaders are those who are able to lead the group and mobilize the members of the group. Through community mobilization they are able to make people aware about the need of SHGs as well as its involvement in rural development. SHGs is such a platform from where members can address the social maladies and mobilizes the resources for rural development. The inherent philosophy of SHGs is to help the community through identifying the problems or needs of the community to rank or order those needs, utilizes the resources (internal or external), and develop the cooperative and collaborative attitude among the SHG members so that they can solve their own problem and develop the community as a whole.

When people live in peace, harmony and abstains from major want (physical, social, economic, spiritual, psychological, political, cultural etc.) then they might come forward to take active participation in community building. Henceforth SHG is giving such opportunity to the women to fulfil their major want through collective action. Peoples' participation would be the only approach to make any programme success. And the success story of the SHGs depends upon peoples participation. Country has experienced lots of failure in many community development and rural development programme because of its bureaucratic nature and non-participation of community people in the programme. Consequently, all the programmes were formulated by the government machinery without involving village people. That is why it was considered as "government's programme and peoples' participation". After series of failure government learnt to formulate popular community development and rural development programme involving village people as a major stakeholder. That is why the success rate of any community development and rural development programme is quite high in present time. And it is happened because of "government's participation in people's programme".

The bar diagram 5.27 reflects that the tallest bar of the diagram represent the majority of the leader respondents 30 (60%) had actively participated in rural/community development activities and the next taller bar diagram represents the majority of the general member respondents 40 (40%) did not participate in rural/ community development activities.

Table 5.28: Opinion of the Respondents regarding Women Earns Respect after Being SHG Member

Types of respondent	*SHG helps to earn respect*			*Total (%)*
	Yes	*No*	*To some extent*	
General member	46 (46%)	24 (24%)	30 (30%)	100 (100%)
Leader	31 (62%)	6 (12%)	13 (26%)	50 (100%)

Source: Field Survey.

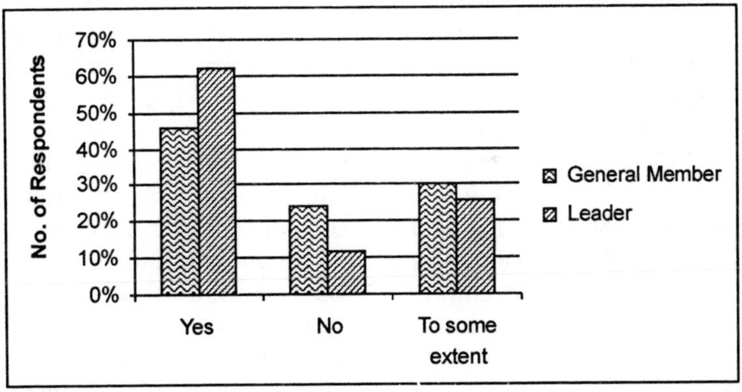

Chart 5.28: Opinion of the Respondents regarding Women Earns Respects After Being SHG Member

It is much longing for the SHG members to become respectable in the community. Here being respected means to gain popularity. Popularity, so called name and fame are an impetus for any SHG which propel the group members towards its goal. It is one of the indicators of being success. It works as ripple effect among the non-SHGs which attracts others to formulate SHGs for the welfare of all. The above table indicates that the majority of the general member respondents 46 (46%) said they were being respected by the community people through involving themselves into the SHGs and its welfaristic activities, followed by 30 (30%) respondents said they were being respected to some extent and remaining 24 (24%) said they yet to be respected while doing SHGs.

On the other hand the majority of the leader respondents 31 (62%) have gained popularity and respected by the community people, followed by 13 (26%) have gained popularity and respect to some extent. Remaining 6 (12%) yet to become popular and respected while doing SHGs.

Table 5.28 clearly suggests that the majority of the general members 46 (46%) and leader respondents 31 (62%) were being respected through associating themselves with the SHGs and it is also significant that low respondents, i.e. 24 (24%) general members and 6 (12%) leader respondents did not get the momentum since the group yet to become popular. It is quite hypothetical that the more quality time are will spend in the SHGs the more popularity and respect are can expect from the community. On the other hand SHGs helped them to become united and works for national integration. Some of the important elements of the SHGs, viz. solidarity, integrity, group sentiment, group dynamic, democratic outlook and transparency in work have allowed the group members to stand against the maladies and ultimately achieve empowerment. It has been seen that the poor women are able to break the poverty cycle through the activities of the SHGs and microfinance. It is obvious that the outlook of the community is very much determined by socio-economic, political, cultural factors. Sometimes, it has also been observed that a community is poor because they want to remain poor. Through the activities of the SHGs, community getting chance of being close and discuss the issues relating to their problem. The role of the SHGs is to organize the community to bring peace and prosperity in the society. Even many community development programme needs active participation of the SHG members. Since women are best resource manager that is why they need to take active participation. It has been observed that if we teach one man then only one person will learn but if we teach one woman then whole family will learn. Using this principle of success, woman must be engaged in community development work since they are the worst sufferer. They have to face all sorts of problems viz. sanitation and toilet facility, health and hygiene, safe drinking water etc. They have also observed that their economic condition is very much associated with the community development or rural development project. That is why rural development projects demand active participation from all corners to make the programme successful. Members of SHGs are also able to rupture the deep rooted problem of society like child marriage, dowry, child labour, alcoholic, gambling, nepotism, HIV/AIDS and so on so forth which help members of SHGs to earn respect. Those who are not getting respect is either remain idle without involving themselves in the development process or did not have much understanding about the importance of SHG.

The sole criteria of earning respect in the family is that women must contribute their labour in the home as well as in the field besides earning wages from outside. Women are considered as multi-task worker who will play the role of producer of children, kitchen manager, care taker of family members, agriculture field manager etc. It has also been observed that those women who contribute their income in the family were given respect. Perhaps earning women influence the member to give respect to them. Those who do not have income by their own are considered themselves powerless. That is why SHGs give an opportunity to women to start their own entrepreneurship by which they can contribute their income to their family.

The bar diagram 5.28 reflects that the tallest bar of the diagram represent the majority of the leader respondents 31 (62%) had earned respect in the society while doing SHG and the next taller bar diagram represent the majority of the general member respondents 46 (46%) had earned respect in the society while doing SHG.

Table 5.28 shows the distribution of respondents in accordance with the decision making in family affairs. The majority of the general member respondents 46 (46%) had low decision making in family affairs followed by 32 (32%) had moderate decision making in family affairs. Rest 16 (16%) and 6 (6%) had high decision making and no decision making in family affairs respectively.

On the other hand the majority of the respondents 17 (34%) had moderate decision making in family affairs followed by 16 (32%), 13 (26%) and 4 (8%) respondents had low, high and no decision making in family affairs respectively.

Table 5.29: Opinion of the Respondents regarding Decision Making in Family Affairs

Types of respondent	*Decision making in family affairs*				*Total (%)*
	High	*Moderate*	*Low*	*No*	
General member	16 (16%)	32 (32%)	46 (46%)	6 (6%)	100 (100%)
Leader	13 (26%)	17 (34%)	16 (32%)	4 (8%)	50 (100%)

Source: Field Survey.

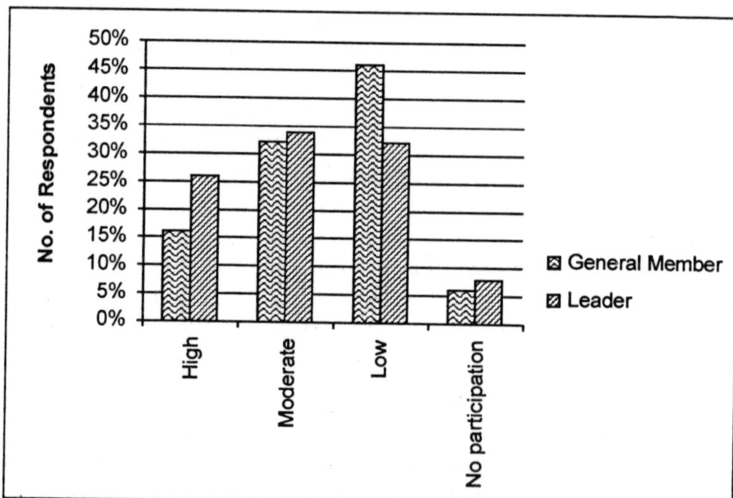

Chart 5.29: Opinion of the Respondents regarding Decision Making in Family Affairs

The trend clearly suggests that the majority of the general member 46 (46%) had low decision making in family affairs whereas the majority of the leader respondents 17 (34%) had moderate decision making in family affairs. It is obvious from the above table that though majority of women were participating in many community welfare programme but in the matter of their welfare (regarding decision making in family planning, choosing right enterprise, assets controlling etc.) the majority of their husband taking decision on behalf of them without involving them in decision making process. But, gradually scenario has been changed and women friendly policies are formulated to change the status of women. Even self help programmes especially SHGs would be the best intervention from the government's part to mainstream the poor and marginalized women by giving them a chance to prove themselves. It is proclaimed that India could not progress until and unless women are given equal representation in all spheres of life. After six decade of exploitation women learn to unite themselves against the exploitation. Slowly but steadily a remarkable change has been seen where large number of women of the SHGs are taking decision in all spheres of life for the welfare of their family.

Decision making is one form of empowerment where women have the right to take decision in any matter of life. SHGs help the women to come together to a platform where they can share their emotion, thought and ideas. They even share their personal problem which happens to their home. While taking decision in certain matter by the women, they must involve their husbands or family members so that the decision becomes amicable one. It creates healthy relations between the husband and wife. It has been seen that women are the best decision maker than their husband in respect of family planning, choosing the right income generation activities, accessing and controlling assets and expenditure. But man always considered themselves to be the best decision maker and do not want to lose the prerogative. Thus patriarchal society always compels them to play subordinate role and misguide them in such a way so that dominancy on women must be perpetuating. Though Government of India through 73rd and 74th amendments of Women Reservation Bill, 1992, which secure 33 per cent seats for women in the panchayat and municipality, still their representation in politics is very negligible. It is because of dogmatic attitude of male dominated society who do not allow their women to contest in the politics so that they can represent the poor and vulnerable of the society to bring desirable social changes.

It is also significant to see that very few general members 6 (6%) and leader 4 (8%) had no decision making in family affairs and these groups belong to muslim community where they were not allowed to take part of any decision making process. The only role of these Muslim women to produce children and take care of the family members. Even they were kept in *purdah* (*Burkha*) to segregate them from outer world.

The bar diagram 5.29 reflects that the tallest bar of the diagram represent the majority of the general member respondents 46 (46%) had low decision making in family affairs and the next taller bar diagram represents the majority of the leader respondents 17 (34%) had moderate decision making in family affairs.

Table 5.30: Opinion of the Respondents regarding Control Over Family Expenses

Types of respondent	*control over family expenses*				*Total (%)*
	High	*Moderate*	*Low*	*No control*	
General member	53 (53%)	32 (32%)	9 (9%)	6 (6%)	100 (100%)
Leader	32 (64%)	12 (24%)	4 (8%)	2 (4%)	50 (100%)

Source: Field Survey.

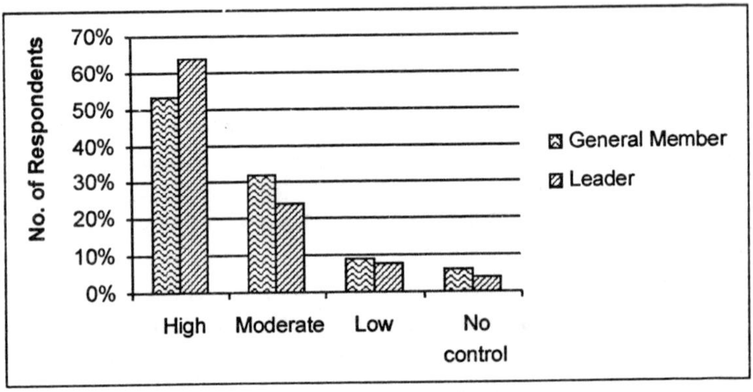

Chart 5.30: Opinion of the Respondents regarding Control Over Family Expenses

A family's perpetuation and sustainability is very much depended on controlling and curtailing the expenses by the family members. Expenses must be done on the basis of income of the family members. Priority must be set for expenses and wastage of money push the family into poverty. Perhaps the majority of the respondents 53 (53%) have high control over family expenses followed by 32 (32%), 9 (9%) and 6 (6%) have moderate control, low control and no control over family expenses respectively. On the other hand the majority of the leader respondents 32 (64%) have high control on family expenses followed by 12 (24%), 4 (8%) and 2 (4%) have moderate, low and no control over family expenses.

The trend clearly suggests that though the majority of the members do not have decision making power but they have full control over family expenses. The majority of the leader 32 (64%) and general member 53 (53%) had high control over family expenses. It has been seen that women have to manage their family with meagre income provided by their husbands. They have to manage all the essential and needful expenses on food, cloths, education, health and entertainment. Women find difficulties to arrange all these things. To manage the family expenses women have developed and upgraded skill of using nature and natural products. If we see the topography of the villages in West Bengal then we will get two types of villages, i.e. villages situated nearby the bushes and jungle or villages situated far from the jungle. Jungle is the best resource provider where women may get forest product, viz. honey, fire wood, fruits, *sal* leaves, latex, medicinal plants etc. It has been observed that rural women are very much dependent on the forest and forest product to manage their family expenses. These forest products help the women to curtail their home expenses since many articles are available in the forest. That is why rural women are investing their spare time to find the forest product. Women hardly cut down plants and trees of the jungle since they know the advantages of jungle. On the other hand the villages do not have bushes or jungle might face lots of challenges to arrange fire wood, medicinal plants, other essential materials etc. They are investing time to collect cow dung, leaves and weeds for fuel etc. Instead of investing money in purchasing water in dry prone areas women take all the hardship to walk long distance to fetch drinking water far from the villages.

Sometimes they were not given any single penny to manage their family and women have to manage the bread and butter of the family by their own. Those women who were deserted or abandoned by the husband or family members still have to manage the children of the family by their own effort. Women always try to save money, food articles and the product which indirectly leads to curtail the expenses. The saving habit was so reinforced to a woman from childhood that they could cope up in any situation. It has also been observed that if some amount is given to women then she definitely invests for her family members. Women rarely spend amount for their entertainment. They always try to keep their amount in safe custody. Women do not have risk bearing attitude in business. That is why very few Indian women become successful entrepreneurs. Whatever the amount they save, try to invest in purchasing jewellry, utensils which are also a kind of savings with future profit. In Indian culture dowry is one of the biggest factor in marriage where bridal parents have to give dowry to the groom, without which a marriage could not be performed. The savings in the form of jewellry and utensils always help to lessen the burden of the bridal parents.

On the other hand, significantly low respondents 6 (6%) general members and 2 (4%) leader had no control over family expenses. It might have several reasons: (i) women did not learn to adapt mechanism to get rid of harsh situation in early life; (ii) women never face such type of situation in early life; (iii) inability of women to control the unprecedented situation etc. It has also been seen that the women who have no control over family expenses could not survive long.

The bar diagram 5.30 reflects that the tallest bar of the diagram represent the majority of the leader respondents 53 (53%) had high control over family expenses and the next taller bar of the diagram represent the majority of the leader respondents 32 (64%) had high control over family expenses (Table 5.30 and Chart 5.30).

Savings and credit of the SHGs has lent the members to become authoritarian in the matter of control over family assets. Controlling assets as well as adding new assets like purchasing land, ornaments, tailoring machines etc. are also the indicators of success. That is why the above table indicates that the majority of the general member respondents 43 (43%) do not have any control over family assets, followed by 27 (27%), 23 (23%) and 7 (7%) respondents have low control, moderate control and high control over family assets respectively. On the other hand majority of the leader respondents 15 (30%) have low control over family assets, followed by 14 (28%), 11 (22%) and 10 (20%) have no control over family assets, moderate control and high control over family assets respectively.

It is quite clear from above trend that the majority of the

Table 5.31: Opinion of the Respondents regarding Control Over Family Assets

Types of respondent	*Control over family assets*				*Total (%)*
	High	*Moderate*	*Low*	*No control*	
General member	7 (7%)	23 (23%)	27 (27%)	43 (43%)	100 (100%)
Leader	11 (22%)	10 (20%)	15 (30%)	14 (28%)	50 (100%)

Source: Field Survey.

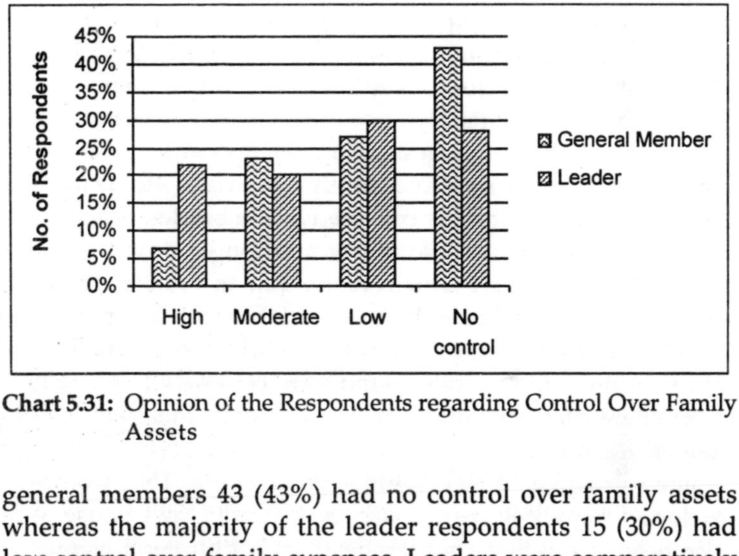

Chart 5.31: Opinion of the Respondents regarding Control Over Family Assets

general members 43 (43%) had no control over family assets whereas the majority of the leader respondents 15 (30%) had low control over family expenses. Leaders were comparatively better position than general members in the matter of controlling of family assets. It is because leaders directly handle group fund as well as bank loan for IGA. That is why they are more vibrant than general members. It has been observed that women's subordinate position is perpetuated and reinforced by their limited access to and control over resources. While it is true that the poor in general have limited access to and control over resources in relation to affluent those who have much access to and control over productive assets. Perhaps women have comparatively less control over such resources than men.

Women thus get doubly marginalized by virtue of being poor and being women.

The typical feature of patriarchal society is that women are not given any importance in the matter of resource controlling and it has been due to long subordination by the male. Women are not involved in this matter though they are the best resource saver as well as resource manager. If we look back to the transition of our society where different culture co-existed and cultural changes taking place. And this paradox that women status largely fallen down in this era. We will get an orthodox scenario that women are forcefully discouraged to become head of the family and even society. It is because patriarchy always wants to dominant on female and do not give any space to them for their development. Thus, long subordination pushes them in abject poverty. Henceforth family encourages baby boy than baby girl because they think boy can sustain the family and do perform all the rituals, funeral rites and cultural activities etc. It has been observed that girl child is considered as a burden of the family because family has to pay hefty amount of dowry for their marriage. As a result female foeticide and female infanticide become natural phenomena. Since bridal parents are giving huge amount of dowry to the groom. That is why the general believes of the bridal family is that in the form of dowry they are given their share of the property to the bride. In this way they are denied from property from their parents' house, and silently women also given their consent to this practice. Thus women are excluded from their own house as well as in-laws house. It has also been found that after the death of her husband women are denied from property and abandoned by the in-laws. However, Constitution of India has given huge relief to the women by securing their property in in-laws house as well as their own house. Unfortunately maximum women are unaware about their property rights.

The bar diagram 5.31 reflects that the tallest bar of the diagram represent the majority of the general member respondents 48 (48%) had no control over family assets and the next taller bar of the diagram represent the majority of the leader respondents 15 (30%) had low control over family assets.

Table 5.32: Opinion of the Respondents regarding Enhancement of Social Status after Associating with SHGs

Types of respondent	*Improvement of social status*				*Total (%)*
	Strongly Agree	*Agree*	*Partially Agree*	*Disagree*	
General member	20 (20%)	34 (34%)	26 (26%)	20 (20%)	100 (100%)
Leader	24 (48%)	18 (36%)	8 (16%)	0 (0%)	50 (100%)

Source: Field Survey.

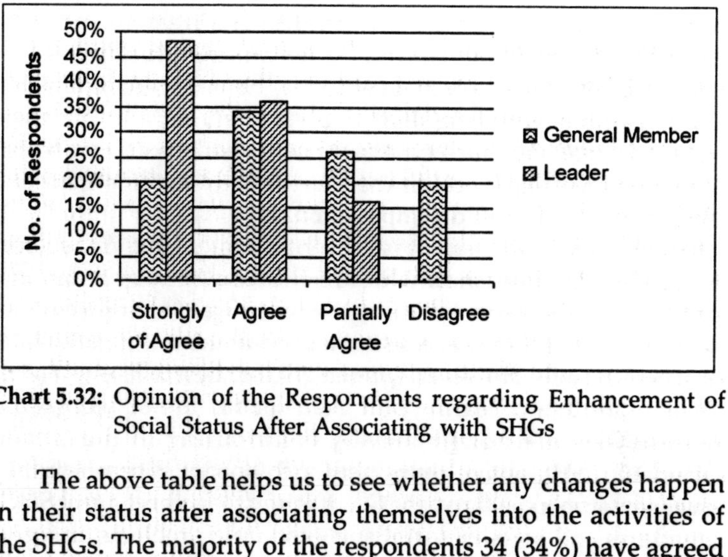

Chart 5.32: Opinion of the Respondents regarding Enhancement of Social Status After Associating with SHGs

The above table helps us to see whether any changes happen in their status after associating themselves into the activities of the SHGs. The majority of the respondents 34 (34%) have agreed that their social status was improved after associating with the SHGs, followed by 26 (26%) have partially agreed on the fact and 20 (20%) have strongly agreed and disagreed about the fact respectively.

On the other hand the majority of the leader respondents 24 (48%) have strongly agreed that their social status was improved after associating with the SHGs, followed by 18 (36%), 8 (16%) respondents have agreed and partially agreed about the fact respectively. No leader respondent has been found disagreed about the fact that their social status improved after associating with the SHGs.

The trend clearly suggests that the majority of the general members 34 (34%) and leader respondents 24 (48%) have agreed as well as strongly agreed about the fact that their social status enhanced after associating with the SHGs. It is, because, SHGs help the women to empower themselves through the process of savings and credit, income generation activities, information sharing, decision making in family planning, decision making in family affairs as well as controlling over assets. Thus they have changed their outlook and attitude of subordination or secondary citizenship. It is also significant that 20 (20%) general member respondents had disagreed the fact that social status improved after the associating with the SHGs because they did not get such exposures which were enjoyed by the leaders. Training, exposure visit and agency visit give the leader an opportunity to meet other resource persons, which definitely helped them to develop and upgrade negotiation skill. Unfortunately general members usually did not have such type of exposure and experience which might become hindrance on the way of their development and subsequently they feel disempowered.

In regard of social status is concern a family as well as society recognizes those women who are financially sound and can contribute to their family. Though women want to contribute to their family but biological constraint prevent them to go to outside for searching jobs. However, women give her best in family affairs, kitchen, and child rearing still their labour is not recognized because they are not financially contributing to the family. Fortunately, SHGs have given them such opportunity where they can generate income through IGA. It is widely accepted that SHGs can address all sorts of social and economic problems and give them a chance for change. It is the force of the affinity group which compels the service providers to listen to them. Perhaps group dynamic and group behaviour attracts others. It is probably a ripple effect where a small number of group members slowly but surely attracts other and motivate them to include in SHGs or helps them to formulate SHGs through their success story in all sphere of life. Being a member as well as spoke person of the SHG she represents the society in all-round development. Thus women of the SHGs earn respect and enhance their social status.

The bar diagram 5.32 reflects that the tallest bar of the diagram represents the majority of the leader respondents 24

(48%) have agreed that social status have been improved after associating with the SHG and the next taller bar of the diagram represents the majority of the general member respondents 34 (34%) have strongly agreed that social status have been improved after associating with the SHGs.

General Member Specific questions: Here the researcher would like to know about the general member's knowledge in the SHGs especially the knowledge in saving and credit, because it is the fundamental of any SHG and their role and functions in the group. Through the following questions the researcher would also like to know the level of involvement in the SHGs. The members formulate SHGs for getting relief from the exploitation, corruption, vulnerability etc. and want to build a just society where they can live happily. Whether the members feel empowered through 'social inclusion' and experience the growth and development opportunity in the SHGs or they feel disempowered through 'social exclusion' and experience more exploitation and vulnerability due to by becoming a member of SHGs. The objective behind formulating general member specific question is to know about the general members' strengths and weaknesses in the group. Whether the group members are proactive towards their action or not. The answers of the following questions help the researcher to draw the conclusion about the attitude and behaviour of the group members towards the SHG.

Table 5.33: Opinion of the Respondents regarding Amount Saved and Deposited Every Month

Amount saved	*Frequency*	*Per cent*
≤Rs. 500	98	98
Rs. 501-800	2	2
Rs. 801-1000	0	0
>Rs. 1000	0	0
Total	**100**	**100**

Source: Field Survey.

Table 5.33 shows the amount saved and deposited by the SHG every month. The majority of the respondents 98 (98%) said their groups have saved Rs. 500 and remaining 2 (2%) said their groups have saved Rs. ≤ 501-800. No respondent has been found

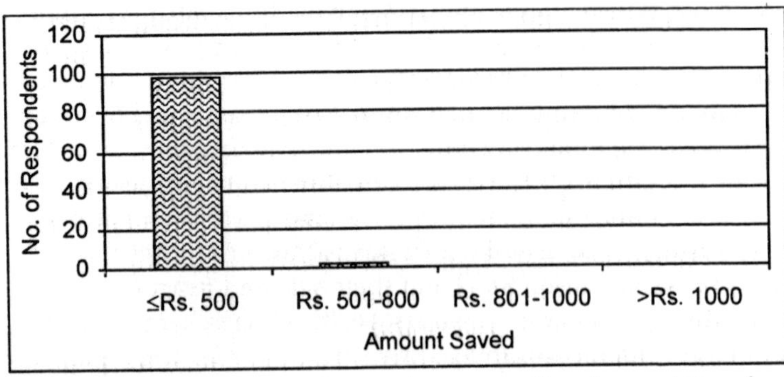

Chart 5.33: Opinion of the Respondents regarding Amount Saved and Deposited Every Month

whose group have saved Rs. 801-1000 and above Rs. 1000 respectively.

The trend clearly suggests that 98 per cent general members deposit their savings in the SHGs expecting to change their economic status. The development of SHG is based on the group fund. So thrift habit is a major development in the domain of self help programme and women of the SHGs have learnt to deposit their savings in time and on regular basis. Savings allowed women to take loan for starting new venture for their economic development and so on total development. The figure also reflects that the majority of the members individually deposit their amount Rs. 50 as their savings and very few of them save more than Rs. 50 individually.

Savings is the elementary of all the development of SHGs. It has been observed that members who deposit their subscription in the group are not getting any financial support from their husband or family members. SHG members need to arrange their subscription by their own. It has been widely practiced in West Bengal that women are habituated to save rice at the time of cooking everyday. At the end of the month they nearly accumulate 4 to 5 kg of rice and they sale it and get nearly Rs. 60 to 70 per month. It helps women to deposit their subscription fee without involving their husband much in SHGs. Though it is a traditional method of savings but it works nearly all the sphere of our life. They imbibe this habit from their ancestors where mother and grandmother used to manage the crisis situation where family is unable to manage the expenses. Apart from this, women offer their labour in agricultural field, doing domestic work or engage in handicrafts or artisan from where they can earn. It has also been seen that women were also doing kitchen gardening and animal husbandry from where they can earn by selling their vegetables and milk and milk product besides domestic use.

Table 5.34 shows the distribution of the respondents in accordance of their mode of savings deposited. The Table shows that the majority of the SHG members 94 (94%) have deposited their savings in monthly basis. Only 6 (6%) respondents have deposited their savings fortnightly. No respondent has been found to deposit their savings bi-weekly or weekly basis. The majority of the SHG members preferred to save monthly basis, because it is easy for them to deposit their savings. It is natural tendency of human being to see the monthly income and accordingly they

Table 5.34: Opinion of the Respondents regarding Mode of Savings Deposited

Mode of savings	*Frequency*	*Percentage (%)*
Bi-weekly	0	0
Weekly	0	0
Fortnightly	6	6
Monthly	94	94
Total	**100**	**100**

Source: Field Survey.

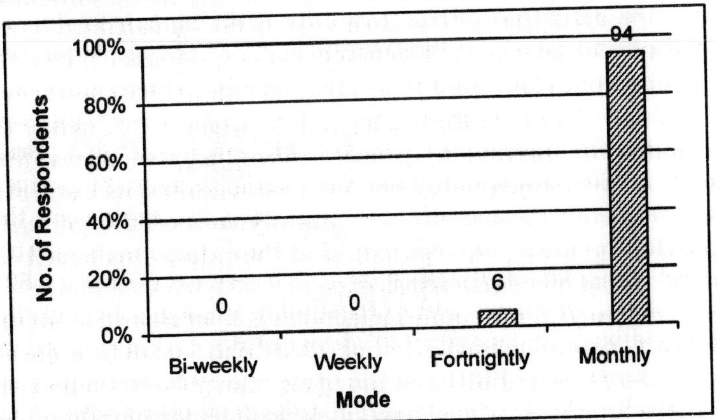

Chart 5.34: Mode of Savings Deposited

plan for their expenditure and savings. Subsequently at the end of the month they usually want to see whether there is anything left or not and accordingly they plan for mode of savings to the SHGs. That is why majority of the group members preferred to deposit their savings at the end of the month or beginning of the month. This gives a clear and broader picture of the women who are still fighting for their existence in the community. It has also been observed that the majority of the women are not financially supported by their husband/parents. Those who were able to deposit their subscription fortnightly either supported by their husband or the women have extra income other than their husbands' income. The women who are helped by their husband are accountable to their husband regarding all sorts of activities happening in the SHGs. They might feel the pressure of being SHG members and want overnight success in entrepreneurship to make profit. It has been observed that their husbands play authoritarian role in day-to-day activities. The women who are responsible for arranging their own subscription might enjoy the group activities and feel proud to become SHG members. Even their husbands were very much reluctant to play any role in the SHGs. Their husbands neither encourage nor discourage them to take part in the SHGs and community development activities.

Mode of saving also determines the economic status of women in the families as well as it also gives synoptic view of their upbringing and behaviour pattern. It has been observed that those who saves on monthly basis have much control on their lives. They are also thoughtful towards their action and allow everybody to take part in decision making process. It has also been observed that those who save fortnightly are much more uncontrolled in nature and try to persuade or influence the member using their money power. They sometimes impose their liking and disliking upon other group members. It is well accepted that the members who are economically well off are generally respected by the group members and their decisions have been considered as strongest decision.

The bar diagram 5.34 reflects that the tallest bar of the diagram represents the majority of the general member respondents 94 (94%) have saved on monthly basis and the smallest bar 6 (6%) of the diagram represents fortnightly saving in the SHGs.

Through Table 5.35 the researcher is willing to know about the duration of the SHGs. Total 100 respondents were interviewed from 50 self help groups under Bolpur-Sriniketan Block. The Table shows that the majority of the general member respondents 62 (62%) said their SHGs had completed 2 to 5 years. Another 20 (20%) respondents said their SHGs had completed 5 years and remaining 18 (18%) respondents said their SHGs yet to complete the time of 2 years.

Table 5.35: Opinion of the Respondents regarding Duration of the Self Help Groups

Age of SHGs	*Frequency*	*Percentage (%)*
Less than 2 years	18	18
2 years to 5 years	62	62
More than 5 years	20	20
Total	**100**	**100**

Source: Field Survey.

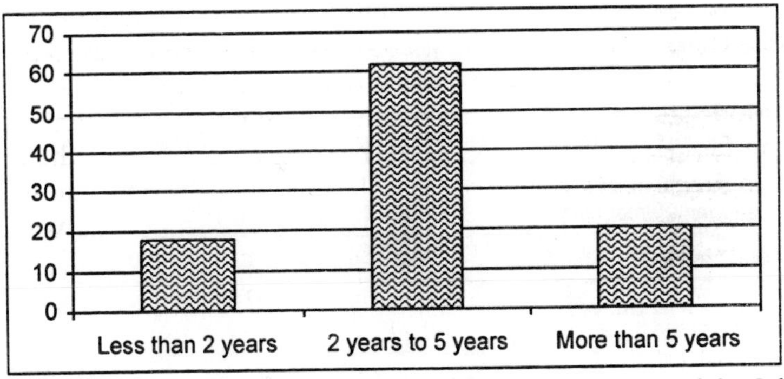

Chart 5.35: Opinion of the Respondents regarding Duration of the Self Help Groups

It has been observed from the study that a SHG needs 2 to 5 years time to become mature in all respect. Within 2 to 5 years members might accumulate their own fund to start inter-loaning which helps the SHGs to tap external credit in near future for income generation activity. Members of the SHGs of 2 to 5 years might become rational and logical towards their action and behaviour and their SHGs can lobby with the panchayat and other service provider for their own benefit as well as benefit of the society. The SHGs completed their 2 to 5 years time period, is very much stable, democratic and motivated towards achieving the goal. They are very much desirous to change their economic, social and political status to achieve empowerment through the activities of the SHGs. On the other hand the SHGs yet to complete their 2 years is not so much stronger in their view point. They have to spend more time with the SHGs in savings and credits, organizing more meetings with the SHG members, discussing the day-to-day problem encounter by the SHG members in the group. It has been observed that the majority of the newly formulated SHGs might not be in a position to leverage the loan to their members for income generation activities or inexperience in handling bank loan which might loss in the joint venture and thus make them more vulnerable.

The number of member in the SHGs determines its success and failure. The Table 5.36 depicts that the majority of the respondents 82 (82%) (41 SHGs out of 50 SHGs) have more than 10 members whereas remaining 18 (18%) respondents (9 SHGs out of 50 SHGs) have less than 10 members in their Self Help Groups.

Table 5.36: Opinion of the Respondents regarding Number of Members in the SHG

Number of members	Frequency	Percentage (%)
Less than 10 members	18	18
More than 10 members	82	82
Total	100	100

Source: Field Survey.

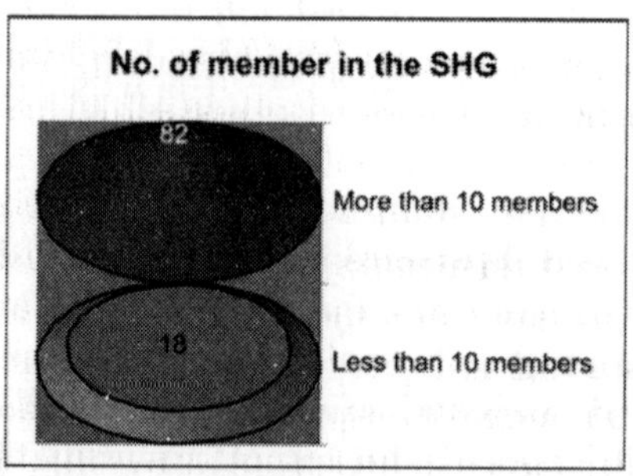

Chart 5.36: Number of Members

According to the NABARD guideline the SHGs having more than 10 members and less than 20 is stable SHG in terms of their own savings and credit policy, decision making in bank loan, decision making in right income generation activities as well as participation in community development etc. The main objective behind keeping 10 to 20 members in a SHG is to make SHG more viable and sustainable so that they can address deep seated social problem and also allow the members to participate in other social responsibility. It has also been observed that few members have joined the SHGs without having adequate information. Henceforth dropout becomes natural phenomenon. That is why more than 10 members are encouraged to form the SHGs so that group can perform its usual task without disrupting the normal functioning and decision making process of the SHGs. If we see the transformation of the society then it is quite clear that the human being usually lives in a group to avoid probable danger of the hostile nature. Subsequently group, community and society emerged and it provides the individual safeguard from any kind of insecurity. As we all know that the individual of the community hardly giving importance by the service provider. And the moment s/he comes under a group, the service providers have to entertain the same individual once rebuked by the service provider. It is all about peer pressure and group effects. Henceforth, single individual is quite handicap of bringing change in one's life while more than one individual can easily bring change in their life. And the tasks become very easy to them. Group dynamic, community sentiment and fellow feeling always help the individual of the group to fight against the anarchy.

Moreover accumulated fund of 10-20 members is quite high than individual savings. Depending on the accumulated fund members can apply for big loan. Even large group (10-20 members) has its own way of giving impact to the society. Large group is more vibrant and visible to the society than small group in terms of savings and credit, income generation activities and community development activity. Henceforth participation of large groups is very much essential to address the deep rooted problem of the society.

Chart 5.36 reflects that the tallest cone of the diagram represent the majority of the general member respondents 82 (82%) have more than 10 members in the SHGs whereas the smallest cone of the diagram represent that only 12 (12%) have less than 10 members in the SHGs.

Table 5.37: Opinion of the Respondents regarding Person Responsible to Organize the Meeting Affairs

Person organize the meeting affairs	*Frequency*	*Percentage (%)*
Leader	96	96
Assistant Leader	3	3
Cashier	0	0
Member	1	1
Total	**100**	**100**

Source: Field Survey.

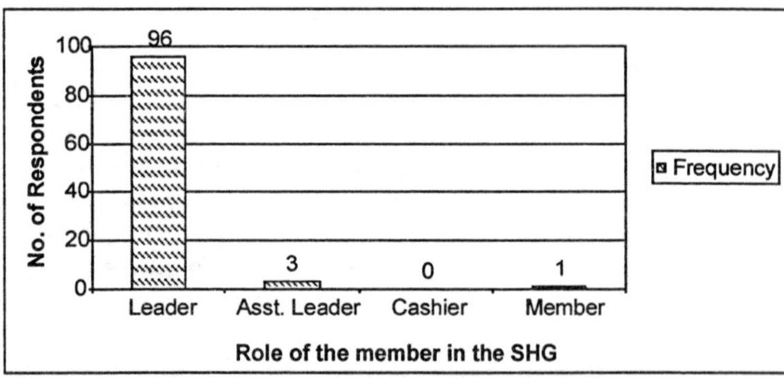

Chart 5.37: Person Responsible for Organizing the Meeting

Management of SHGs and its daily affairs is very vital and critical task for the office bearers. Until and unless they have the cooperation and coordination among themselves the group will not achieve the desire goal. In this regard the above Table shows the distribution of the respondents with respect to person responsible to organize the meeting affairs. The majority of the respondents 96 (96%) said leader calls the meeting affairs and the next higher percentage 3 (3%) said assistant leader calls the meeting affairs. A very negligible respondent 1 (1%) said member calls the meeting affairs if situation demands. No respondent had been found from the cashier to organize the meetings.

The trend clearly suggests that the majority of leader respondents organized the meeting affairs because it is the leaders' discretion and in the resolution it was unanimously decided by the group to give some extra power and responsibility to the leader, assistant leader and cashier. Before being office bearer of the SHGs the members has to pass some kind of mechanism called selection, election and nomination procedure. Leaders have enjoyed exclusive power to call meetings and taking decisions on behalf of the group. But sometimes assistant leader has to play the role of an acting leader in absence of leader. If situation demands then general members also call the meeting at the time of urgency when they find manipulation in accounting part, nexus among the leader and political parties, favourism, unconducive environment for growth etc.

Perhaps selection method is the best procedure among the three methods of selecting the leaders. Selection is done on the basis of certain qualifications of the individual like education, honesty, knowledge, patience and perseverance and proactive. Sometimes a leader has to play autocratic, democratic and *laissez faire* leadership together according to the need of SHG. It has been also observed that rotational leadership is very much desirable and effective to make leadership transparent, accountable and liable to the SHGs. More than two years' leadership makes the leader stagnant, bias and sometimes corrupt. That is why rotational leadership is very much desirable. Rotational leadership prevents corruption, nepotism, political infighting, political nexus and subgroup in SHG etc. Leadership should be such who shows the way and means of doing things and stand beside the members at the time of crisis. The philosophy of leadership should be "for the people, of the people and by the people" for performing any sorts of work. A leader should give credit to the whole group for success and should be responsible for failure. A leader should give an equal opportunity to the potential members to develop leadership. A leader should capacitate the follower in such a way that each becomes self-sufficient and takes prompt decision.

The bar diagram 5.30 reflects that the tallest bar of the diagram represents the majority of the general member respondents 96 (96%) have responded that leader has the power to organize the SHG meetings and the smallest bar 1 (1%) of the diagram represents that the member of the SHG has the power to organize the meeting.

Leader specific question: The researcher formulated few questions for the leader to know about their procedure or style of work which may or may not help the group to achieve the desires goal. Through the following answers of the question helps the researcher to identify the techniques and skills of the leaders which propels the group to the success. The objective behind formulating leaders' specific question is to know about the leaders' strengths and weaknesses in the group. The following questions help the researcher to draw the conclusion about the attitude and behaviour of the leaders towards the SHG. It has also been observed that leaders are more empowered than general member. If so then what helped the leaders to become empowered. Finding out all these queries is the major concern of the researcher through this section.

The maintenance of accounting part of the SHGs needs meticulousness and perfection. It can tie up whole group with single thread. And to do so everybody needs to be conscious about the matter. Table 5.38 shows the distribution of respondents in accordance with maintenance of account. And it has been seen that the majority of the respondents 42 (84%) have maintained account of the SHGs just after finishing up the meetings followed by 6 (12%) and 2 (4%) have maintained account the very next day and before next meeting respectively. None of the respondents have been found to maintain the group account in any other way.

The trend clearly suggests that the majority of the leaders of the SHGs had maintained group account just after finishing up the meeting because it is very easy to write down all the evidences and observations when group members are in front. If it is kept for maintaining for some other day then it would not

Table 5.38: Opinion of the Respondents regarding Time of Maintaining Group Accounts

Time of maintaining group account	*Frequency*	*Percentage (%)*
Just after finishing up the meeting	42	84
The very next day	6	12
Before next meeting	2	4
Any other	0	0
Total	**50**	**100**

Source: Field Survey.

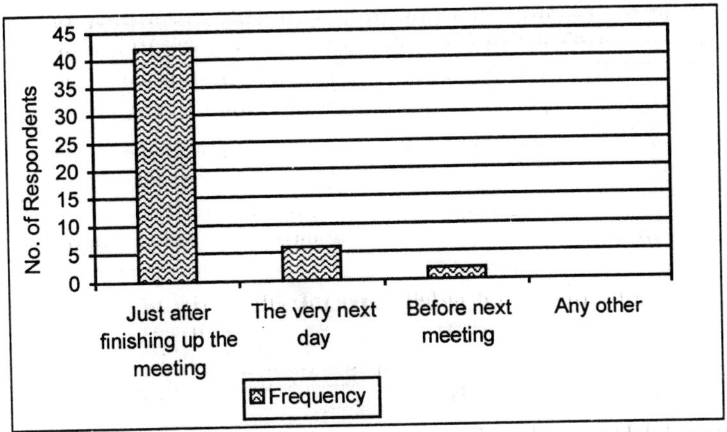

Chart 5.38: Opinion of the Respondents regarding Time of Maintaining Group Accounts

be possible to write down all the observations and it creates some sort of mistrust among the group members. Since accounting parts is really one of the sensitive part which needs utmost care to handle so it is better to maintain the account in front of all the members and if possible collect each and everybody's signature as evidence.

It is really good practice where leader maintains group account just after finishing up the meeting. In a group meeting besides maintaining group account there are other agenda also subject to discussion. Every member should have something to say regarding the success and failure about the SHG. To place an agenda before the group and get the agenda passed unanimously is very difficult where more than 10 members are participating in the decision making procedure. Since the meeting is the only medium to express their feeling, everybody should contribute their suggestion in the meeting so that no matter should remain hidden or secret. Members of the group also supplement and adding up with the agenda if something is missing. In that way the whole process should continue in front of the members so that no misconception takes place. After that no group member can blame to the group leader for any kind of disaster, because she puts the best possible way of maintaining group account.

Table 5.39: Opinion of the Respondents regarding Person Responsible for Maintaining Group Accounts

Person responsible for maintaining group account	*Frequency*	*Percentage (%)*
Leader	7	14
Asst. Leader	4	8
Cashier	39	78
Any other	0	0
Total	**50**	**100**

Source: Field Survey.

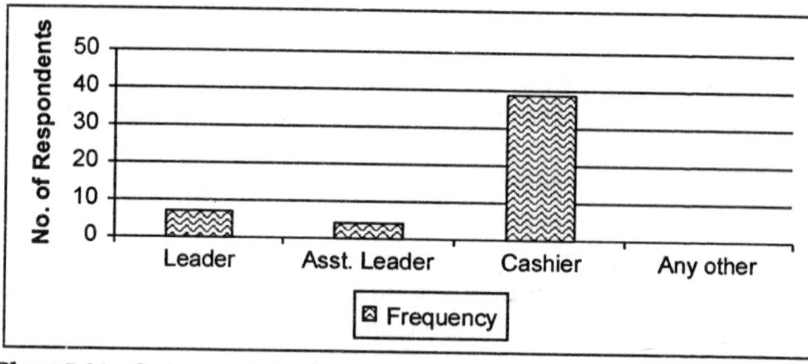

Chart 5.39: Opinion of the Respondents regarding Person Responsible for Maintaining Group Accounts

Maintaining group account is very serious work and the responsible person should be proactive in this matter. Otherwise it will let down the whole group. Table 5.39 shows the distribution of respondents in accordance with the person responsible for maintaining the group account. The majority of the respondents 39 (78%) said cashier was responsible for maintaining the group account followed by 7 (14%) and 4 (8%) said leaders and assistant leaders were responsible for maintaining the group account respectively. None of the respondents had been found in any other category to maintain the group account.

The trend clearly suggests that the majority of the cashier maintained the account because they had been assigned to do such kind of jobs. That is why cashiers must be those who could pursue their work independently without getting influenced by others. Cashier should be smart and proactive. It has been observed that many SHGs dismantle because of inappropriate way of maintaining group account. Cashiers sometimes used group's fund for their personal use. Even they are not bothered to disseminate the information related to the savings and credit. Henceforth, the group members lost their faith on the SHGs. The cashiers must redress the grievances of the individual members of the SHGs in group meetings. Subsequently, if any dispute arises out of maintaining group account must be resolved immediately so that no mistrust occurs in the long run. She should maintain the group pass book as well as individual pass book in front of the group members and they should be made understand about their status in savings and credit. Since it is a very crucial part of whole activity that is why cashier should be careful while handling these jobs. Even cashier is such a key person who first identify whether their group is mentally and physically prepare or not to handle the bank loan for setting new enterprise. Therefore, if anyone of the group member become defaulter then the whole group will be in stake. That is why cashier is such person who must identify the strengths and weaknesses of the individual members in the group regarding timely deposit of individual subscription, timely refund bank loan etc. If the members having such problem then cashier must rectify them so that the group become healthy one to use bank loan in appropriate way and make profit out of it. The office bearer must be educated and must have some command on the general members. The respondents were asked about the type of bank account they have. All the respondents replied that they have savings accounts in the name of their respective groups. The savings and credit activities of the SHGs are operated through the account of the group, therefore, the knowledge of the SHG member about their savings and credit status is very important aspect. In many cases individual members of the SHG have their pass book and they have full knowledge about their savings and credit status. It has been found during the study that in majority of the groups the SHG bank transaction is maintained by the respective cashiers of the groups but in few cases it has also been seen that the leader and assistant leader are sharing the responsibility along with the cashier. It has also been observed that few groups manage their accounting part by the students or educated person from outside of the group and to do so they have to incur lots of expenses. It grew over dependency on others in the matter of maintaining account.

Table 5.40: Opinion of the Respondents regarding Problem faced by the SHGs

Types of problem	*Frequency*	*Percentage (%)*
Societal	4	8
Familial	23	46
Technical	4	8
Financial	8	16
Political	11	22
Total	**50**	**100**

Source: Field Survey.

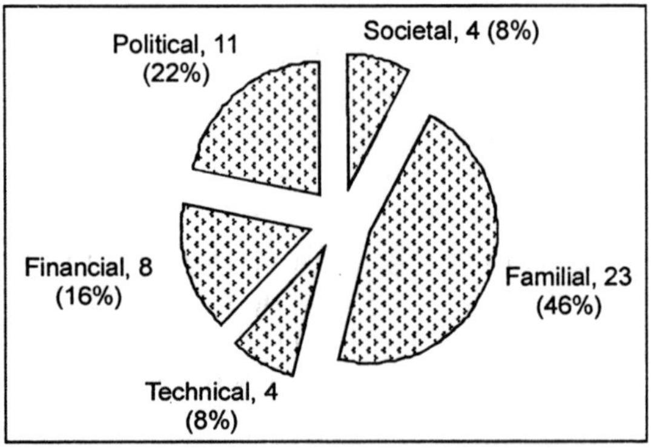

Chart 5.40: Problem faced by the SHGs

Through Table 5.40 the responses regarding problem faced by the members during day-to-day affair of the SHGs have been expressed categorically. The majority of the respondents 23 (46%) have faced familial problem. Due to over indulgence in household responsibility they could not spend much time to the SHG activity as required. It has also been seen that family members do not extend their cooperation and encouragement to undertake group activities. The next higher respondents 11 (22%) have encountered lots of political pressure since all the political parties want to get SHGs as their medium of political campaign. Even they also pressurize the group members to contribute donation on regular basis to the party fund from their bank loan or common fund as the panchayat pradhan of political party has influenced the bank manager to provide them loan. The next higher percentage 8 (16%) respondents have faced financial problem because their husband or father did not contribute to the SHGs or the members were the sole bread earner of the family and the remaining 4 (8%) respondents have faced technical problem where they did not have functional knowledge about the SHGs and societal problem where religious orthodoxy and community sentiment did not allow women to participate in the activities of the SHG respectively.

Moreover irrational behaviour, religious orthodoxy and dogmatic attitude of the family members let down the women who are participating or willing to participate in the SHGs. Even they are not allowed to go outside and take part in community development or rural developmental activities. The main reasons behind women are not allowing to take part in the group activities largely because of misinterpretation about the SHGs by the patriarchal society. They assumed SHGs as a time wasting and gossiping agency where the members are taught to interfere unnecessarily in the family matter. Through the SHGs women willing to confer power and prestige in the society and it leads to the problem for the person with vested interest. Patriarchy always considers women as a secondary citizen and prevents them to become empower and in so doing they could be dominated. Women are united themselves through SHGs to regain their power and prestige in the family as well as in the society which they have lost in the medieval and modern society. They want equal participation of women in any sort of decision making. It is basically a power conflict between men and women. And the patriarchal society always in a fear of losing the absolute power which they have enjoyed earlier. There are other reasons too, viz. denial of information, resources, education, health etc. which make the women disempowered. These evil practices have been seen in all segments of the community irrespective of educated and economically well of. The patriarchal society never gives space to the women where they can grow and lead healthy life.

The pie chart 5.40 reflects that the major portion of the chart represents that the majority of the leader respondents 23 (46%) have faced familial problem of doing SHG activities whereas the smallest pie of the Chart 4 (8%) represent leaders have faced technical as well as societal problem while doing SHG activities.

Table 5.41: Opinion of the Respondents regarding Knowledge about the Panchayat and its Function

Knowledge about the panchayat	*Frequency*	*Percentage (%)*
High	7	14
Moderate	8	16
Low	26	52
No knowledge	9	18
Total	**50**	**100**

Source: Field Survey.

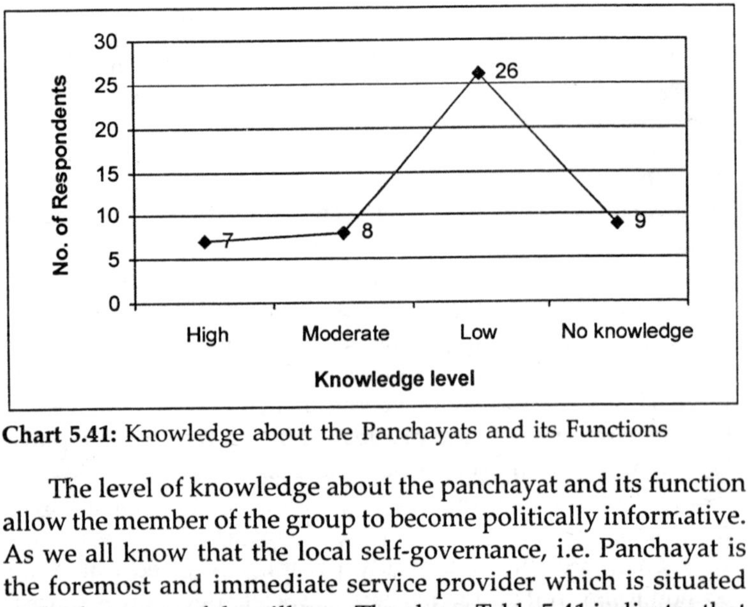

Chart 5.41: Knowledge about the Panchayats and its Functions

The level of knowledge about the panchayat and its function allow the member of the group to become politically informative. As we all know that the local self-governance, i.e. Panchayat is the foremost and immediate service provider which is situated at the door step of the villager. The above Table 5.41 indicates that the majority of the respondents 26 (52%) have very low knowledge regarding panchayat and its function. Since SHGs of NABARD model do not require much intervention of panchayat that is why they usually do not visit the panchayat. It might be one of the reasons for low knowledge regarding panchayat. They considered panchayat as a political arena where political members and followers are given preferences in terms of services. It has been seen that panchayat render services to those who follow and support the agenda of the ruling party of the panchayat. The rural masses are compelled to attend the political rallies and meeting called by the ruling parties to get benefit from the panchayat. Those who are not turn out to the rallies or meeting never be able to get the services and resources. Even corruption and nepotism are widely practiced in the panchayat that is why women very much reluctant to go panchayat for getting services or schemes. The next higher percentage 9 (18%) have no knowledge about the panchayat and its functioning because they do not find any suitability to visit panchayat and they also think that panchayat is the place for men only. It has been observed that majority of the Muslim women were not allowed to visit the panchayat to avail resources. That is why they might not have the knowledge about the panchayat and its functioning. On the other hand 8 (16%) and 7 (14%) respondents have moderate knowledge about the panchayat and its function and high knowledge about the panchayat and its function respectively. The respondents who have moderate and high knowledge about the panchayat and its function have great access to the panchayat. Generally, tribal women, women belong to Scheduled Caste and general category except Muslim frequently visits the panchayats to clutch the resources. They have experienced that their total development is very much dependent on the services and schemes rendered by the panchayats. They might understand that panchayat is the only institution which is available to their door step rendering services to the needy and poor. It is such institution of the rural side where people are directly related and getting hassle free services. It has also been observed that those are getting benefits from the panchayat definitely having someone in the panchayat who look after the matter. It might be possible that either any individual of the family of the group member is associated with the panchayat as a service holder or the family belongs to ruling party who negotiate for the SHGs. Sometimes the women of the SHGs directly elected by the rural masses hope to get best possible services from them. Even SHGs also encourage women to contest in the panchayat poll so that they could bring women friendly schemes and services.

Chart 5.41 of line diagram reflects that the highest point of the line diagram represents the majority of the leader respondents 26 (52%) have low level of knowledge about panchayat and its functioning, whereas the lowest point of the line 7 (14%) leader respondents have high knowledge about the panchayat and its functioning.

Table 5.42: Person Responsible for Taking Decision on Bank Loan for Income Generation Activity (IGA)

Decision about loan for IGA	*Frequency*	*Percentage (%)*
Leaders	9	18.0
Members	5	10.0
Both (Leader and General Member)	36	72.0
Any other	0	0
Total	**50**	**100.0**

Source: Field Survey.

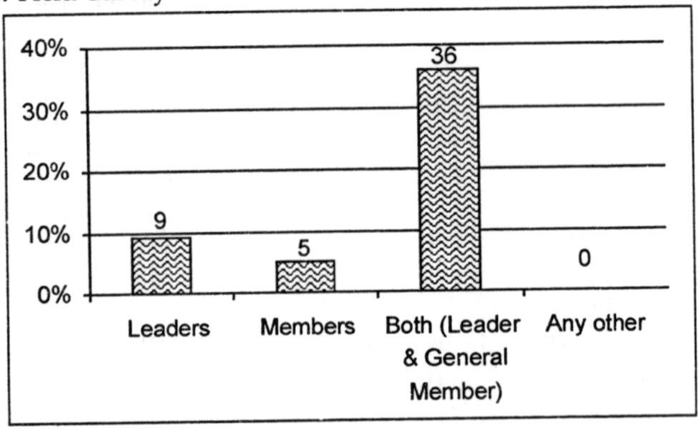

Chart 5.42: Decision about the Bank Loan for IGA

Table 5.42 shows the distribution of respondents in accordance with the person responsible for taking decision on bank loan for income generation activities. The majority of the respondents 36 (72%) said both (the leaders and the general members together) the respondents have decided on bank loan for income generation activities. There are two procedures of getting loan, i.e. (i) inter-loaning—getting loan from group's own accumulated fund which is also called preparatory stage of getting bank loan and (ii) loan from micro-finance institutions such as banks, post office etc. or institutions like Ujjiban, Bandhan etc. Loan is such a sensitive matter that there is always a chance of default if it is not considered seriously. It is quite general practice among the group members of Bolpur-Sriniketan Community Development Block that after availing loan the members of the group divided the loan among themselves so that they can start their individual enterprises. On the other hand 9 (18%) respondents said only leaders have the power to decide about bank loan for income generation activities and the next higher percentage 5 (10%) respondents said only general members decide bank loan for income generation activities. No other respondents from any other category have been found to decide bank loan for income generation activities.

The best practice is that to achieve group goal the majority of leader and general members of the SHGs must obey the bye-laws of the group so that cohesion among the group members must be maintained. Group decision is absolute to prevail on everybody and must be respected by all the members irrespective of leader and general member. So, before going to take decision on bank loan; members should have thorough discussion among themselves about the advantages and disadvantages of bank loan. Leaders of the group must consider few factors while applying for bank loan, viz. (i) member must understand the objectives of the SHG; (ii) members must have experience in inter-loaning; (iii) members must be mature enough to handle the bank loan; (iv) members must have various options in profitable joint venture before applying for bank loan; (v) in no circumstance bank loan will be given to their husband or to the people living outside the village; (vi) in no circumstances bank loan is kept ideal without using it in IGA; (vii) identify the probable risk lying with the joint venture, i.e. market, raw material etc., and (viii) identify the mechanism to control the damage if occurs, i.e. formulating emergency fund in the group from where group can repay the bank loan to avoid bank defaulter. The leaders of the SHGs takes decision unanimously regarding any matter so that cooperative and collaborative attitude must be manifested. It is also suggested to the group member that before going to take decision on bank loan the members of a group should have detailed knowledge about the loan and its repayment procedure and if possible the consequences of being defaulter.

It is very difficult for the lay person to get bank loan without any collators or mortgage. But Self Help Group and bank linkage programme of NABARD made it possible for the poor to become bankable and credit worthy. It has also been observed that members form SHGs to get bank loan only since they need not to deposit any collators. Once they have the bank loan they are not bothering to repay the loan. And it happens because they do not have proper information about the SHGs. Some way or the other it defames the SHGs and poor reluctant to form SHGs. The SHGs who are matured enough in all respects should go for bank loan. Sometimes, it has also been observed that bank manager leverages the loan to the immature SHGs only to avail incentives given by the NABARD. A very unique scenario has been found in the district of Birbhum regarding income generation activity. The majority of the SHGs are doing individual income generation activity. It means several members of one SHGs are doing several income generation activities. It is really undesirable because they are usually breaking the philosophy of SHG where they supposed to do common venture. Individual venture requires same amount of pressure and time like joint venture. The members of group are doing individual income generation activity because they are unable to become united. They fail to convince the other group members in the matter of common venture. They thought common venture creates unnecessary chaos in the group in the matter of division of labour and distribution of profit. It has also been seen that those prefer individual venture their group is not sustaining in the long run. No sooner than later their group dismantles like anything. All the time they bear some kind of doubt in their mind against one another regarding individual venture and leg pulling is quite common phenomena. The principle of cooperation, collaboration and democracy hardly been seen in such types of SHGs.

The bar diagram 5.42 reflects that the tallest bar of the diagram represents the majority of the leader respondents 36 (72%) had agreed that both the leader and general member together decided the bank loan for IGA, whereas the smallest bar diagram represents that only 5 (10%) leaders believed that only general member decided about the bank loan for IGA.

Decision taken for income generation activities lays great risk. And the person who takes decision in favour of the group may become hero or escape goat. So decision taken in this regard require thorough knowledge about the entrepreneurship. The majority of the respondents 35 (70%) said both (the leaders and the general members together) the respondents have taken decision for income generation activities. Since it is the collective effort of the group to

Table 5.43: Person Responsible for Decision Making in IG Activities

Decision in IG Activities	*Frequency*	*Percentage (%)*
Leaders	10	20.0
Members	5	10.0
Both (Leader and General Member)	35	70.0
Any other	0	0
Total	**50**	**100.0**

Source: Field Survey.

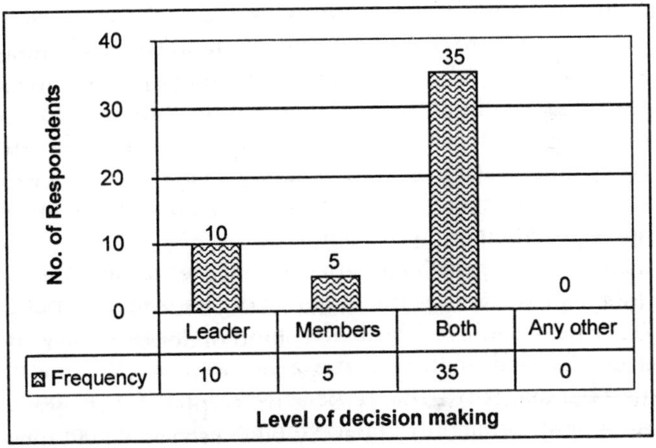

Chart 5.43: Decision Making in IGA

eradicate poverty and secure better future in the society, so democratic decision making is highly desirable. Each individual has her own domain of knowledge about the income generation activities and leader should give respect to their individuality and jointly take such income generation activities which give more profit without taking much hazard. While taking decision of income generation activities few important things should be prerequisite to encounter like demand and supply, availability of low cost inputs and risk factors of the venture. The next higher percentage 10 (20%) said only leaders have the prerogative to decide about income generation activities and the next higher percentage 5 (10%) said only members have the prerogative to decide about income generation activities. None of the respondents of any other category has been found to take decision on income generation activities. But, the trend clearly suggests that the majority of the members irrespective of leaders and general members have taken the decision on income generation activities. Collective decision always gives energy, confident and pleasure to the members of the group. They feel warmth and empowered as being decision maker. It is much sought that every member should contribute her view or decision towards selecting profit making income generation activities. Selection of profit making IGA is really a challenging work. SHG must go for such IGA where risk bearing factors are less. By doing so the SHGs earn strength, stability and prestige in the group, community and society at large. SHGs should not consider large IGA at the initial stage because women hardly have experience about the venture. If they have done any mistake in the venture then this mistake must not let down the whole group. The small IGA will give women an opportunity to practice and learn venture and if they do mistake then they must learn from that mistakes so that common venture should not be in stake. The profits out of the venture make the women self-reliant and self-confident.

The bar diagram 5.43 reflects that the tallest bar of the diagram represents that the majority of the leader respondents 35 (70%) have believed both the general member and leader together decided about income generation activities and the smallest bar diagram 3 (6%) represents that very low respondents of leader agreed that only general member decided about income generation activities.

Table 5.44: Opinion of the Respondents regarding Mechanism of Ensuring Maximum Attendance in the Meeting of SHG

Mechanism of ensuring maximum attendance	*Frequency*	*Percentage (%)*
Impose penalties	15	30.0
Persuasion	30	60.0
Throwing bad words	3	6.0
No action taken	2	4.0
Any other	0	0
Total	**50**	**100.0**

Source: Field Survey.

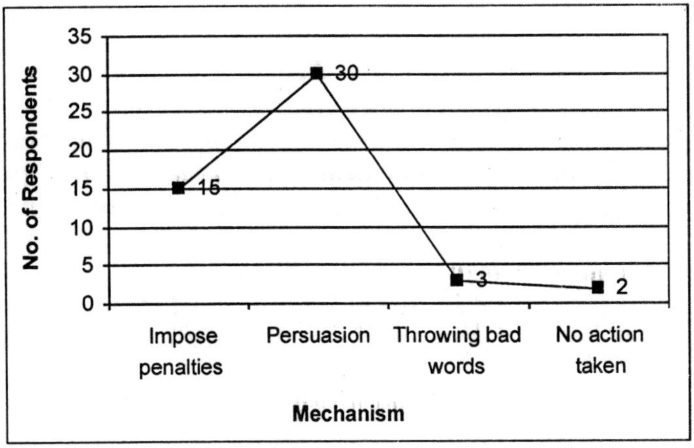

Chart 5.44: Mechanism for Ensuring Maximum Attendance

The Table 5.44 reflects with the mechanism for ensuring maximum attendance in the group meeting. The majority of the respondents 30 (60%) said persuasion to the members about the importance of group meeting would be the only option to ensure maximum attendance. The next higher percentage 15 (30%) said imposing penalty to those who are not serious about the group meeting would be the only option. Another 3 (6%) said throwing bad words would sometimes to be very much effective to those who are not at all serious about their group meeting. Only 2 (4%) respondents said no action should be taken against the members who are not regular to the group meeting. None of the respondents had been found to suggest any other mechanism to ensure maximum attendance in the group meeting.

The trend clearly suggests that the majority of the respondents believed persuasion is the only option to retain and ensure maximum attendance because women are usually facing lots of problem to attend the group meetings still they have tried their level best to attend the group meetings. Therefore, if the members are penalized or inflicted with insulting words then it might become very difficult for them to associate with the group. Perhaps groups have to find out some way out to ensure maximum attendance for those who are truant by nature. Leader has to explore innovative ideas to make the meeting interesting. To retain members in the group, leaders must use creative ideas, viz. role play, drama, quiz contest, game and sports etc. These entire programmes must have some emotional content and must bear some moral values. To make the group members attentive in group meeting they must be given some task to find out some familial as well as community problem and subsequently encourage them to suggest solutions. It has been observed that due to intervention of women self help group many issues like alcoholism, gambling, wife battering, dowry, infanticide, female foeticide, child marriage, child labour, HIV/AIDS, human trafficking etc. have been addressed successfully.

Apart from that they should bring external members of the SHG to share their experiences especially their success stories. Sometimes they should bring bank official or NGO staff who makes the SHG members updated with the latest information. All those efforts definitely make the member curious about attending the meeting. Informative, educative and communicative (IEC) material would be very good option to make people understand about the importance of SHG in regard to eradicate poverty. Sometimes DRDC official also arrange meeting with other SHGs to strengthen their knowledge as well as capacitate them so that they never think of to quit.

Chart 5.44 of line diagram reflects that the highest point of the line diagram represent the majority of the leader respondents 30 (60%) had believed persuasion will help to ensure maximum attendance where as the lowest point of the line 2 (4%) responded no action should be taken to ensure maximum attendance in the group meeting.

Table 5.45: Opinion of the Respondents regarding Procedure of Loan Disbursement

Procedure of loan disbursement	*Frequency*	*Percentage (%)*
Need based and rotation wise	35	70.0
Personal likings and disliking	2	4.0
Influential members	10	20.0
Any other	3	6.0
Total	**50**	**100.0**

Source: Field Survey.

Table 5.45 shows the distribution of respondents in accordance with the procedure of loan disbursement. The majority

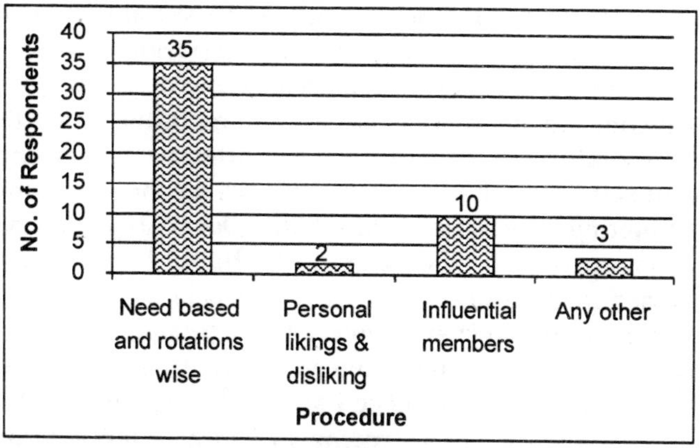

Chart 5.45: Procedures of Loan Disbursement

of the respondents 35 (70%) said loan must be disbursed according to the need based and rotation wise. The next higher percentage 10 (20%) respondents have complaint that the loan was disbursed to the influential members in the group who hold some political affiliation. The next higher percentage 3 (6%) said it could be any other loan which is equally distributed among the members. Remaining 2 (4%) respondents said the loan had been given to the members on personal liking and disliking.

The trend clearly suggests that more than half of the respondents have believed that loan must be circulated on need based and rotation-wise so that everybody should have equal access to the loan for their betterment. Every member comes to join SHG with some expectation to eradicate poverty and from that point of view everybody needs loan. The peculiarity of the SHG is that loan is given to the group members without collateral security but in the case of individual loaner bank needs collateral security. At the time of formation of the SHGs some of the basic principles and bye-laws have been constituted collectively to maintain democracy in the group. It has been decided in the group that loan must be given priority basis. And the loan which is given on need based and rotation-wise is largely fulfilling the said criteria. The most affected and vulnerable member of the SHG will be given priority while disbursing loan. At the time of giving loan it is obligatory for all the members to repay the loan with interest. In the context of West Bengal, maximum SHGs disbursing the bank loan among the group members are according to the suitability of IGA. Though temporarily it avoids conflict of choosing of IGA but in the long run SHGs loose the pace of development. Member concentrated on individual development rather than group development. Group loses its basic character of cooperation and collaboration. Though it has been collectively decided that loan should be given on priority basis but should also be decided that if emergency occurred then loan should be given to that particular affected individual. It has also been observed that some SHGs have their emergency fund created by their own saving apart from their regular savings. It is because sometime SHGs may face emergency need like health, education, marriage purpose, renovating or repairing housing, sometimes repay individual loan and so on so forth.

The bar diagram 5.45 supports the table and reflects that the tallest bar of the diagram represent the majority of the leader respondents 35 (70%) have responded that the loan must be distributed according to need based and rotation-wise, subsequently next bar of the diagram represent the majority of the leader respondents 10 (20%) believed that the loan was distributed to the influential members, the next taller bar diagram 3 (6%) represent it may be any other like equal distribution and smallest diagram represent 2 (4%) loan was given on personal liking and disliking.

Table 5.46: Opinion of the Respondents regarding Mechanism for Collecting Money from Defaulter

Mechanism for collecting money	*Frequency*	*Percentage (%)*
Peer pressure	33	66.0
Penalty impose	13	26.0
Any other	4	8.0
Persuasion	0	0
Total	**50**	**100.0**

Source: Field Survey.

The mechanism for collecting money from the defaulters must be ensured for the continuity of the SHGs. It is very sensitive issue which needs to handle carefully. Through the above table

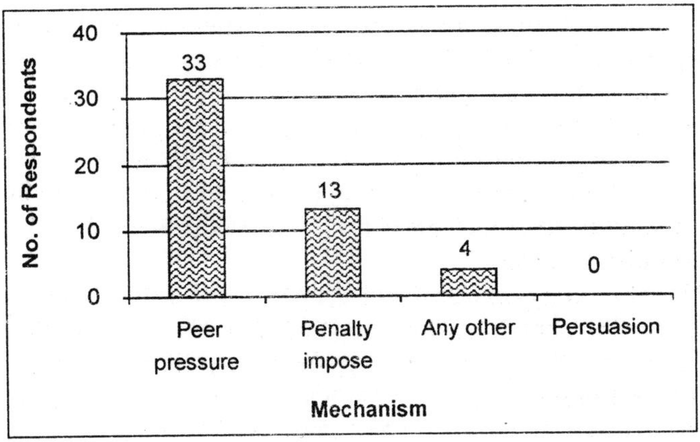

Chart 5.46: Mechanism for Collecting Money from Defaulter

the responses have been expressed categorically. The majority of the respondents 33 (66%) said that the peer pressure is the only option for getting loan back from the defaulter. The next higher percentage 13 (26%) said that the imposing the penalty is the only option for getting loan back and remaining 4 (8%) said it could be any other like encroaching their property, lodge case against the defaulter etc. None of the respondents had been found to persuade the members to get back the bank loan.

The trend clearly suggests that the majority of the respondents believed in peer pressure which would be the effective mechanism to collect default money. Perhaps Microfinance Institutions (MFI) using the same principle to get back their loan from the defaulter. Since individual growth and development is very much dependent on the collective action of the group so everybody should be conscious about each other. Members should be proactive of their thought. Group should be given utmost priority than any individual. So leaders should be very much conscious about selecting effective members who can contribute to their knowledge, information and labour to the group so that group must push towards the development.

SHGs are constituted with more than 10 and less than 20 people. So it is natural that group dynamic plays an important role in group development. In the forming stage the group members should be purposefully chosen to avoid the problem of default. Before forming the SHGs women must follow the guideline of the NABARD where it is clearly articulated that a group must be homogeneous one residing in the same place, belonging to the same caste, creed, sex and religion. It helps the SHGs to avoid unnecessary clash to each other. It also helps the SHGs to choose active, effective, honest, industrious members who will dedicate themselves for the development of group and community at large.

The bar diagram 5.37 reflects that the tallest bar of the diagram represent the majority of the leader respondents 33 (66%) had agreed about peer pressure for collecting money from the defaulter, followed by 13 (26 %) believed imposing penalty will work effective, followed by 4 (8%) believed it may be any other like encroaching personal property. No respondents have been found in persuasion category to collect the money from the defaulter.

6

Social Work Intervention

Modern age is called an age of cooperation, collaboration, correlation and coordination. Nothing can exist in this world in isolation. Every branch of knowledge is correlated, interdependent and has derivation of development and growth. This is true in case of social work and social sciences because social work deals with the problems of human beings and problems cannot be understood without the knowledge of psychology, sociology, political, ethnicity of human beings and the society at large. It is becoming increasingly perceptible to the social workers that the problems of personality and human adjustment require the integration of our knowledge of biological organism, society and culture. No social worker can ignore the significance of sociological, psychological, anthropological, economic data in the study and the solution of their problems. Social work practices are sometimes suspect, sometimes viewed with ambivalence by the public; they need to be continually validated and proven. Social work aims to improve and facilitate the working of society, the environment of relationship and social institutions developed from relationships, in which human beings live. Henceforth, social work tries to improve social life increasing cooperation among human beings and solidarity in society. The most used formulation currently is the international definition of social work devised jointly by the *International Federation of Social Workers (IFSW)* and supported by the *International Association of Schools of Social Work (IASSW)*: "The social work profession promotes social change, problem-solving in human relationship and the empowerment and liberation of people to enhance well-being."

Utilizing theories of human behaviour and social systems, social work intervenes at the points where people interact with the environment. Principles of Human Rights and Social Justice are fundamental to social work" (IFSW, 2000). The above definition has three key elements of social work; (a) social change, (b) problem solving in human relationships, and (c) liberation of people to enhance well-being.

To deal with the problem of the individual, group and community at large social worker must have the meticulous knowledge of the foundation of social work practice. The social work practice helps the social workers to identify deep rooted problem lying with the individual as well as environment. A little effort has been thrust to know the occurrence of the exact problem of the person and environment through the Figure 7.1 which helps the social worker to do the needful to solve the problem.

Figure 6.1 has been constituted with five important elements—Purpose, Sanction, Values, Knowledge and Skills. Let's have a synoptic view on each of the elements.

Purpose: The primary purpose of social work continues to the enhancement of social functioning. Social worker enables individuals, groups, families and communities to function more effectively within their various environments. Social workers strive to eliminate discrimination and to create just special environment. The ways in which social workers implement their purpose take different forms, approaches, and methodologies. Workers engage in direct practice with client in such roles as counsellor, enabler, broker, case manager, and advocate. They may also assume various indirect practice roles, such as supervisors, managers, administrators, teachers, researcher, and consultants. They work to prevent, resolve, or minimize human problems.

Sanction: The authority and permissions that sanction the practice of social workers in society come from several different sources. These include—(a) governmental agency boards with legal regulation responsibility; (b) public or private human service agencies; and (c) the organized profession.

Values: The values of the social work profession are rooted in a belief in the dignity and worth of every human being, and recognition of the need for a democratic and caring society.

SOCIAL WORK		
PERSON IN ENVIRONMENT		
PURPOSE		
To enhance the social functioning of individuals, families, groups, and communities in their environment		
SANCTION		
Clients, Private/Public Agencies, Profession, Government (Laws)		
VALUES		
1. Dignity and worth of every person		
2. Practice Principle		
3. Code of Ethics		
4. Democratic, caring society		
	KNOWLEDGE	
Developmental/life cycle	Socialization	Organizational theory
Biological	Role	Political Science
Psychological	Behavioural therapy	Legislative process
Psychosocial	Communication	Social Policy
Cognitive	Stress/Conflict	Cultural Anthropology
Moral	Systems	Community resources
Spiritual	Group process	Public/Private services
Self Actualization/ Self-Awareness	Population at risk	Social welfare
	SKILLS	
Relationship skills	Problem solving skills	Political skills
Listening	Problem identifying	Advocating
Responding	Data collecting	Bargaining
Information giving	Planning	Organizing
Referring	Implementing	Demonstrating

Fig. 6.1: A Holistic Conceptualization of the Foundation for Social Work Practice

Knowledge: To carry their commitment into action, social workers need to understand persons and environment and their interdependence. Professional social work is selected for an understanding of behaviours and needs of human systems within the context of their diverse culture and environment. More specifically, the workers need to know about the various systems that constitute their work environment. To gain knowledge about the profession and social welfare polices and services, social workers study theories relevant to practice.

Skill: Guided by values and knowledge, a social worker executes a series of activities within the framework of a method with client related system to achieve identified goals. These activities constitute the skills of the worker. Social workers are known for using interpersonal relationships in a helping process. In addition, problem solving, goal setting, and task defining are commonly identifies as central to practice.

The SHGs are formulated to achieve empowerment and it is not possible without microfinance. But in reality a very few SHGs are completing their life cycle to achieve empowerment. Perhaps women do not have adequate knowledge about the SHGs or micro credit and is not easily available which let down the SHGs at premature stage. Until and unless the SHGs and microfinance becoming complementary to each other, the women empowerment will remain secluded. So, the duty and responsibility of social workers to use social work practice which is shown in the diagram to identify the problem related to SHGs and microfinance so that something must be done to achieve empowerment.

Undoubtedly we require through knowledge about the social group to understand the SHGs satisfactorily. Self Help Group is a group concept which requires social group work method to deal with the problems of the SHGs. Therefore, we are bound to know the tools, techniques and skills of social group work to handle the SHGs. "Social group work is a method of social work which helps individuals to enhance their social functioning through purposeful group experience and to cope more effectively with their personal, group or community problems" (Konopka, 1963). Social group work has the knowledge of individuals, group, community behaviour and skill of working with the group members. Leader is made aware about the factors of human behaviour, such as role of heredity, environment, learning, socialization, motivation and perception. Leader of the group must have skill in participation with the group, dealing with group feeling, using agency and community resources for achieving target of the SHGs. The leaders enable the groups to function in such a way that both group interaction and programme activities contribute to the growth of the individual, and the achievement of desirable goal. The objectives of SHGs are:

1. To help the individuals use groups to further their development into emotionally balanced, intellectually free and physically fit persons.
2. To help the groups to achieve the ends in the economic, political and social democracy.
3. To bring highest possible development of human personality dedicated and devoted to the democratic ideals.
4. To bring changes in internal personality encourages accepting new roles, bringing closeness in the relations among group members, and improving the condition of systems and also in communication process.

In this particular work, we put our best effort for congregation, substantial and relevant information from primary as well as secondary sources. After gathering information for the respondents using interview schedule for data collection, we identified a good number of problems in self help group. It was also divulged through investigation that the concept of professional social work is not very popular in this region, i.e. West Bengal. Social work is a broad as well as century old subject. It includes many approaches such as preventive, promotive, curative and ameliorative. It is such an inter-disciplinary practice profession which conglomerate of developmental psychology, sociology, social economics, social medicines, social policy and planning, social welfare administration and so on so forth. A lot of research and development in this particular issue has been made over a long period of time, which has helped in establishing it as a profession. Gradually, it has also been established that social work promotes the general welfare of the society, from local to global levels and the development of people, their communities, and their environment. Social work should advocate better living conditions conducive to the fulfilment of basic human needs and should promote social, economical, political and cultural values and institutions that are compatible with the realization of social justice. Considering the above mentioned points, self help group, microfinance and women empowerment would be an ideal field of practice for social work professionals because of the existence of abundant social problem.

Considering the discussion with the respondents and the available literature, we found the following as the fundamental problems of the Self Help Group, Microfinance and Women Empowerment:

1. Low level of education among the group members.
2. Lack of awareness among the group members about the schemes related to rural development.
3. Problem of alcoholism and gambling among the husbands of the group members.
4. Unhygienic working condition and family environment of the group members.
5. Non-availability of alternative employment opportunities for the group members.
6. Active role played by the money lenders for indebtedness among the community members.
7. Identification of proper income generation activities and its market for supplying the product.
8. Lack of skills about the enterprise.
9. Absenteeism in group meeting and dreadful effect of bank loan default.
10. Political manoeuvering between the group members and political leaders.
11. Nepotism between the leaders and group members regarding loan disbursement.
12. Seclusion of the poorest among the group members in the community.
13. Lack of awareness among the group members about human trafficking.
14. Lack of awareness regarding HIV?AIDS through migration.
15. Lack of awareness among the group members about the evil effects of dowry, child marriage, child labour, female infanticide and female foeticide.
16. Lack of awareness among the group members about the women friendly laws and enactments.
17. Lack of awareness about the evil effects of environmental degradation.

18. Lack of awareness regarding their constitutional rights (Human Rights) and duties.

Apart from the above, group members also experience other kinds of problems related to physical, psychological and emotional in their life. Self Help Group is such a platform where the professional social worker might play a multidimensional role. Social welfare, social services, social justice, dignity and worth of the person, the importance of human relationships, integrity and competence are some of the issues that social workers deal with.

The National Association of Social Workers (NASW) makes it clear that the social workers who are involved in developmental work through Self Help Group, Microfinance and Women Empowerment should be guided by the professional values and ethics of social work. Social workers should carefuliy examine relevant issues and their possible impact on the individuals before deciding on a course of action. Along with these social workers should facilitate informed participation by the inmates of the Self Help Group in shaping social policies and social instructions through active participation, consultation and training and development.

The researchers also found the following elementary functions the social worker might play with the Self Help Groups for their empowerment and sustainable growth.

- Conducting awareness programmes on different issues like dowry, child marriage, alcoholism, HIV/AIDS, legal aid etc.
- Arranging primary and vocational and continuing education for the SHG members.
- Conducting health education programme through awareness on preventive and social medicine.
- Developing Information, Education and Communication (IEC) materials for better publication and promotion of SHG.

Social workers provide interventions to individuals, families and groups in order to assist them with their needs and issues. Interventions are intended to and clients in alleviating problems impeding their well-being. Interventions used by the social workers are those that are identified as potentially helpful on the basis of the social worker's ongoing assessment of the client.

Social work interventions are selected on the basis of the issues, needs and strengths of the individual member of the Self Help Group. These are determined as a result of a psychological assessment conducted by the social worker. In initial meetings with group members, the social worker will obtain extensive information from the group members in order to develop a detailed and comprehensive understanding of the Self Help Groups, in which interventions, action, steps and desired outcomes specified. A time frame will be established for each outcome, with a means to measure the group member's progress towards achieving his/her goals on a regular basis identified. Henceforth, the diagram of 'A Holistic Conceptualization of the Foundation of Social Work Practice' would help the social worker to draw cordial plan to sought result oriented solution with shortest period of time.

NASW has identified a number of super specialty areas in social groups where social workers might work. It influences the types of interventions selected for use with the individuals. Ares of practice include aging among the group members, alcohol and substance abuse, adjustment problem, socio-cultural and economic problem, absenteeism, borrowing from the moneylender, loan defaulter, superstitions etc. Interventions can include: psychotherapy (individual, couples, families and groups), group therapy, role playing, system theory, counselling, case management, crisis intervention, relaxation training, anger management, stress management etc.

Social worker works with the different stages of development of the Self Help Group besides helping them to use micro-credit from microfinance institutions. The social workers help the under privileged sections to organize themselves for formulating Self Help Groups and if requires the members of the group will be provided or developed the literature of regional language related to the SHGs. Social workers must be knowing the strengths and weaknesses of the individual group member and help the members to use group dynamics to achieve the group goals. The social worker must provide the group member latest information regarding the programmes and policies so that they make use of all these things. The social worker must show trust on the group members so that they might feel empowered. She/he must enable the group members in number of areas i.e. bank linkage, inter-loaning, selecting right venture, marketing, abolishing money lenders, participation in community development activities, removing social stigma and evil practices etc. These programme and service areas vary on the type of problems that clients bring to a particular setting, representing specialization in social work. Thus, the function of social work interventions is determined by the types of issues and needs which clients bring to the social work setting as well as the social worker's specialization area.

The degree to which social work interventions are effective is determined by the degree to which client goals and outcomes are achieved. When goals and outcomes are achieved as demonstrated by the results of the work done between the social worker and the client, their interventions used are then recognized as effective.

When providing services and interventions, social workers have been criticized in a number of areas and are not always viewed in positive light. Social workers are often thought to be untrained, uncaring and disruptive in the lives of clients. It was found that clients frequently complain that little social support is provided by social workers and prevention services are rarely available. Clients continue to feel stigmatized and looked down upon after working with a social worker. Their remains a need for continued efforts to improve and strengthen the role of social workers as they intervene in the lives of those with whom they work.

However, the importance of professional social workers is undoubtedly growing day by day because of its scientific and systematic nature. Philanthropic and humanitarian are the important factors of social work which play crucial role in helping the individuals to overcome their problems by their own. It is such profession which condemns the act of the individuals not the actors and thus makes the profession noble one. Creating self-worth is the important aspect of this profession. It is the only profession which rehabilitates the sufferer and reinforces some of the skills and techniques for their perpetuation.

7

Major Findings

1. The majority of the leader respondents, i.e. 58 per cent and general member respondents, i.e. 57 per cent were in the age group of 26-35 years. It is also significant that 2 per cent general member respondents and leader respondents were the age group of 50 years and above.
2. The majority of the leader respondents, i.e. 88 per cent and general member respondents i.e. 81 per cent of the self help groups were married. On the other hand, it is also significant that only 5 per cent general member respondents were single and no leader respondents have been found single.
3. Cent per cent (100%) leader respondents had attained primary school whereas nearly 70 per cent general member respondents did not have primary schooling.
4. The majority of the leader respondents, i.e. 70 per cent had preferred small family size and having less than five members in the family whereas the majority of the general member respondents, i.e. 66 per cent had preferred large family size having more than five members in the family.
5. The majority of the leader respondents, i.e. 78 per cent and general member respondents, i.e. 76 per cent of the self help group were belonged to nuclear family. On the other hand, it is also important to see that 22 per cent leader respondents and 24 per cent general member respondents were belonged to joint family respectively.
6. The majority of the respondents, i.e. 54 per cent each from

leader and general members belonged to SC. It is also significant that only 4 per cent general member respondents and 2 per cent leader respondents belonged to OBC.

7. The majority of the general members 62 per cent and the leader respondents 58 per cent did not face resistance from their family members for forming the SHGs.
8. The majority of the general members 73 per cent and leader respondents 70 per cent have attended the meeting regularly organized by the SHGs and it is also significant to see that 10 per cent general members and 18 per cent leader respondents not at all attended the meeting.
9. The majority of the general member respondents, i.e. 66 per cent and leader respondents, i.e. 50 per cent have attended the group meeting twice in a month. It is also significant that a very low respondent, 2 per cent each from general members and leaders never attended the group meeting.
10. The majority of leader respondents (40%) got training in tailoring/kantha stitch/batik printing whereas the majority of the general members (38%) got training in domestication of small ruminants/animal husbandry. It is also significant that no single respondent from the leader and general member had shown interest in food processing or craftsmanship/artisan.
11. The majority of leader respondents and general member respondents (56%) each have joined SHG to eradicate poverty and for better future respectively.
12. The majority of leader respondents (44%) and general member respondents (37%) were getting information about SHG from panchayat members and neighbours.
13. The majority of leader respondents (78%) and general member respondents (46%) have annual income between Rs. 8000-10000 after being associated with SHG. Therefore, if we compare Tables 5.9 and 5.10 then it is quite clear that nearly 70 per cent of women have enhanced their annual income up to the level of Rs. 2000 from Rs. 6000-8000 to Rs. 8000-10000 after joining SHG.
14. The majority of general members (66%) and leader respondents (52%) have received training from local NGOs.

15. The majority of leader respondents (60%) participated in community development activities whereas the majority of the general member respondents (40%) did not participate in the said activities.
16. The majority of general members (55%) and leader respondents (67%) preferred to get credit from NGOs (private microfinance institutions, i.e. Ujjiban, Badhan etc.) for income generation activities.
17. The majority of general member respondents (81%) and leader respondents (80%) preferred to have savings and credit facility from rural bank.
18. The majority of the general member respondents (89%) and leader respondents (88%) preferred formal credit sources for income generation activities.
19. The majority of leader respondents (62%) and general member respondents (46%) have earned respect through getting associate themselves with SHGs.
20. The majority of general member respondents and leader respondents (78%) each have taken loan for income generation activities.
21. The majority of the general member respondents and leader respondents (78%) each one was doing different income generation activities.
22. The majority of leader respondents (40%) and general member respondents (27%) have taken income generation activities as tailoring/kantha stitch/batik fabric.
23. The majority of general member respondents (86%) and leader respondents (78%) never failed to repay loan.
24. The majority of general member respondents (83%) have moderate knowledge about functioning of the SHGs whereas the majority of the leader respondents (58%) have profound knowledge about the functioning of SHGs.
25. The majority of the general member respondents (65%) and leader respondents (60%) have deposited their saving in the SHGs common fund timely and regularly. It is also important to see that significantly low respondents from general members (21%) and leader respondents (16%) have failed to deposit their saving in the common fund of the SHGs.
26. The majority of the general member respondents (46%)

have less decision making power in family affairs whereas leader respondents (34%) have more decision making power in family affairs.

27. The majority of leader respondents (64%) and general member respondents (53%) have greater control over family expenses.
28. The majority of leader respondents (72%) said that both the leaders and the general members do take decision for loan in income generation activities.
29. The majority of the leader respondents (70%) said that both the leaders and the general members do take decision for loan in income generation activities.
30. The majority of leader respondents (84%) maintain account of SHGs just after finishing up the meetings.
31. The majority of leader respondents (78%) said that cashier is the person who is responsible for maintaining the account.
32. The majority of the leader respondents (46%) have faced familial problem while under taking SHG activities.
33. The majority of the leader respondents (52%) have very low knowledge regarding panchyat and its function.
34. The majority of the general members (94%) deposit their savings in monthly basis.
35. The majority of the general member respondents (62%) said that the members of their SHGs are under the age group of 20-25 years.
36. The majority of the general member respondents (82%) (41 SHGs out of 50 SHGs) said that their SHGs have more than 10 members in the group.
37. The majority of the general member respondents (96%) said leader calls the meeting affairs for the group.
38. The majority of the general member respondents (43%) have no control over family assets as compare to 30 per cent leader respondents who have less control over family assets.
39. The majority of the general member respondents (98%) said that their SHGs deposit less than Rs. 500 or Rs. 500 monthly as savings.
40. The majority of leader respondents (48%) and the general member respondents (34%) have strongly agreed about

the fact that social status has been improved after getting associated with SHGs.

41. The majority of the leader respondents (66%) said that peer pressure is the only option for getting loan back from the defaulter.
42. The majority of the leader respondents (70%) said that the loan must be distributed according to the need base and rotation-wise.
43. The majority of the leader respondents (60%) said that persuading the members about the importance of group meeting would be the only option to ensure maximum attendance.

8

Conclusions and Suggestions

In rural area of Birbhum District, the poorest among the poor are women. The women empowerment through self help programme could help to prevent the feminization of poverty. In the last six decades of development efforts, the existence of people of Birbhum District of West Bengal in a state of social, economical, political and information disempowerment is considered as a major constraint to overall development. There is an essential demand for the integrated development, which should encompass development in all spheres, which covers status, equality, security, complete physical, mental and social well-being of women. A lot of developmental efforts has been initiated by the government but could not mainstream the poor women. Till date no developmental programme bring about holistic development in a sustainable manner. Henceforth, the number of people Below Poverty Line (BPL) has increased alarmingly over the period. Even though many participatory programmes, which are meant for inclusive growth also failed to bring sustainability. The latest development strategy introduced was self help group by NABARD. Realizing its usefulness and potentiality, the number of SHGs are increasing day by day and it is being introduced in every development programme.

The major thrust of SHGs to empower poor women socially, economically, physically and mentally through different activities of SHGs. Empowerment process starts when they decided to join SHGs. Simultaneously, they become integral part of different activities performed by SHGs for their development. Initially they learn to collect various information about SHGS from other SHGs and NGO worker. Once they are satisfied with the information then they start participating in the SHGs. They share their emotion and experience during group meetings. They participate in capacity building programme whenever they need to develop themselves. They have also taken the opportunity to frequently visit and meet government agencies, panchayat, block office, police station, bank etc. to mobilize the resources. Group meetings also help to finalize the decision of loan, income generation activities and participation in community development programme. Through SHGs the poor women are able to break the vicious circle of poverty and unemployment.

The Study revealed that SHGs have great impact on the lives of women of Bolpur-Sriniketan Block of Birbhum District in West Bengal. It also reveals that majority of the women of SHGs have achieved consciousness about the role and function of SHGs, local self-governance, bank, cooperatives and other service providers. They are also showing great amount of courage for achieving self-reliance through adopting small family norm and family planning. They have also become able to take decision of family affairs, economic matter, child health, education and family welfare. They have conferred the power of choice and upgrading negotiation and bargaining skill helps to become empower. Subsequently, control over family expenses, and family assets etc. Also indicates women's status in the family as well as in the community. After lots of discussion with the SHGs, women respond that they feel the advantages of SHGs which helps the members to overcome many deep rooted problems, i.e. economic, social, political and physical. When women were asked about the participation in politics or in panchayat they responded very positively and willing to compete in the politics for the betterment of the society. They really eager to represent the women and want to implement women related schemes for the betterment of women. The study also reflected that empowerment is an aggregate of certain dependent variables such as savings and credit, decision making in loan and income generation activities, decision making in family affairs, decision making in control over family expenses and family assets, family size and family type and social participation in community development activities. Thus SHGs' ultimate solution is to fight against all the discrimination and violation of women.

On the basis of major findings, following suggestions are made towards empowering the women through SHGs and microfinance:

1. As many women do not have adequate knowledge about SHGS, they should be provided literature with case studies in regional language so that they could have at least theoretical knowledge about the SHGs and not become burden on the SHGs or *vice versa*.
2. As micro-credit gives women an opportunity to change their economic status through savings and credit policy but few commercial banks are reluctant to give loan to the mature SHGs. So that they could start their enterprise and can break the long chain of poverty and unemployment.
3. Members should be very analytical and logical while taking loan. They also have to be cautious about the proper selection of income generating activities. Otherwise they might become loan defaulters which make women more vulnerable.
4. Since Birbhum District is not agriculturally developed, therefore, emphasis must be given on promotion of horticulture and kitchen gardening with government support as their income generating activities.
5. The NGOs and Government should give them a fair amount of chance to market their product and help them to send their product in exhibition and workshops.
6. The study reveals the majority of the group leaders are much informative and empowered than the general members and fair amount of chances are, therefore, nepotism, favourism and corruption. So emphasis should be given to rotational leadership among the group members in an interval of two years.
7. The study also depicted that majority of general members are illiterate, so non-formal education would be very much effective for understanding group activities specially group savings and credit policy which avoid unnecessary conflict among the group members. It also helps to retain members in the group.
8. Attending meeting should be made compulsory so that people should get benefit out of SHGs.

9. At least one leader of SHGs should be incorporated with the rural development programme to avoid the failure of the programme.
10. A block level federation of SHG members can strengthen the movement of a large extent as well as encourage the population to come forward and join in active politics.
11. Periodical training at regular interval for the SHG members should be imparted so that they could enjoy the group thoroughly to reduce the dropout.
12. Community based micro-enterprises like poultry farming, food processing, leaves plate making, batic, fabric work etc. would be most viable economic activities, which helps the beneficiaries drive out from the poverty trap. That is why product should be produced according to local demand using local inputs. Entrepreneurial training and exposure visit would be added value to the SHGs for procuring quality of product.
13. Empowering one means disempowering others so everybody should be brought to the periphery of SHGs.
14. Role of the media should be more proactive and should broadcast the news on SHGs now and again to make rural women aware and make the programme interesting.
15. Since SHG is the only option to inculcate social, economic and political development; SHG should be given more emphasis as a medium of rural development.
16. Government should take initiative to reduce the exorbitant rate of interest charged by the bank to the SHGs on bank loan. Since women belong to the poorest of poor, they should be given such type of relaxation.
17. Government should provide a few incentives or rewards to the excellent SHGs.
18. Since majority of women does not have control over assets so government should take initiative to reduce the disparity between men and women in the matter of controlling assets. Only legislations would not be effective until and unless the SHGs are involved to campaign against the maladies and injustice against the women.
19. Further research should be encouraged to make the policies favouring women SHGs.

Bibliography

Ackerly, B.A. (1995). Testing the tools of development: credit programmes, loan involvement and women's empowerment, in Getting Institutions Right for Women in Development, *IDS Bulletin*, Vol. 26(3)3.

Agarwal, Bina (1989). Rural Women Poverty and Natural Resources: Sustenance, Sustainability and Struggle for Change, *Economic and Political Weekly*, Vol. 24 (43): 46-65.

Aguiar, Mark, Hurst, Erik (2007). Measuring trends in leisure: the allocation of time over five decades, *the Quarterly Journal of Economics, Oxford Journals*, 122 (3): 969-1006, doi: 101162/qjec.122.3.969. pdf

Ahmed, M.A. (1999). Women Empowerment: Self Help Groups, *Kurukshetra*, April, Vol. 47(2): 19, 20 and 49.

Aiyar, M. Shankar (2008). A Social Revolution: Panchayati Raj, Kurudshetra, Vol. 55(5): 43-46.

Amin, M. Mir. (2008). Entrepreneurship Development: An Approach to Economic Empowerment of Women, *Kurukshetra*, Vol. 56(11): 29-33.

Annas. J. (1993). Women and the Quality of Life: Two Norms or One?, in *The Quality of Life*, edited by Martha C. Nussbaum and Amartaya Sen.

Approach Paper to Ninth Five Year Plan, Centre for Monitoring Indian Economy, Bombay, India, Chakroborty, S., Mandal, B., Das, C., and Satish, S. (1993).

Armendariz de Aghion, and B. and J. Morduch (2005). *The Economics of Microfinance*, MIT Press.

Beteille, Andre (1999). Empowering through the expansion of the civil, political and social rights of citizenship, *EPW*, Vol. 34, Issue No. 10-11, 6 March, 1999.

ali, Swain, R. (2006). Can microfinance do it? Women Empowerment and the Self Help Group Bank Linkage Programme in India, *draft*, Department of Economics, Uppsala University.

I ıli, Swain, R. (2006). *Microfinance and Women's Empowerment*, Sida Working Paper, Division of Market Development, Sida, Stockholm.

B ındhyopadhyay, D, Yughandhar, B.N. and Mukherjee, Amitava (2000),

"Convergencce of Programmes by Empowering SHGs and PRIs", *Economic and Political Weekly,* June 29.

Barish, H. (1971). Self Help Groups In: *Encyclopaedia of Social Work,* 16th issue, Vol. II. National Assoc. Social Workers, New York, pp. 1163-1169.

Basu, P. and Srivastava, P. (2005). Scaling-up Microfinance for India's Rural Poor, *World Bank Policy Research Working Paper 3646,* WB, Washington DC.

Bifulco, R. (2002). Addressing Self-Selection Bias in Quasi-Experimental Evaluations of Whole –School Reform, *Evaluation Review,* Vol. 26(5): 545-572.

BRAC (Bangladesh Rural Advancement Committee) (1991). *Rural development programme and rural credit project: Annual report,* Dhaka.

Buvinic, Mayra (2001). The Psychology of Donor Support, *World Development,* Vol. 17(7): 1045-1057.

Carr, M., Chen, M. and Jabvala, R. (2000). *Speaking Out, Women's Economic Empowerment in South Asia,* IT Publications, London.

Chakravarty, S., Shukla, G. and Suresh, C.P. (2007). Tribal Welfare and Development in India: Past, Present and Strategies with Special Reference to Agriculture and Forestry, *Kurukshetra,* Vol. 56t(1): 33-39.

Chanana, Karuna (ed.) (1988). *Socialization, Education and women: Exploration in Gender Identity,* Orient Longman Ltd.

Chatterjee, Sankar (2003). Networking SGSY, Banks and SHGs: Initiatives in Uttar Pradesh, *Kurukshetra,* February, Vol. 51(4):. 27-29.

Chattopadhyay, Arundhati (2006). Empowering Women, *Yojana,* Vol. 50: 30-34.

Chen, Martha Alter and Donald Snodgrass (2012). *An Assessment of the Impact of SEWA Bank in India: Baseline Findings.* Harvard Institute for International Development, http://www.mip.org

Cheston, S. and Kuhn, L. (2015). Empowering Women through Microfinance, *Draft,* Opportunity International a Microcredit Summit-5, New York, 10-13 November, available at http://microcreditsummit.org/papers/papers.html.

Coleman B. (1999). The Impact of group lending in Northeast Thailand, *Journal of Development Economics,* Vol. 60(2): 105-142.

Consultative Group to Assist the Poor (CGAP) (2002). Microfinance and the Millennium Development Goals, *Donor Brief no. 9,* Consultative Group to Assist the Poor, Washington DC.

Dalla Costa, Mariagrosa, James, Selma (2012). *The power of women and the subversion of the community,* Bristol, England: Falling Water Press. OCLC 67881986.

Damayanthi, U.T. (1999). Development of Women and Children in Rural Areas—An Impact Study, *The Asian Economic Review,* August, Vol. 41(2): 349-357.

Dodkey, M.D. (1999). SHGs and Micro Credit, Sustaining Rural Women, Social Welfare, *March*, Vol. 45(12): 19-20.

Dr. Kaushik, V. and Ms. Kumari, S. (2008). Risk and Hindrances in Growth of Women Entrepreneurship in Rural Areas, *Kurukshetra*, Vol. 56(3): 12-16.

Dr. Loganathan, P. and Ashokan, R. (2006). Inter Regional Development of Self Help Groups in India, *Kurukshetra*, Vol. 54(11): 9-12.

Dr. Premavathy, N. and Kadharlal, A. (2008). Government initiatives for women entrepreneurial development in Tamil Nadu, *Kurukshetra*, Vol. 56(3): 17-21.

Dr. Ramachandran, T. and Balakrishnan, S. (2008). Impact of Self Help Group on Women's Empowerment/A study in Kanyakumari District, *Kurukshetra*, Vol. 57(2): 31-34.

Dr. Samad, M. Abdul (2008). Women Empowerment and Panchayati Raj Institutions in Kerala, *Kurukshetra*, Vol. 55(5): 37-42.

Dr. Sharma, S. (2008). Empowering Women through Education: Strategy for Sustainable Rural Development, *Kurukshetra*, Vol. 56(3): 3-5.

Dr. Singh, Deepali, and Dr. Ansari, A. Nafees (2008). The Empowerment of Indian Women with reference to Five Years Plans, *Kurukshetra*, Vol. 56(11): 13-17.

Dr. Singh, Indrabhhushan and Dr. Kumari, Usha (2007). Jeevika Mega Project: Empowerment of Rural Poor in Bihar, *Kurukshetra*, Vol. 56(2): 14-17.

Dr. Singh, Indrabhhushan and Dr. Kumari, Usha (2008). Rural Development and Women Empowerment, *Kurukshetra*, Vol. 55(5): 3-8.

Dr. Singh, S. and Rathore, M. (2008). Women Enterprise: A Step Towards Success, *Kurukshetra*, Vol. 56(3): 8-11.

Dr. Soundarapandian, M. (2006). Microfinance for rural entrepreneurs, *Kurukshetra*, Vol. 54(11): 14-16.

Dr. Suneetha, R. (2008). Is DWCRA Programme Empowering the Rural Women, *Kurukshetra*, Vol. 55(5): 17-20.

Dr. Tyagi, S. (2008). Strategic model for effective functioning of SHG, *Kurukshetra*, Vol. 57(2): 17-19.

Fisher, T. and Sriram, MS. (2002). *Beyond Micro-Credit: Putting Development Bank into Microfinance*, Vistar Publications, New Delhi.

Federici, Silvia (2010). *Wage Against House Work*: Wall Press.

Folbre, Nancy (2010). *Who pays for the kids?: Gender and the Structures of Constraints*. London, New York: Routledge.

Freedman, David H. (1992). New theory on how the aggressive egg attracts sperm, *Discover Magazine*, Kalmpach Publishing, 6 (13): 55.

George, N.D. (2008). Issues and Strategies of Self Help Group, *Yojana*, Vol. 52: 41-43.

Gilman, C.P. (1898). *Women and economics: a study of the economic relation between men and women as a factor in social evolution*. Boston: Small, Maynard, & Co. OCLC 26987247

Goetz, A. and Gupta, R. Sen (1996). Who takes the credit? Gender, power, and control over loan use in rural credit programmes in Bangladesh, *World Development*, Vol. 24(1).

Gopalakrishnan, B.K. (1998). SHGs and Social Defense, *Social Welfare*, January, Vol. 44(10): 30-34.

Gore, M.S. (1985). *Social Aspects of Development*, Rawat Publications, Jaipur.

Grootaert, C. (2003). On the relationship between empowerment, social capital and community driven development, *World Bank Working Paper no. 33074*, WB, Washington, DC.

Harford, Tim. (2008). The Battle for the Soul of Microfinance, *Financial Times*, 6 December.

Hartmann, Heidi (1981). The unhappy marriage of Marxism and Feminism: towards a more progressive union, in Sargent, Lydia, Women and revolution: a discussion of the unhappy marriage of Marxism and Feminism, South END PRESS *Political Controversies Series*, Boston, Massachusetts: South End Press, pp. 1-42.

Hashemi, S.M., Schuler, S.R. and Riley, A.P. (2012). Rural Credit Programmes and Women's Empowerment in Bangladesh, *World Development*, Vol. 24(4): 635-653.

Holvoet, N. (2005). The Impact of Microfinance on Decision-Making Agency: Evidence from South India, *Development and Change*, Vol. 36(1).

Hulme, D. and Mosley, P. (1996). *Finance Against Poverty*, London: Routledge.

Humm, Maggie (1992). *Modern feminisms: Political, Literary, and Cultural*. New York: Columbia University Press.

Humm, Maggie (1990). *The dictionary of feminist theory*. Columbus: Ohio State University Press. pp. 278.

India (2005). *A reference manual*, Res., Ref. and Trg. Divn., Min. of Infmn. And Publicity, GoI, New Delhi.

Jain, Ritu (2003). Socio-Economic Impact Through Self Help Groups, *Yojana*, Vol. 47(7): 11-12.

Jayesh, Ranjan., Sanghi, N.K., Jawali, B.G., Rao, A.P. and Reddy, K. (2002). Organization of men SHGs in rural areas—A felt need of the hour. In: A journey through watersheds. *MANAGE*. Vol. 1(3).

Jeyanthi, Gayatri R. (2002). *SHGs in Kanyakumari District*, M.Phil., dissertation submitted to Alagappa University, Karaikudi, T.N.

Jeyaraman, R. *et al.* (2004). Role of Self help Groups in Fisher Women Development, *Peninsular Economist*, Vol. XII(2): 197-200.

Jha, Abhaskumar (2004). "Lending to the Poor: Designs for Credit", *EPW*, Vol. XXXV, No. 8 abd 9.

Jha, Kalinath (2005). *Modernizing Women-Searching their Identities*, Rawat Publications, Jaipur, India.

Joshi, N.C. (2008). Women Welfare-A Priority On The Government's Agenda, *Kurukshetra,* Vol. 56(11): 7-9.

Kabeer, N. (2013). Resources, agency, achievements: reflections on the measurement of women's empowerment, discussing Women's Empowerment—Theory and Practice, *SIDA Studies No. 3.*

Kabeer, N. (2001). Conflicts over Credit: Re-Evaluating the Empowerment Potential of Loans to Women in Rural Bangladesh. *World Development, Vol. 29(1):* 63-84.

Kabeer, N. (2000). *The power to choose: Bangladeshi women and labour market decisions in London and Dhaka,* London: Verso.

Kabeer, N. (1998). Money can't buy me love": re-evaluating gender, credit and empowerment in rural Bangladesh, *Discussion Paper No. 363,* Institute of Development Studies. Brighton, U.K.

Kandiyoti, D. (2000). *Women and Rural Development Policies: the Changing Agenda,* Institute of Development Studies, Brighton, UK.

Katz, A.H. (1965). Application of self help concept in current social welfare. *Journal of Social Work.* Vol. 10(3): 68-74.

Khullar, K.K. (2007). Mahila Samakhya: Empowerment of Women through Education, *Kurukshetra,* Vol. 55(5): 9-11.

Kokila K. (2001). Credit Groups for Women workers:, *Social Welfare,* May, Vol. 48(2): 23-25.

Konopka, G. (1963). *Social Group Work: A Helping Process,* Prentice Hall, Englewood Cliffs, pp. 29.

Kour, Amarjeet (2008). Self Help Group (SHG) and rural development, *Kurukshetra,* Vol. 57(2): 25-30.

Krishna A. (2003). Social Capital, Community Driven Development, and Empowerment: A short note on concepts and operations, *World Bank working paper 33077,* WB, Washington, DC.

Krishana, Vijaya, R. and Das, Amarnath, R. (2003). Self Help Groups—A Study in A.P. District, *HRD Times,* May.

Kuhn, J. (1985). The role of Non Governmental Organisations in promoting self help organizations. *Sem. Paper, Druchari tranz, Paffen holz, Bomheins.* pp. 264-266.

Kumar, Shashi. Bhushan (2010). Women's Reservation Bill.2008: A Landmark Measure to Empower Women. *Chronicle*: Vol. XX(5).

Lalitha, N. (1998). Micro Finance: Rural NGOs and Banks Networking, *Social Welfare,* October, Vol. 45(7): 13-17.

Lalitha, N. and Nagarajan, B.S. (2000). *Self help Groups in Rural Development,* Dominant Publishers and Distributors, New Delhi.

Likert, R. (1932). A technique for measurement of attitude. Archives *Pscyhol.* 140.

Luker, Kristin (1996). *Dubious conceptions: the politics of teenage pregnancy,* Cambridge, Massachusetts: Harvard University Press.

MacFarquhar, Neil (2011). Making money out of poor people?, *The Hindu,* 15th April.

Malhotra, A., Schuler, S.R. and Boender, Carol (2002). Measuring Women's Empowerment as a Variable in International Development, *Background Paper for World Bank Workshop on Poverty and Gender: New Perspectives.*

Manimekalai, N. and Rajeswari, G. (2002). Grassroots Entrepreneurship through Self Help Groups (SHGs). *SEDMI Journal*, Vol. 29: 2.

Martin, O. (1990). Translating the self help concept into action in Indonesia. *International Asian Focus*, Vol. 21(3-4): 235-244.

Mathew, P.M. (2008). FM and Financial Inclusion, *Yojana*, Vol. 52: 37-40.

Marx, Karl Engels, Frederick (1848). *The Communist Manifesto*, Moscow: Foreign Languages Publishing House. OCLC 919388374. View online.

Marx, Karl (1859). *A Contribution to the Critique of Political Economy.* Progress Publisher, Moscow.

Mayoux, L. (1997). The Magic Ingredient? Microfinance and Women's Empowerment, *A Brief Paper prepared for the Micro Credit Summit*, Washington

Mayoux, L. (2001). Tackling the Down Side: Social Capital, Women's Empowerment and Micro-Finance in Cameroon, *Development and Change*, Vol. 32.

McCormack, J., Walsh, M. and Nelson, C. (1986). Women's Group Enterprises—A study of the structure and opportunity on the Kenya coast, *Report of USAID*, Human Resource Division, World Education Inc., Boston, US.

Mehra, R. (1997). Women Empowerment and Economic Development, *The Annals of the American Academy of Political and Social Science*, Vol. 554: 136-149.

Meyer, B.D. (1995). Natural and Quasi-Experiments in Economics, *Journal of Business and Economic Statistics*, Vol. 13(2): 151-161.

Miller, D.C. (1971). *Handbook of Research Design and Social Measurement.* David Mckay, New York.

Mishra, Swarswati (2002). *Status of Indian women*, Gyan Publishing Home, New Delhi, pp-107-108.

Mohanty, C.T.; Russo, A. and Torres L. (1991). Under western eyes: feminist scholarship and colonial discourses. In *Third World Women and the Politics of Feminism*, Indiana University Press: Cambridge.

Montgomery, R. (1999). Disciplining or Protecting the poor? Avoiding the social costs or peer pressure in Microcredit schemes, *Journal of International Development*, Vol. 8(2), Wiley, U.K.

Morduch, J. (1999). Does Microfinance Really Help the Poor? New Evidence from Flagship Programmes in Bangladesh. *Mimeo.* Princeton University. Princeton.

Muhammad, Anu (2013). Grameen and Microcredit: A Tale of Corporate Success, *Economic and Political Weekly*, August, Vol. XLIV(35): 35.

Mukherji, P.N. (1977). Social movement and social change: Towards conceptual clarification and theoretical framework. *Soc. Bull.* Vol. 26(1).

Murugan, K.R. and Dharmalingam, B. (2000). Self Help Groups/New women's movement in T.N. *Soc. Welfare,* Vol. 47(5): 9-12.

MYRADA (2002). Impact of Self Help Groups (Group Processes) on the Social Empowerment Status of Women Members in Southern India, *paper presented at the Seminar on SHG Bank Linkage Programme,* New Delhi.

NABARD (1992). *Credit needs of the rural poor—Role of self help groups and their linkage with formal credit institutions.* NABARD, Mumbai.

NABARD (1992). *Foundation for development cooperation: Banking with the poor.* NABARD, Mumbai.

NABARD (1995). *Role of self help groups and their linkage with formal credit institutions.* NABARD, Mumbai.

NABARD (1998). *Self help group concept, Vijaya Bank.* NABARD, Bangalore.

NABARD (2005). *Progress of SHG—Bank Linkage in India, 2004-2005,* Microcredit Innovations Department, NABARD, Mumbai

NABARD (2005). *Programme of SHG-Bank Linkage in India,* Micro credit Innovations Department, Mumbai.

Nair, Tara. S. (1998). Meeting the Credit Needs of the Micro Enterprise Sector: Issues in Focus, *The Indian Journal of Labour Economics,* July-September, Vol. 41(3): 531-538.

Naranaswamy, N.S. Manivel and B. Bhaskar (2003). Networking SHGs and Cooperatives—An Analysis of strengths and Weaknesses, *Journal of Rural Development.* Vol. 22:3.

Narashimban, Sakunatala (1999). *Empowering Women: An Alternative Strategy for Rural India,* New Delhi: Sage Publications India Pvt. Ltd.

Narayanaswamy, B.; Samanta, R.K. and Gowda, Narayana, K. (2007). *Self Help Groups*—Key to Empowerment of Rural Women, The Women Press Publication, Delhi, ISBN-81-89110-17-9.

Naqvi, Hena (2008). The path of women's empowerment in India *Kurukshetra,* Vol. 56(11): 26-28.

Nayak, Krupasindhu (2008). Sustainable development for vulnerable poor, *Kurukshetra,* Vol. 56(5): 8-11.

Nayyar, Reva (2006). Towards Gender Equity, Yojana, Vol. 50: 14-17.

Nussbaum, M.C. (2000). *Women and Human Development: The Capabilities Approach.* Cambridge University Press: Cambridge.

Panda, Snehlata (2008). Political Empowerment of Tribal Women in Orissa, *Kurudshetra,* Vol. 55(5): 29-32.

Parekh, R. and Mehta, K. (1992). *Empowerment of Rural Women: A case study of Udwada,* Proc. Of the National Consultation on gender issues in credit in the rural non-farm sector, 14-15th September, organised by SNDT Women's University, Bombay.

Patil, Pratibha. Devisingh (2008). Empowered Women/Empowered Nation, *Yojana,* Vol. 52: 5-7.

Pitt, M. and Khandker, S.R. (1998). The Impact of Group-Based Credit Programmes on Poor Households in Bangladesh: Does the Gender of the Participant Matter? *Journal of Political Economy*, Vol. 106: 958-96.

Prasad, H. (1995). DWCRA-Successful case studies. *J. of Rural Development*. Vol. 14(1): 65-67.

Prof. Panhannavar, A.Y. (2008). Self Help Groups and rural poverty, *Kurukshetra*, Vol. 57(2): 12-16.

Puhazhendi, V. and Badatya, K.C. (2002). SHG Bank Linkage Programme for Rural Poor—An Impact Assessment, *paper presented at the seminar on SHG bank linkage programme* at New Delhi, Micro Credit Innovations Department, NABARD, Mumbai

Puhazhendi, V. and Satyasai, K.J.S. (2001). Economic and social empowerment of rural poor through SHGs, *Indian Journal of Agricultural Economics*, Vol. 56(3): 26-28.

Qazi, M. (1999). Self help groups—A novel approach to rural development. *State Bank of India Monthly Rev.*, Vol. 36(9): 460-465.

Rahaman, A. (2014). *Women and Micro credit in Rural Bangladesh: An anthropological study of Grameen Bank lending*, Boulder, West View Press.

Rahman, A. (1999). Microcredit initiatives for equitable and sustainable development: who pays?, *World Development*, Vol. 27(1): 35-38.

Rajagopalan, B.K. (1998). SHGs and social defense. *Soc. Welfare*, Vol. 44(2): 30-54.

Rosemary Radford Ruether (1983). *Sexism and God-talk: Toward a feminist Theology*, Beacon Press, ISBN 080701205X

Rajamohan, S. (2003). Activities of Self Help Groups in Virudhunagar District—A Study, *TNJC*, pp. 25-29.

Raghavendra, H.G. (2002). "Comparative study on performance of Women Self Help Groups organized by two NGOs in Kolar District." M.Sc. (Agri) Thesis, University of Agricultural Sciences, Bangalore.

Raman, T.S. (1997). *Assessing Empowerment of Rural Women: A study with the marginal farmers of Andhra Pradesh*, Sivam Publications, Hyderabad, India.

Ramesh, K. (1997). *Banking with the poor*, National Institute of Bank Management, Pune, Royal Tropical Institute, Koenraad Verhangen, The Netherlands.

Rao, V.M. (2003). "Women Self Help Groups, Profiles from Andhra Pradesh and Karnataka", *Kurukshetra*, Vol. 50(6): 26-32.

Renjitha, M.H. (2003). "Empowerment of Rural Women through Self Help Groups: A critical analysis". M.Sc. (Agri) Thesis, IARI, New Delhi.

Robinson, Marguerite (2001). *The MICROFINANCE Revolution: Sustainable finance for the poor*, Washington, DC: The World Bank,. pp. xlvii, 304.

Rose, K. (1992). *Where Women are Leaders: The SEWA Movement in India,*

Vistar Publications (An Division of Sage Publications India), New Delhi, India.

Roy, K.C., Tisdell, C.A. and Blomquist, H.C. (1996). *Economic Development and Women in the World Community*, Praeger Publisher, West Port, USA.

Rubin, Gayle (1975). The Traffic in Women: Notes on the 'Political Enonomy' of Sex, in Reiter, Rayna (ed.). *Toward an Anthropology of Women*. New York: Monthly Review Press.

Russell Hochschild, Arlie, Machung, Anne (2003). *The second shift: working families and the revolution at home*. New York: Penguin Books.

Russell Hochschild, Arlie (2001). *The time bind: when work becomes home and home becomes work*. New York: Henry Holt & Co.

Sabyasachi Das (2003). Self Help Groups and Micro Credit Synergic Integration, *Kurukshetra*, Vol. 51(10): 25-28.

Sapna (1997). *Social Mobilization-Group formation, Micro credit experience in poverty eradication, Training Module*, South Asian Perspective Network Association, Kathmandu, Nepal, pp. 1-18.

Satir, Virginia (2014). Introduction to for our future, for our family, in Pairs Foundation, for our Future, for our family: participants handbook, Broward County, Florida: Paris Foundation P.6 (Participants handbook for Paris 30 hours curriculum for Supporting Healthy Marriages) Cited with permission (2012112710011715), Preview on ISSUU.

Schreiner, M. (1999). *Aspects of Outreach: A Framework for the Discussion of the Social Benefits of Microfinance, draft*, Centre for Social Development, Washington University in St. Louis.

Schiebinger, Londa (1999). Medicine, in Schiebinger, Londa, *Has feminism changed science?* Cambridge, Massachusetts: Havard University Press.

Scoggins, A. (2005). *Women's empowerment through micro-finance? The case of the micro credit project for women*, Occasional Paper No.2, CMF [Case Studies of Pokhara Municipality, Dang District and Khokana Village Development Committee] Website: http://www.cmfnepal. org/downloadoc/occapapno_2.doc.

Selvakumar, M. and Sundar, R. (2007). Swarnajayanti Gram Swarozgar Yojana (SGSY)-Tool for Poverty Eradication, *Kurukshetra*, Vol. 56(2): 18-24.

Sen, A.K. (1997). Gender and Co-operative Conflict, in I. Tinker (edited.) *Persistent Inequalities*, Oxford University Press, New Delhi.

Sen, A.K. and Nussbaum, M.C. (ed.) (1993). *Capability and Well-Being, in The Quality of Life*.

Sen, A.K. (1990). *Commodities and Capabilities*, Amsterdam: The Netherlands.

Shankar, Savita and Asher, M.G. (2013). Regulating Microfinance: A

Suggested Framework, *Economic and Political Weekly*, January 2, Vol. XLV(1): 15.

Shankar, Savita and Asher, M.G. (2008). The Microfinance Bill, *Yojana*, Vol. 52: 56-58.

Sharma, Sheetal (2006). Educated Women, Empowered Women, *Yojana*, Vol. 50: 52-57.

Shylendra, H.S. (1999). Micro-finance and self help groups. A study of the experience of two leading NGOs-SEWA and AKRSP in Gujarat, *Search Bull*. Vol. 14(3): 56-78.

Sylendra, H.S. (2008). Role of Self Help Groups, *Yojana*, Vol. 52: 25-28.

Simanowitz, Anton and Walker, Alice (2002). Ensuring impact: reaching the poorest while building financially self sufficient institutions, and showing improvement in the lives of the poorest women and their families, *unpublished background paper for the Micro Credit Summit* + 5, New York, 10-13 November, available at <http://www.microcredit summit.org/papers/papers.htm>.

Singh, O.R. (2001). Education and Women's Empowerment. *Social Welfare*, Vol. 48(1): 35-36.

Sinha, Archana (2004). Micro Finance for Women's Empowerment: A Perspective, *Kurukshetra*, Vol. 52(6): 31-38.

Sinha, F. and Patole, M. (2002). Microfinance and the Poverty of Financial Services: How the Poor in India could be better served, *Working Paper Series*, Finance and Development Research Programme, Institute for Development Policy and Management, University of Manchester.

Smith, S. (1995). *Accountability on Development Organization, Experiences of Women Organizations in India*, Sage Publications, New Delhi, India.

Snehalatha, M. (1994). *A study on the impact of thrift and credit groups in improving the status of rural women*. M.Sc. (Agri) Thesis. Andhra Pradesh Agricultural University, Hyderabad.

Snehalatha, M. and Reddy, M.N. (1998). Impact of thrift and credit groups in income generation of rural women, *Journal of Extn. Edn*. Vol. 9(2): 2031-2032.

Sriram, M.S. (2008). Commercialisation of Microfinance, *Yojana*, Vol. 52: 33-36.

Tangirala, H.S.K. (2008). SHG is a tool of economic development of cooperative and its members, *Kurukshetra*, Vol. 57(2): 22-24.

Todd, H. (Ed.) (1996). *Cloning Grameen Bank: Replicating a Poverty Reduction Model in India, Nepal and Vietnam*, IT Publications, London, UK.

Trecker, H.B. (1955). *Social Group Work: Principles and Practices* Association Press, New York, pp. 5.

Tripathy, K.K. (2006). Microcredit Interventions and Poverty Alleviation, *Kurukshetra*, Vol. 54(11): 4-8.

Tyagi, L.K. (1999). Poverty eradication through self help group promotion. *IASSI*. Vol. 18(1): 57-63.

U.N.D.P. (2001). *Empowerment of Women throughout the life cycle as a transformative strategy for poverty eradication* (EGM/POV/2001/REPORT).

UNCDF (2005). *Microfinance and the MDGs, A reader's guide to the Millennium Project Reports and Other UN Documents,* United Nations Capital Development Fund, New York.

UNDP (1995). *Human Development Report, Gender and Human Development,* Oxford University Press, New York.

United Nations Human Development Report (2004). *Section 28: Gender, Work Burden, and Time Allocation.*

Verma, Renu (2008). Microfinance and Empowerment of Rural Women, *Kurukshetra,* Vol. 56(11): 3-5.

Viswanath, V. (1995). *NGOs and Women's Development in Rural South India. A comparative Analysis,* Westview Press, Oxford, UK.

Viswanathan Maithili (1994). *Women and Society,* Vol. 1, Print well Publications, Jaipur, India.

Vyas, M. (2003). Self help initiatives—Towards improving quality of life in a changing community context. *IASSI,* Vol. 21: 3-4.

World Bank (2001). *Engendering Development: Through Gender Equality in Rights, Resources, and Voice—Summary,* Washington. www.worldbank.org/gender/prr/engendersummary.pdf

World Bank (2003). *Social Capital, Empowerment, and Community Driven Development.* An 80-minute video presented by Ruth Alsop, Rob Chase and Dan Owen. http://info.worldbank.org/etools/bspan/PresentationView.asp?PID=936&EID=482.

World Bank Report (1990). *Strategies for enhancing the role of operations, Country–wide studies,* Bangladesh.

Young, Cathy (2000). *The Mama Lion at the Gate,* Salon. Com. Salon. Retrieved July 8, 2008.

Yunus, Muhammad (1997). Towards creating a poverty-free world. *Lecture delivered at Institute of Social Science,* New Delhi.

Yunus, Muhammad (2002). *Grameen Bank II: designed to open new possibilities,* available at http://www.grameeninfo.org/bank/bank2.html, 8th Nov. 2002.

Yunus, Muhammad (2008). Give the man Credit: An interview, *Yojana,* Vol. 52: 7-10.

Yorukoglu, Mehmet, Greenwood, Jermy and Seshadri, Ananth (2005). Engines of Liberation, Oxford University Press, *Review of Economic Studies,* 72(01): 109 133.

Zaman, H. (2001). *Assessing the poverty and vulnerability impact of micro-credit in Bangladesh: a case study of BRAC,* unpublished background paper for World Bank, World Development Report 2000/2001 (Washington, World Bank).

Websites

http://en.wikipedia.org/wiki/Birbhum_district dated 6/7/2010 time 11.45 am

http://wbdemo5.nic.in/writereaddata/Directoryof_District_Block_GPs (RevisedMarch-2008).doc. Retrieved 2008-12-16.

http://en.wikipedia.org/wiki/grameen_bank

www.istr.org/conferences/toronto/workingpaper/handy.femida.pdf.

Status of Indian Women. http://en.wikipedia.org/wiki/women_in_India

Information related to demography of Birbhum district: search date: 25.10.2011 at 11 am http://censusindia.gov.in/2011-prov-results/ensus2011_paper1_states.html

Grameen Bank-16 decisions for Microfinance <http.//en.wikipedia.org/wiki/Grameen_Bank>

Index